The Stinehour Press

The Stinehour Press

A BIBLIOGRAPHICAL CHECKLIST

OF THE FIRST THIRTY YEARS

Selected and Compiled by
DAVID FARRELL

with an Introduction by
RODERICK STINEHOUR

Meriden - Stinehour Press

LUNENBURG · VERMONT

Limited to 1,200 numbered copies

Distributed by
BEV CHANEY JR. BOOKS
73 CROTON AVENUE, OSSINING, NEW YORK 10562

CONTENTS

INTRODUCTION

THIS VOLUME records what was produced at The Stinehour Press during the first thirty years of its existence—
work that represents the growth of the Press in pursuit of its
objective to print useful books and periodicals of scholarly
and literary value. The checklist does not contain *all* that
was printed—most of what can best be described as "job
printing" has been excluded, along with certain lesser work
not considered significant to the Press's development. An
attempt has thus been made to keep the list from being un-
bearably long; but as it is, attention to the one thousand six
items herein described has taken time and energy during
several years in the busy life of David Farrell, and I am most
grateful to him for his care and his professional dedication
given to this long and demanding task.

While much can be gleaned from what David Farrell sets
forth in this volume (such as the identity of the customers of
the Press, when they used its services, and for what kind of
publications), this does not of course, in and of itself, constitute
a history of The Stinehour Press. Indeed, there are no plans
for encouraging the writing of such a history at this time.
Three decades is, after all, but the formative period in an
enterprise such as this. However, I am so often asked how
The Stinehour Press came into being, located in Lunenburg,
Vermont, that perhaps an informal and quite personal ac-

count of the circumstances leading to the Press's founding might appropriately be offered here.

In order to begin at the beginning I must reach back at least to 1943 and to my graduation that year from the Whitefield, New Hampshire, high school. Whitefield, a small town on the northern edge of the White Mountains, is situated only about twelve miles from Lunenburg. (Nonetheless, I do not recall ever setting foot in that town, on the west side of the Connecticut River, at any time during my high-school years.) A few weeks after graduation, that June, I left Whitefield on the morning train, with orders to join a class of Naval Aviation Cadets then being formed at Dartmouth College in Hanover, New Hampshire, some seventy miles southward. Four years of wartime service, in various places, then intervened before I returned homeward again, in July of 1947, to accept employment with the Connecticut Valley Air Service.

It turned out that operating a flying service at a remote North Country outpost was a precarious undertaking, and prospects for the business's future soon seemed doubtful, at best. Happily, however, my progress in developing an ever-closer friendship that summer with my former high-school classmate Elizabeth Maguire was more successful, and as leaves turned in autumnal splendor we announced our intention to be married in December. The Christmas blizzard of 1947 was of memorable proportions, but our wedding on December twenty-seventh proceeded as planned, and afterwards we left, on schedule, for a month-long honeymoon in far-off Florida.

Our return to New Hampshire in February was attended by an unexpected complication for me. I found that I had no job. The Connecticut Valley Air Service, by then facing foreclosure by its creditors, had no money for payroll or for anything else. Fortunately, Elizabeth Maguire Stinehour, a qualified substitute teacher, was kept fairly busy at the local high school, so the newly wed couple did not starve that first winter of their married life; but with his flying career so abruptly ended, the husband badly needed to find employment, in a place of limited opportunity. (The area's economy was based on the extensive forest lands, as well as on a short tourist season during the summer months. Paper mills, furniture factories, and wood-harvesting operations were the largest year-round employers.)

One evening "Minan" and I sat at our kitchen table, analyzing and discussing our situation. First of all, we were, we knew, country people who wanted to continue to live in our rural northern homeland. Our material needs and our financial expectations were modest, and very secondary to other considerations relative to the kind of family life we envisioned for ourselves. I, for my part, wanted work that would be intellectually exhilarating, as well as demanding as a craft —perhaps architecture, but certainly involving the making of something that would be useful and, if possible, handsome. We started to draw up a list of possibilities and, short though the list was, printing was on it.

Several of the surrounding small towns had weekly newspapers, with shops for printing them, as well as for doing supplementary job printing. I started making the rounds of these establishments, interviewing the editors and hoping to be hired in some capacity, however lowly. The results were dismal, as most of the proprietors were quick to point out my lack of experience. In order to counter this I showed, I remember, one successful editor some sketches and a few architectural perspectives that I had done, and I expressed my interest in design. "Design," he responded, "is never considered in this shop."

As I was about to give up what appeared to be a fruitless line of investigation, I was told of a one-man printing shop, the Bisbee Press, located on a farm in Lunenburg, Vermont. Although what I heard about the Bisbee Press did not sound at all promising, I decided to go for a visit. It was a fateful decision.

Ernest Bisbee was a lean, white-haired man with rimless glasses, a cap always perched to one side of his head, and a pencil behind one ear. I remember his forthright stare and crisp, spare talk, his red suspenders, and his old-fashioned courtesy. The shop was in a small outbuilding that was overshadowed by a large red barn. Close by it was a shingled house, the residence of Mr. and Mrs. Bisbee. The shop's interior was bright, neat, and filled with fascinating machines and tools. The furnishings and woodwork were painted a cheery orange, and a marvelous odor combining printer's ink and wood smoke permeated this wonder-filled, intriguing place.

There were four presses lined up along the front windows of the shop. Two were Golding hand-fed platen presses, another a Kluge automatic platen, and the fourth a Miehle vertical cylinder. All were provided with Vermont granite imposing stones and workbenches. Along the inside walls of the room, from floor to ceiling, were racks containing cases of foundry type. As he showed me around, Mr. Bisbee explained the workings of the mysterious contraptions and how the intricate tools were used to put print onto paper. Ultimately, he even admitted to having perhaps some interest in the prospect of employing an apprentice. When we parted he said he would check the references I had given him. A week later he called me and said that I could come to work for him.

I knew at once, on my very first day in the Bisbee shop, that I had found my life's occupation. There was no doubt. The job was demanding and the details to be mastered seemed infinite. Setting type was an absorbing study in itself —and, of course, only the beginning. Makeup, lockup, press makeready and operation, paper selection and preparation, the varieties of printer's inks! It made my head spin, as I came to realize that learning to fly a Navy fighter aircraft was mere child's play compared with one's trying to learn the trade of printer. Ernest Bisbee proved, however, to be a patient teacher, and that gave me confidence to proceed, step by step, from beginning to logical end.

There were many small jobs that filtered into the shop, jobs that provided the satisfaction of accomplishment. We were supplying the basic printing needs of local tradesmen and businesses: envelopes, invoices, letterheads, forms, advertising flyers, labels, tickets, posters, booklets, and folders. Many customers came into the shop to drop off their orders and to talk with Mr. Bisbee about what they wanted, but most of our routine orders arrived by mail. And, in those days, there was no telephone in the shop, so Mrs. Bisbee would have to bring over occasional phone messages from the house.

My apprenticeship at Bisbee Press began in February of

1948, and by the following summer I had mastered the basic operations of the shop and could creditably produce small jobs on my own. Most of the work given the Press to print was relatively straightforward and could be accomplished by using hand methods. Type was handset and the work was run off on one of the hand-fed jobbers. Paper was cut on a hand-powered guillotine papercutter, and all folding and other finishing was accomplished by hand. Mr. Bisbee and I worked side by side, he explaining and directing, and I gradually extending my usefulness.

During my lunch hour I, early on, discovered a small shelf of books in the back of the shop, and thereafter began to read printer's manuals, type specimen books, trade magazines, and histories of printing. This inspirational extension of workaday labors slowly deepened my understanding of the foundations and rich traditions of this ancient craft that I was now pursuing. It also made me aware of how much more there was to learn—and to doubt that all of my learning could be done at Ernest Bisbee's country shop.

In discussions with my employer, the possibility of my attending a printing school during the winter months was discussed. Between us we had somehow heard about some courses relating to printing that were offered at Dartmouth College. Accordingly, one warm and sunny summer's day I went down to Hanover to investigate. In those days Dartmouth was a quiet place in summer, and there were few people around as I went up the stairs of the administration building, Parkhurst Hall, to make inquiries at the Registrar's office.

There were indeed within the curriculum, I was told, two

courses that dealt with printing, and there existed something called the Graphic Arts Workshop, as well. Registrar Conant was interested in my previous Dartmouth relationship, from my Naval training days, and he encouraged me to think about fall enrollment as a member of the Class of 1950. He even suggested that I meet with Professor Ray Nash in order to discover whether he would accept me as a student in his printing and arts of the book classes. A quickly made phone call established that the professor was in fact in his Baker Library office at that moment and that he would see me. Accordingly, I went across the street to the library for a meeting—one that was to have the greatest influence on the direction of my life.

In the fall of 1948 I began two years of combined liberal arts and "vocational" education as a student at Dartmouth College. Minan, expecting our first child, stayed behind in Whitefield until October, when Stephen was born. Then, mother and son joined me in Hanover. While at college I continued a close relationship with Ernest Bisbee. I worked with him at Lunenburg in between-semester vacation breaks and during the summer months. We also maintained a lively correspondence. But, then, word of his sudden death reached me in March of my senior year. (He had died in the shop of a heart attack.) Shortly after that, I began commuting regularly to Lunenburg in order to help Louise Bisbee with unfinished business, including the completion of orders for spring delivery.

The Bisbees had no immediate family, and Mrs. Bisbee soon concluded that she had no reason to stay on at the farm. She decided to sell the property and to move into town. I suppose it was inevitable that Minan and I should dream of buying the Bisbee farm, which could provide the country home we were looking for, as well as a means of livelihood and of following the career I had chosen for myself. Mrs. Bisbee was encouraging of our aspirations, and she offered us liberal terms. Nevertheless, the raising of the necessary money from our local banks was difficult and discouraging. In the end, we succeeded only because my Dartmouth mentor, Professor Nash, lent me the sum of our down payment. Thus, after my graduation from college, in June of 1950, we headed back north to a new life as proprietors of the Bisbee Press and as householders on the upper reaches of the Connecticut River, in Vermont's Northeast Kingdom.

* * *

THE EVOLUTION of the name of the Press needs, perhaps, some explanation. I had, while still working in the Graphic Arts Workshop at Dartmouth, decided to call the press that I was about to establish at Lunenburg the "North Country Press." My plan was to continue using the Bisbee name for the job-work part of the business, while at the same time looking for the customers and the means to produce, as the North Country Press, the kind of printing I really wanted to do. I anticipated that gradually, as things progressed, the North Country Press imprint and activity would dominate. However, a serious hitch in this projection developed in 1953, with the arrival of a registered letter from a law firm on the other side of the state. I then learned of another North Country Press, long established at Essex Junction, Vermont, and of its objection to my now presuming to trade on its name and good reputation. The North Country Press of Lunenburg died abruptly at that point, and "The Stinehour Press" came into being in its place, continuing for nearly thirty years to be the name of our business. Then, in 1977 The Stinehour Press and The Meriden Gravure Company of Meriden, Connecticut, merged to form a single corporation, but both continued to do business under their individual names for several years. Late in 1979 the imprint Meriden-Stinehour Inc. first appeared, and by 1980 the designation Meriden-Stinehour Press came into being.

*   *   *

THE GROWTH and development of The Stinehour Press has, as I have always gratefully acknowledged, reflected the character, personality, and commitment of the people associated with it. Both by dint of effort and good fortune I have been allied with some extraordinary collaborators over the years. First and foremost, my lovely wife and chief associate

Elizabeth Stinehour

She has always supplied the greatest support and encouragement. Also, I have had as a steadfast, sympathetic, and supportive co-worker, my brother

Laurence Stinehour

He was the first employee of the Press, and he continues to be committed to the ideals of its establishment. Another associate from the earliest days who has significantly contributed to the course and direction of the Press is

Freeman Keith

a highly valued colleague who has become, as well, an indispensable friend. These three are members of the "founding group"—employees of the first five years—who by their skills, dedication, and intelligence gave purpose and direction to the fledgling Press, and who to this day influence the way it functions. Other members of that group are

> Harwood Wentzell
> Carrie Haley
> Evelyn Smith
> Sinclair Hitchings

For these earliest fellow workers, as well as for those who subsequently joined the endeavor, I have the most profound respect and admiration. Their contributions are tangibly embodied in the works enumerated in this Checklist.—"By the work one knows the workmen."—It is with gratitude for their efforts and accomplishments that I record here the following names:

David Anderson	David Benson	Werner Brudi
Floyd Arnold	Sally Benson	William Burton
Dana Arsenault	Douglas Biow	Paul Cargill
Joyce Arsenault	Michael Blake	Elizabeth Chase
Michael Arsenault	Genese Blanchette	Linda Cloutier
Rene Arsenault	Harold Bockus	Martha Cobbs
Steven Arsenault	Ann Stinehour Bottoms	Doreen Cooper
Thomas Arsenault	Herve Bouchard	Edward Coxey
Dana Atchley	Peter Bougie	Calvin Crawford
Constance Bacher	Louise Boyle	Vincent Currier
Roland Baird	Kenneth Brisson	Roger Daigle
Philip Barra	Ashley Broberg	Joan Day
Warren Bean	Norman Brooks	Raymond Delcamp
Frank Bender	Harriette Brown	Donald Donahue

Jean Downing
Edward J. Driscoll
Edward L. Driscoll
Lana Duda
Aloysius Eastman
Peter Elliott
Walter Ellison
Marie Emde
Linda Ernest
James Flanagan
Robert Foote
Douglas Frizzell
Neil Frizzell
Chisholm Gentry
Mary Gilbert
Elmer Gilman
Elaine Ginger
Yves Girard
David Godine
Marie Laura Green
Virginia Green
Richard Grefe
Sally Griffin
Fred Haggett, Jr.
Linda Hall
James Hamilton
Evan Hammond
Peter Haraty
Diane Harpell
Howard Harris
Harold Hartshorn
Stephen Harvard
Marla Hazen
Josiah Hill
Edward Hinchliffe
Mae Hinckley

Grace Hinkley
Phyllis Hodgdon
Paul Hoffmann
Glenn Hogan
Mary Holcomb
Katy Homans
James Houle
Florence Howard
Julia Peacock Howe
Lynda Howells
Darrell Hyder
Joseph Jackson
Fay Jennings
Cameron Keith
Christopher Keith
Cynthia Keith
Margaret Keith
Neil Kelley
Jeanette Kenney
Patricia Kenney
James Keough
Michael Kip
Lydia Koppang
Owen Koppang
Ralph Kyper
Marilyn Carr LaCroix
Marjorie LaValley
Beatrice Lewis
Paul Lewis
Richard Lynch
Gertrude LeClere
Suzanne Maes
Muriel Mahn
Leonard Malenowski
William McClaughry
Marcus McCorison, Jr.

John McCormack
Robert McCoy
Edith McKeon
David McLean
Sarah McMann
Robert Marchewka
John Melanson
Bruce Michel
Mitchell Moody
Susan Moody
Chester Moulton
Lucille Moulton
Harry Mueller
John Nash
Erik Nilsen
Daniel Olmstead
Derek O'Malley-Keyes
Margaret Stinehour
  O'Malley-Keyes
Werner Pfeiffer
Hester Phelps
Marilyn Pond
Nila Powers
Susan Powers
William Powers, Jr.
Kari Prager
Georgia Pugh
Jonathan Quay
Alan Rich
David Ritscher
Donald Riff
William Robarts
Janice Haley Ronish
Donald Sanborn
Patricia Sanborn
Willis Silver

Darlene Sterling	Stephen Stinehour	Elizabeth Weistrop
Tom Stevelt	William Stinehour	Larry Welch
Ann Stewart	Chester Stockwell	Freda Wentzell
Dwight Stiles	Evelyn Stolhandske	Susan Wentzell
Craig Stinehour	Stephen Thomas	Timothy Wentzell
Christopher Stinehour	Wayne Thompson	Carol Wheelock
John Stinehour	Thomas Thomson	Eleanor White
Katherine Stinehour	Timothy Towle	Rosemary White
Mary Stinehour	Stephen Tucker	Edna Whyte
Maxwell Stinehour	Amy Turner	Jeffrey Wortman
Patricia Stinehour	W. de Groot	Peter Yeamans
Patrick Stinehour	van Embden	Beth Young
Peter Stinehour	Wendy Watson	Judith Young
Phyllis Stinehour	Alfons Weidacher	Edward Zaremba, Jr.

From the time of its incorporation, in 1957, and onward through the rest of its first thirty years, the Press was also served, as members of its Board of Directors, by Ray Nash, Harold Hugo, and Edward Lathem. First becoming part of my life during undergraduate days at Dartmouth College, these three men, as close friends and confidants, were essential to the growth and direction of the Press.

*   *   *

HAEC OLIM MEMINISSE JUVABIT

is the motto of the Press. The source is Virgil, and roughly translated it says, "In time to come you will enjoy recalling these things." This book is the record of the work of three decades—the foundation for the decades ahead. For some of us the perusal of this list will recall old friends and former days; for others it may entail useful discovery.

RODERICK STINEHOUR

COMPILER'S NOTE

THIS CHECKLIST describes 1,006 publications printed at The Stinehour Press from 1950 through 1979. Included in separate appendices are 64 serial titles, of which at least one issue was printed at the Press during this period, and a compilation of "Writings Related to The Stinehour Press." The coverage of the publication and serial listings is intended to be comprehensive, within limits described below, but the section of "Writings . . ." is very likely incomplete, as it records only those items collected in the files of the Press at Lunenburg or preserved within its archives at the Dartmouth College Library.

The elements of the bibliographic descriptions are these: Title / Author, editor, compiler, illustrator / Place of publication / Publisher / Publication date / Special information concerning the item's text or format / Notes, including format dimensions, pagination, presence of illustrations or a bibliography; number of copies; method of affixing signatures to the case; material and color of the cover; and finally the Stinehour "job number," where available, in parentheses (a number useful for investigation in the Press archives, where production materials are filed by it).

The bibliographic descriptions of serial titles, being simpler in nature, will be found to be self-explanatory. Several publications issued only occasionally, as well as certain serials, have been excluded if they were recurring publications of institutions represented by other more significant items in the checklist. In this category are bulletins and catalogs of Dartmouth College, for example, and book-dealers' catalogs. Publications for which Stinehour provided merely captions or set only small amounts of type are also excluded, as are most personal and ephemeral publications, such as social invitations or programs for memorial services and, of course, stationery, order forms, and other business materials.

In some cases, titles for items have been abbreviated for clarity. No attempt has been made to record precise title-page transcriptions or to describe printing types, ink colors, the kind or quality of the paper, or the ornamentation. Whenever possible, information for the checklist's descriptive entries was obtained from the publications themselves, and all but two or three items have been personally examined by the compiler. Information derived from any other source has been set off in square brackets.

I believe it should be recorded that I first became interested in The Stinehour Press when, as Curator of Rare Book and Map Collections at the University of Kentucky, I was responsible for managing and developing collections of modern press books. Later I studied printing by hand with Carolyn Hammer and Gabriel Rummonds and, when Mrs. Hammer retired, became Co-Director of the King Library Press. One of our programs brought to the Library numbers of distinguished designers and printers. It was during one of those seminars, in discussion with Stephen Harvard, that I became aware that a bibliography of The Stinehour Press was long overdue. With assistance from the University of Kentucky, Indiana University, and The Stinehour Press I was able to complete the checklist now published herein.

DAVID FARRELL

Bloomington, Indiana
October 1986

AN ILLUSTRATED
BIBLIOGRAPHICAL
CHECKLIST

CHECKLIST

[1950]

1

THOREAU MCDONALD'S DRAWINGS FOR DARTMOUTH. With notes by Ray Nash. Lunenburg, Vt., North Country Press, 1950.

Printed by Roderick D. Stinehour at the Graphic Arts Workshop, Dartmouth College, May 1950.

$4\frac{3}{4} \times 3\frac{3}{4}$ inches; [16] pages including 5 pages with illustrations on Japanese tissue tipped in.
200 copies; untrimmed; handsewn into light brown paper cover.

[1952]

2

NOTES ON PRINTING AND GRAPHIC ARTS. Lunenburg, Vt., North Country Press, 1952.

9×6 inches; unpaged; folder. Unbound.

3

THE WATERVILLE VALLEY: A STORY OF A RESORT IN THE NEW HAMPSHIRE MOUNTAINS. By Nathaniel L. Goodrich. Lunenburg, Vt., The North Country Press, 1952.

$9\frac{1}{4} \times 6\frac{1}{4}$ inches; xiii+77+[8] pages of plates; decorated endleaves. 600 copies bound in blue paper and blue quarter cloth over boards; gold-stamped spine.

4

AN ADDRESS BY DANIEL WEBSTER BEFORE THE FACULTY
AND STUDENTS OF DARTMOUTH COLLEGE ON JULY 21,
1828. Hanover, N.H., Dartmouth College Library, Division
of Special Collections, Archives Department, 1953.

7¾×5¼ inches; 10 pages.
500 copies handsewn into decorated green paper cover.

5

BAKER MEMORIAL LIBRARY, 1928–1953. Hanover, N.H.,
Dartmouth College, [1953].

Cover title.
7¼×5½ inches; [4] pages; single folded leaf.
2,000 copies; unbound.

6

DARTMOUTH MOUNTAINEERING CLUB: JOURNAL, 1953.
[Hanover, N.H.], 1953.

9¼×6¼ inches; 39 pages (lacks pages 1–2); illustrated.
Saddlewire stitched into printed yellow paper cover.

7

DON'T JOIN THE BOOK BURNERS. By Dwight David Eisenhower. [Hanover, N.H., Dartmouth College, 1953.]

Excerpt from the remarks of the President of the United States at the
Dartmouth College Commencement on 14 June 1953.
15×11¾ inches; broadside.
2,000 copies; untrimmed; unbound.

8

FOUR ADDRESSES BY JOHN SLOAN DICKEY. Hanover,
N.H., Dartmouth College, [1953].

9½×6 inches; 30 pages.
Saddlewire stitched into gray paper cover.

9

FRANKLIN PIERCE OF NEW HAMPSHIRE BECOMES 14TH PRESIDENT OF THE UNITED STATES. Bethlehem, N.H., The Lloyd Hills Press . . . for the State of New Hampshire Recreation Division, [1953].

7¼×4¾ inches; 12 pages; portrait.
Saddlewire stitched into printed gray and white paper cover.

10

ON GOING TO LIVE IN NEW HAMPSHIRE. By Paul Scott Mowrer. Lancaster, N.H., Printed by the Bisbee Press for Wake-Brook House, 1953.

8¾×5¾ inches; 109 pages.
Printed yellow cloth and red quarter cloth over boards; labels pasted on on cover and spine.

[1954]

11

ANCIENT ART IN AMERICAN PRIVATE COLLECTIONS. Cambridge, Mass., Fogg Art Museum of Harvard University, 1954.

10½×7½ inches; 43 pages + 100 pages of plates numbered 1 to XCIX [*sic*] + [3] pages.
500 copies Smythsewn and glued into printed light brown paper cover.

12

A BESTIARY BY TOULOUSE-LAUTREC. Foreword by Philip Hofer. Chicago, Ill., The Art Institute of Chicago and the Department of Printing and Graphic Arts, Harvard Library, 1954 (Fogg Museum Picture Book Number 3).

7¾×5¼ inches; 46+[1] pages including 18 pages of plates; portrait.
Smythsewn and glued into printed green paper cover.

13

COUNTRY LIFE IN ANCIENT EGYPT. [By William Stevenson Smith.] Boston, Mass., Museum of Fine Arts, [1954] (Museum of Fine Arts Picture Book Number 2).

$8\frac{1}{2} \times 5\frac{1}{2}$ inches; [32] pages including 28 pages of plates.
Saddlewire stitched into printed brown paper cover.

14

A DRAWING BOOK ALPHABET. By Edward Lear. Cambridge, Mass., The Harvard College Library, 1954.

$8\frac{1}{2} \times 5\frac{1}{2}$ inches; 16 pages; facsimile.
Saddlewire stitched into printed blue paper cover.

15

THE HUNTERS; OR THE SUFFERINGS OF HUGH AND FRANCIS, IN THE WILDERNESS. A TRUE STORY. [Introduction by Richard W. Morin.] Lunenburg, Vt., The Stinehour Press, 1954.

$5\frac{3}{4} \times 3\frac{3}{4}$ inches; 45 pages numbered [i] to xvi+17 to 45; illustrated.
100 copies bound in blue paper and quarter cloth over boards; goldstamped spine; wrapper.

16

AN ILLUSTRATION BY WILLIAM BLAKE FOR THE "CIRCLE OF THE TRAITORS" [from] DANTE'S INFERNO, CANTO XXXII. A monograph by Philip Hofer. Meriden, Conn., Meriden Gravure Company, 1954.

$9\frac{1}{4} \times 12\frac{1}{4}$ inches; [12] pages including 3 leaves of plates numbered I to III.
400 copies handsewn into printed red paper cover.

17

MR. EMERSON WRITES A LETTER ABOUT WALDEN. Edited with brief notes by Herbert Faulkner West. Hanover,

N.H., The Thoreau Society and the Friends of the Dartmouth Library, 1954.

9 ×6 inches; [20] pages; facsimile.
1,000 copies handsewn into brown paper cover.

18

THE RENAISSANCE SOCIETY OF AMERICA: DIRECTORY OF FOUNDER MEMBERS. New York, N.Y., Renaissance Society of America, 1954.

Cover title.
9¼ ×6 inches; [2]+17 pages.
2,000 copies saddlewire stitched into white paper cover.

19

VOX HUMANA. By Johannes Alexander Gaertner. Lunenburgiae Vermontensium, Prelum Typographicum Stinehourianum, 1954.

7¼ ×4¾ inches; [4]+xxviii pages.
Light green paper and quarter leather over boards; gold-stamped spine.
Also issued in light brown paper cover over boards.

[1955]

20

AMERICAN MARINE PAINTINGS. Boston, Mass., Museum of Fine Arts, 1955 (Picture Book Number 7).

5½ ×8½ inches; [4] pages + 29 pages of plates.
Saddlewire stitched into printed blue and white paper cover.

21

A BIBLIOGRAPHY OF FATHER RICHARD'S PRESS IN DETROIT. By A. H. Greenly. Ann Arbor, Mich., William L. Clements Library, 1955.

10 ×6½ inches; x+48 pages; illustrated.
750 copies bound in decorated paper and blue quarter cloth over boards; gold-stamped spine.

22

BOOK OF LYRICS. By Witter Bynner, New York, N.Y., Alfred A. Knopf, 1955.

First edition.
8¾×5½ inches; [14]+125 pages.
1,750 copies bound in yellow paper and gray quarter cloth over boards; blind-stamped cover; wrapper.

23

A CHRISTMAS NUMBER OF THE BEN BUCKHURST CHRONICLE, 1865. [New York, N.Y., Privately printed], Christmas 1955.

Cover title; "With best wishes . . . [from] George Arents."
11¾×7¾ inches; [12] pages; facsimile.
350 copies saddlewire stitched and handsewn into printed white paper cover.

24

DARTMOUTH 1840–1845. A Reminiscence by Samuel Hopkins Willey. [Hanover, N.H.], Archives Department, Dartmouth College Library, 1955.

7¾×5 inches; [4]+15 pages.
1,000 copies handsewn into blue paper cover.

25

THE FIFTY BEST HISTORIC AMERICAN HOUSES. By Ralph E. Carpenter, Jr. New York, N.Y., E. P. Dutton and Co. (A Mowbra Hall Press Book), 1955.

8½×5½ inches; 112 pages; illustrated.
Red cloth over boards; gold-stamped cover and spine; wrapper.

26

THE HAPPY HYPOCRITE: A FAIRY TALE FOR TIRED MEN. By Max Beerbohm. New Fairfield, Conn., Bruce Rogers October House, 1955.

Designed by Bruce Rogers.
7¾×4¾ inches; 81 pages.

600 copies bound in printed violet paper and violet quarter cloth over boards; gold-stamped spine.

27

MARTIN J. HEADE, 1819–1904, AS REPRESENTED IN THE M. AND M. KAROLIK COLLECTION OF AMERICAN PAINTING, 1815–1865. Prepared by Richard B. K. McLanathan. Boston, Mass., Museum of Fine Arts, 1955 (Picture Book Number 5).

$5\frac{1}{2} \times 8\frac{1}{2}$ inches; [32] pages including 26 pages of plates. Saddlewire stitched into light green paper cover.

28

MODERN PRINTS. Selected by Peter A. Wick. [Boston, Mass.], Museum of Fine Arts, 1955 (Picture Book Number 4).

$8\frac{1}{2} \times 5\frac{1}{2}$ inches; [32] pages including 29 pages of plates; illustrated. Saddlewire stitched into printed yellow paper cover.

29

NEW HAMPSHIRE. A poem by Robert Frost. Illustrated with a woodcut by J. J. Lankes. Hanover, N.H., New Dresden Press, 1955.

First separate edition of the poem.
$7\frac{1}{2} \times 5\frac{1}{4}$ inches; [4]+19 pages.
750 copies printed on untrimmed Arches paper, numbered and signed, and bound in brown paper and light brown quarter cloth over boards; gold-stamped cover and label on spine. Issued with 2,000 copies of a prospectus ($7\frac{1}{2} \times 5\frac{1}{4}$ inches printed on [6] pages of untrimmed Arches paper, illustrated with Lankes' woodcut) sewn into a brown paper folder.

30

THE NOBLER RISK AND OTHER SERMONS OF AMBROSE WHITE VERNON. Selected and edited by Roy B. Chamberlin. Hanover, N.H., Dartmouth Publications, 1955.

$9\frac{1}{2} \times 6\frac{1}{4}$ inches; xvii+148 pages; frontispiece portrait.
500 copies bound in red cloth over boards; gold-stamped cover and spine.

31

QUEEN TOMYRIS AND THE HEAD OF CYRUS: PETER PAUL
RUBENS. Prepared by Richard B. K. McLanathan. Boston,
Mass., The Museum of Fine Arts, 1955 (Picture Book No. 6).

8½×5½ inches; [3] pages + 12 pages of plates.
Saddlewire stitched into printed paper cover.

32

WHAT'S IN A NAME. By Charles L. Youmans. Illustrated
by Claude L. Brusseau. Lancaster, N.H., The Bisbee Press,
1955.

7¾×5 inches; xi+79 pages.
500 copies bound in blue cloth over boards; gold-stamped spine.

⌈1956⌉

33

ANCIENT COINS. Cambridge, Mass., Fogg Art Museum of
Harvard University, 1956 (Fogg Picture Book Number 4).

5¼×7¾ inches; [40] pages; illustrated.
Smythsewn and glued into printed black paper cover.

34

ANIMALS IN PAINTINGS FROM ASIA. Prepared by Robert
Treat Paine, Jr. Boston, Mass., Museum of Fine Arts, 1956
(Picture Book Number 9).

8½×5½ inches; 32 pages including 28 pages of plates.
Saddlewire stitched into printed red and gold paper cover.

35

THE ART OF BEN SHAHN. Cambridge, Mass., Fogg Art
Museum, Harvard University, 1956.

5×7½ inches; [12] pages.
1,000 copies saddlewire stitched; self-covered.

36

DRAWINGS AND OIL SKETCHES BY P. P. RUBENS FROM
AMERICAN COLLECTIONS. [Introduction by Agnes Mongan.] Cambridge, Mass., Fogg Art Museum, Harvard University; New York, N.Y., The Pierpont Morgan Library,
1956.

11 ×8¼ inches; 42 pages + 32 pages of plates numbered 1 to XXXII.
Smythsewn and glued into light blue paper cover.

37

THE ELIOT CHURCH OF NEWTON: ITS HOUSES OF WOR-
SHIP 1845–1956. By Arthur Hardy Lord. Newton, Mass.,
The Eliot Church of Newton, 1956.

7¾×5 inches; 38 pages; illustrated.
600 copies saddlewire stitched into blue paper cover.

38

FITZ HUGH LANE. Prepared by Richard B. K. McLanathan. Boston, Mass., Museum of Fine Arts, 1956 (Picture
Book Number 8).

5½×8½ inches; [32] pages including 23 pages of plates.
Saddlewire stitched into printed white paper cover.

39

LECTURES ON MOTOR ANOMALIES. By A. Bielschowsky,
M.D. With a foreword by Walter B. Lancaster, M.D.
Hanover, N.H., Dartmouth Publications, 1956.

9¼×6¼ inches; 186 pages; illustrated.
1,000 copies Smythsewn and glued into light yellow paper cover.

40

LOWELL HOUSE AFTER TWENTY-FIVE YEARS. Cambridge, Mass., Privately printed for the Senior Common
Room, 1956.

9¼×6 inches; 23 pages; illustrated.
100 copies handsewn into printed green paper cover.

41

THE NEW-ENGLAND COURANT: A SELECTION OF CER-
TAIN ISSUES CONTAINING WRITINGS OF BENJAMIN FRANK-
LIN . . . IN HONOR OF THE 250TH ANNIVERSARY OF HIS
BIRTH. Introduction by Perry Miller. Boston, Mass., The
American Academy of Arts and Sciences, 1956.

12½×9 inches; 9 pages + [134] pages of facsimile.
500 copies bound in dark blue cloth over boards; gold-stamped cover
and spine.

42

PAUL REVERE, GOLDSMITH (1735–1818). By Kathryn
C. Buhler. Edited by Richard B. K. McLanathan. Boston,
Mass., Museum of Fine Arts, 1956.

11 ×8½ inches; [48] pages including 38 pages of plates.
Smythsewn and glued into printed cream paper cover.

43

PERRAULT'S TALES OF MOTHER GOOSE. Introduction
and critical text by Jacques Barchilon. New York, N.Y., The
Pierpont Morgan Library, 1956.

Includes the "dedication manuscript of 1695" in facsimile.
8¾×6¼ inches; Vol. I: Text, 162 pages; illustrated. Vol. II: Facsimile,
124 pages.
600 numbered sets bound in decorated paper and light brown quarter
cloth over boards; gold-stamped spine; together in a slipcase. Copies 1
to 250 colored by hand in pochoir by the Maria Bittner Studio.

44

THE RAVEN. A poem by Edgar Allan Poe. With illustrations by Edouard Manet. Prepared by Anne Blake Freedberg. Boston, Mass., Museum of Fine Arts, 1956 (Picture
Book Number 10).

8½×5½ inches; [16] pages including 4 pages of plates; facsimile.
Saddlewire stitched into printed white paper cover.

45

SARGENT'S BOSTON. With an essay and a biographical summary and a complete checklist of Sargent's portraits. By David McKibbin. Boston, Mass., Museum of Fine Arts, 1956.

10¼×7¼ inches; 132+[4] pages including 3 pages of colored plates. Green linen cloth over boards; gold-stamped cover and spine. Also issued Smythsewn and glued into printed paper cover.

46

SCENES FROM THE BIBLE DRAWN BY ROBERT CRUIKSHANK. [New York, N.Y., Privately printed], Christmas 1956.

Cover title; "with best wishes . . . from George Arents."
9×12 inches; [18] pages including 6 pages of plates.
325 copies saddlewire stitched and handsewn into printed green paper cover.

47

THE STYVESANT STAIRCASE, AYRAULT HOUSE, NEWPORT. [Newport, R.I.], Privately printed, 1956.

8¾×6¼ inches; 12+[2] pages; illustrated.
150 copies printed on untrimmed paper; handsewn into brown paper cover.

48

A VISIT TO ROME IN 1764. [Introduction by Philip Hofer.] Cambridge, Mass., Fogg Art Museum and Harvard College Library, 1956 (Fogg Museum Picture Book Number 5).

7½×5¼ inches; 13+[19] pages including 16 pages of plates; facsimile. Smythsewn and glued into printed white paper cover.

[1957]

49

DAY AND NIGHT IN THE FOUR SEASONS: SKETCHES BY

HOKUSAI, 1760–1849. Prepared by Kojiro Tomita. Boston, Mass., Museum of Fine Arts, 1957 (Picture Book Number 14).

8½×11 inches; [32] pages including 24 pages of plates.
Saddlewire stitched into printed cream paper cover.

50

THE GREAT STONE FACE. By Nathaniel Hawthorne. With a foreword by Stearns Morse. Drawings by John Nash. Lunenburg, Vt., The Stinehour Press, 1957.

7½×5¼ inches; xi+34 pages; illustrated.
Smythsewn and glued into white paper cover; wrapper.

51

THE HANOVER SCENE. By William H. McCarter. Drawings by John R. Nash. Hanover, N.H., Dartmouth Publications, 1957.

9½×6 inches; 96 pages; illustrated.
Printed gray paper and green quarter cloth over boards.

52

A HISTORY OF MILTON. By Edward Pierce Hamilton. Milton, Mass., Milton Historical Society, 1957.

10¼×7¼ inches; xv+275+[3] pages + [25] leaves of plates; maps.
1,200 copies bound in green cloth over boards; gold-stamped cover and spine.

53

JOHN HOWARD BENSON AND HIS WORK, 1901–1956. By Philip Hofer, with a preface by Lawrence C. Wroth and an introduction by Rudolph Ruzicka. New York, N.Y., The Typophiles, 1957 (Typophile Chap Book Number 31).

Designed by Rudolph Ruzicka.
7×4¾ inches; x+[2]+56+[2] pages; illustrated.
625 copies bound in printed paper and quarter cloth over boards; gold-stamped spine.

54

JOURNEY OF A JOHNNY-COME-LATELY. By David Bradley. Hanover, N.H., Dartmouth Publications, 1957.

9½ ×6¼ inches; xv+213+[3] pages; frontispiece.
Green cloth over boards; gold-stamped cover and spine.

55

MODERN PAINTING, DRAWING, AND SCULPTURE COL-LECTED BY LOUISE AND JOSEPH PULITZER, JR. Catalogue by Charles Scott Chetham. Cambridge, Mass., Fogg Art Museum, 1957.

Also issued as a catalogue published by Knoedler and Co., New York, and the Fogg Art Museum.
[Vol. I]: 11 ×8¼ inches; 172 pages including plates numbered 1 to 64.
1,500 copies Smythsewn and glued into printed white paper cover; together with Vol. II in a red paper–covered box; label on spine (see item 84).

56

MOUNT VERNON SILVER. By Kathryn C. Buhler. Mt. Vernon, Va., The Mount Vernon Ladies' Association of the Union, 1957.

8½ ×5½ inches; 75 pages; illustrated.
Smythsewn and glued into blue paper cover; silver-stamped cover and spine.

57

ON COLLECTING. By C[urtis] O B[aer]. [Lunenburg, Vt., Privately printed, 1957.]

Cover title.
9 ×6 inches; 11 pages.
Saddlewire stitched into white paper cover.

58

PICASSO: GRAPHIC ART. Cambridge, Mass., The Fogg Art Museum, Harvard University, 1957.

Issued separately by The Art Institute of Chicago.

$7\frac{3}{4}\times5\frac{1}{4}$ inches; [32] pages including 28 pages of plates numbered 1 to 28.
Smythsewn and glued into printed blue paper cover.

59

THE RELIC AND OTHER POEMS. By Robert Hillyer. New York, N.Y., Alfred A. Knopf, 1957.

Title page wood engraving by Leonard Baskin.
$8\frac{1}{2}\times5\frac{3}{4}$ inches; [14]+93+[3] pages.
Smythsewn and glued into maroon cloth over boards; blind-stamped cover and gold-stamped spine; blue wrapper.

60

SHIP MODELS. By Richard B. K. McLanathan. Boston, Mass., Museum of Fine Arts, 1957.

Cover design by Carl Zahn.
$11\times8\frac{1}{2}$ inches; [48] pages including 39 pages of plates.
Smythsewn and glued into printed blue paper cover.

61

THE SPEE CLUB OF HARVARD. [Cambridge, Mass., The Spee Club], 1957.

$9\frac{1}{4}\times6\frac{1}{4}$ inches; 63 pages.
500 copies bound in red cloth over boards; blind-stamped cover and gold-stamped spine.

62

THE STINEHOUR PRESS: NOTES ON ITS FIRST FIVE YEARS. By Sinclair Hitchings. With a selective list of printing, a gathering of sample pages, and drawings by John R. Nash. Lunenburg, Vt., The Stinehour Press, 1957.

9×6 inches; 47 pages + [6] leaves from Stinehour Press imprints tipped in; illustrated.
Smythsewn and glued into light orange paper cover.

63

TEN DAYS JOURNAL. By Sinclair Hitchings. Drawings by John Nash. Hanover, N.H., [Privately printed], Christmas 1957.

"Smugglers' Notch to Sherburne Pass, July 23 to August 4, 1956, on the Long Trail."
9×6 inches; [2]+28+[1] pages.
Handsewn into green paper cover and glued into printed green wrapper.

64

THOREAU AND THE WILD APPETITE. By Kenneth Allen Robinson. Wood engravings by J. J. Lankes. Hanover, N.H., Westholm Publications, 1957.

Also appeared in an edition published by the Thoreau Society and Friends of the Dartmouth College Library (title page varies) in 1957.
9½×6¼ inches; 29+[3] pages.
150 copies signed by the author; bound in printed paper and black quarter cloth over boards.

65

A TRIBUTE TO WILLIAM EMERSON. [Lunenburg, Vt., Privately printed, 1957.]

10¼×7½ inches; [32] pages including 6 pages of plates; colored frontispiece portrait.
750 copies bound in brown-gray paper over boards; gold-stamped cover and spine; acetate wrapper.

66

WALTHAM INDUSTRIES: A COLLECTION OF EARLY FIRMS AND FOUNDERS. By Edmund L. Sanderson. Waltham, Mass., Published by the Waltham Historical Society, Inc., in cooperation with the Waltham Chamber of Commerce, 1957 (Waltham Historical Society Publication Number 6).

9¼×6¼ inches; xiii+164 pages + [13] leaves of plates.
750 copies bound in green cloth over boards; gold-stamped spine.

67

WILLIAM BULMER AND THE SHAKESPEARE PRESS: A BI-
OGRAPHY OF WILLIAM BULMER FROM A DICTIONARY
OF PRINTERS AND PRINTING BY C. H. TIMPERLEY,
LONDON, 1839. With an Introductory Note on the Bulmer-
Martin Types by Laurance B. Seigfried. Original wood
engravings by John De Pol. Syracuse, N.Y., Syracuse Uni-
versity Press, 1957.

Designed by Harvey Satenstein.
7¼×4¾ inches; [4]+34+[2] pages; frontispiece portrait.
Black cloth over boards; gold-stamped spine and label pasted on cover;
printed acetate wrapper.

[1958]

68

AMERICAN SILVER IN THE HENRY FRANCIS DU PONT
WINTERTHUR MUSEUM. By Martha Gandy Fales, with
photographs by Gilbert Ask. [Winterthur], Del., Winterthur
Museum, 1958.

11¼×8¾ inches; [29] leaves; illustrated.
Red cloth over boards; gold-stamped cover and spine.

69

ANNUAL MEETING OF THE GARDEN CLUB OF AMERICA.
York, Me., 1958.

8½×5½ inches; 48 pages numbered 3 to 45; illustrated; maps.
Smythsewn and glued into printed white paper cover.

70

THE BUILDING OF THE TVA: AN ILLUSTRATED HISTORY.
By John H. Kyle. Baton Rouge, La., Louisiana State
University Press, 1958.

10¼×7¼ inches; x+[4]+162 pages; illustrated.
Red-brown cloth over boards; blind-stamped cover; wrapper.

71

CARL O. SCHNIEWIND, 1900–1957. Commemorative
Address by Frederick B. Adams, Jr. Chicago, Ill., The
Art Institute of Chicago, 1958.

Catalogue of the Carl O. Schniewind Memorial Exhibition of Prints
and Drawings. Designed by Suzette M. Zurcher.
8¾×6½ inches; [38] pages including 17 pages of plates; frontispiece
portrait.
1,000 copies Smythsewn and glued into brown and white paper cover.

72

THE CHURCH OF THE HOLY TRINITY. Jefferson, N.H.,
The Church of the Holy Trinity, [1958].

Cover title.
7½×5 inches; 11 pages; illustrated.
Saddlewire stitched into printed gray paper cover.

73

COCKTAIL PARTIES MADE EASY. By Mary Dodge Silk.
Whitefield, N.H., [Privately printed], 1958.

6×9 inches; 42+[2] pages; illustrated.
Plastic spiral bound in printed white paper cover.

74

THE DARK HOUSES. By Donald Hall. New York, N.Y.,
The Viking Press, 1958.

8½×5¾ inches; 63 pages.
Printed white paper and black quarter cloth over boards; silver-stamped
spine; wrapper.

75

DEDICATION EXERCISES: BISSELL HALL; BROWN HALL;
COHEN HALL; LITTLE HALL. Hanover, N.H., Dartmouth
College, 1958.

Cover title.
9×4¾ inches; [18] pages including 1 plate.
Saddlewire stitched into untrimmed paper cover.

76

DOCTOR WELLS OF VERMONT. By Donald Bartlett.
Hanover, N.H., Dartmouth Publications, 1958.

9 × 6 inches; 16 pages.
Saddlewire stitched into printed brown paper cover.

77

DRAWINGS FROM THE COLLECTION OF CURTIS O. BAER.
Cambridge, Mass., The Fogg Art Museum, 1958.

9 × 6 inches; 75+[1] pages + [48] pages of plates numbered 1 to 61.
Smythsewn and glued into printed brown paper cover.

78

EARLY NEW ENGLAND SILVER LENT FROM THE MARK
BORTMAN COLLECTION. Northampton, Mass., Smith
College Museum of Art, 1958.

9¼ × 6 inches; 23+[1] pages including 4 pages of plates.
Saddlewire stitched into printed blue paper cover.

79

EARLY OWNERS OF THE PARSON BARNARD HOUSE AND
THEIR TIMES. By Horatio Rogers, M.D. North Andover,
Mass., North Andover Historical Society, 1958.

Cover title.
9 × 6 inches; 15+[1] pages; bibliography.
Saddlewire stitched into printed white paper cover.

80

A FEW PARAGRAPHS ON PRINTING IN VERMONT. . . . By
Rowland E. Robinson. Lunenburg, Vt., [The Stinehour
Press], Christmas 1958.

Excerpt from *Vermont: A Study of Independence* (1897).
6½ × 3¾ inches; [8] pages.
200 copies printed for friends of the Press; handsewn into printed blue
paper cover.

81

A HANDBOOK OF STYLE. [Preface by C. Freeman Keith.] Lunenburg, Vt., The Stinehour Press, [1958].

9×6 inches; 8 pages.
Saddlewire stitched without cover.

82

KOLLWITZ: CATALOGUE OF THE EXHIBITION AND COLLECTION OF THIRTY-FOUR PRINTS AND ONE DRAWING. With an essay by Leonard Baskin. Northampton, Mass., Smith College Museum of Art, 1958.

9¼×6 inches; 22 pages; illustrated; bibliography.
Saddlewire stitched into white paper cover; glassine wrapper.

83

A LETTER TO MY CHILDREN. By William G. Saltonstall. Lunenburg, Vt., Privately published, 1958.

9¼×6⅛ inches; 50 pages including [2] pages of plates.
Light blue paper and dark blue quarter cloth over boards; label pasted on cover; gold-stamped spine. Also issued handsewn into blue paper cover; label pasted on cover.

84

MODERN PAINTING, DRAWING, AND SCULPTURE COLLECTED BY LOUISE AND JOSEPH PULITZER, JR. Catalogue by Charles Scott Chetham et al. Cambridge, Mass., Fogg Art Museum, 1958.

Vol. II: 11×8¼ inches; 155 pages numbered [173] to 327 including plates numbered 65 to 128.
Smythsewn and glued into printed white paper cover; together with [Vol. I] in a red paper–covered box; label on spine. (See item 55.)

85

RANDALL JARRELL: A BIBLIOGRAPHY. Compiled by

Charles M. Adams. Chapel Hill, N.C., University of North Carolina Press, 1958.

9¼×6¼ inches; 72 pages.
Printed red paper and red quarter cloth over boards; gold-stamped spine and labels on cover.

86

A SELECTIVE BIBLIOGRAPHY OF IMPORTANT BOOKS, PAMPHLETS AND BROADSIDES RELATING TO MICHIGAN HISTORY. Bibliography and notes by Albert Harry Greenly. Lunenburg, Vt., The Stinehour Press, 1958.

10×6½ inches; xvii+165 pages + [26] pages of plates.
500 copies Smythsewn and glued into light brown buckram and dark brown quarter buckram over boards; gold-stamped spine.

87

75 AROMATIC YEARS OF LEAVITT AND PEIRCE IN THE RECOLLECTION OF 31 HARVARD MEN. Cambridge, Mass., Leavitt and Peirce, 1958.

9½×6¼ inches; 50 pages including 9 pages of photographs and facsimiles.
Saddlewire stitched and glued into light brown paper and quarter cloth over boards; gold-stamped spine. Also issued saddlewire stitched into printed light brown or light green paper cover. (56445)

88

SOME HISTORICAL ROMAN COINS FROM THE HENRY FAIRBANKS COLLECTION OF GREEK AND ROMAN COINS AT DARTMOUTH COLLEGE. By Edward Lee Terrace. Hanover, N.H., Dartmouth Publications, 1958.

9×6 inches; 44 pages + [4] pages of plates.
Saddlewire stitched into blue paper cover.

89

THIRTEEN DARTMOUTH POEMS. Selected [with a foreword] by Richard Eberhart. Hanover, N.H., The Charles Butcher Fund, 1958.

7¾×6¾ inches; [24] pages.
150 copies handsewn into printed blue paper cover.

90

TREASON OF THE BLACKEST DYE. Ann Arbor, [Mich.], The William L. Clements Library, 1958.

Letter from "Moore" [Benedict Arnold] to "Captain John Anderson" [Major André] dated 15 July 1780.
12 × 9 inches; 10 pages including 3 pages of facsimile.
700 copies printed for The Clements Library Associates; saddlewire stitched into printed black paper cover.

91

WILLIAM HENRY HUDSON'S DIARY CONCERNING HIS VOYAGE FROM BUENOS AIRES TO SOUTHAMPTON. With notes by Dr. Jorge Casares. Hanover, N.H., Westholm Publications, 1958.

7½ × 4¾ inches; 40 pages numbered [i] to ix, [10] to 34, [35 to 40]; frontispiece portrait.
250 copies printed on untrimmed handmade Amalfi paper; bound in orange cloth over boards; gold-stamped cover and spine.

92

WILLIAM HICKLING PRESCOTT, 1796–1859. [Washington, D.C., United States Information Service, 1958.]

"Una Exposición Preparada . . . por la Harvard University Press, la Escuela de Diseño de la Universidad de Harvard y la Massachusetts Historical Society."
7½ × 5¼ inches; [5] pages + [8] pages of plates.
Saddlewire stitched into gray paper cover.

[1959]

93

THE EPISCOPAL CHURCH AT HARVARD AND RADCLIFFE. [Cambridge, Mass., Privately printed, 1959.]

Cover title.
8¼ × 5½ inches; [8] pages; illustrated.
Saddlewire stitched into blue-gray paper cover.

94

Good Reading for Youth. Concord, N.H., New Hampshire State Library, 1959.

9×6 inches; 72 pages; illustrated.
Smythsewn and glued into printed white paper cover.

95

History of the Diocese of Massachusetts, 1810–1872. By Joseph Breed Berry. Boston, Mass., The Diocesan Library, 1959.

10×6½ inches; vi+[6]+252 pages; frontispiece portrait.
Red cloth over boards; gold-stamped cover and spine.

96

Lake Champlain and the Upper Hudson Valley. By Edward P. Hamilton. Ticonderoga, N.Y., Fort Ticonderoga Association, 1959.

9¼×6¼ inches; 47 pages; illustrated (some colored).
Printed paper over boards.

97

Louisiana State University: A Pictorial Record of the First Hundred Years. Edited by V. L. Bedsole and Oscar Richard. [Introduction by T. Harry Williams.] Baton Rouge, La., Louisiana State University Press, 1959.

Designed by Oscar Richard.
9½×7¼ inches; 112 pages.
Blue cloth over boards; gold-stamped cover and spine; wrapper.

98

Modigliani: Drawings from the Collection of Stefa and Leon Brillouin. [Introduction by Agnes Mongan.] Cambridge, Mass., Fogg Art Museum, 1959.

10×7¼ inches; 36 pages + 32 pages of plates.
Smythsewn and glued into printed light blue paper cover.

99

PAINTINGS FROM SMITH ALUMNAE COLLECTIONS. North-ampton, Mass., Smith College Museum of Art, 1959.

9×6 inches; 102+[6] pages including 45 pages of plates.
Smythsewn and glued into brown paper cover.

100

THIRTY DARTMOUTH POEMS. Selected by Richard Eberhart. Hanover, N.H., The Charles Butcher Fund, 1959.

9×6 inches; 39 pages.
150 copies handsewn into white paper cover and glued into gray paper wrapper.

101

YANKEE DOODLE. [By S. Foster Damon. Providence, R.I., Brown University], 1959.

Keepsake for the Annual Meeting of the Bibliographical Society of America.
12¼×8 inches; 12 pages; illustrated (facsimiles).
1,050 copies handsewn into printed cream paper cover.

[1960]

102

THE AMERICAN SCHOLAR PRINTER. By Ray Nash. [Lunenburg, Vt., The Stinehour Press], 1960.

"An oration delivered before the Harvard Chapter of Phi Beta Kappa in Sanders Theatre, Cambridge, 13 June 1960."
8½×6 inches; 16 pages.
Saddlewire stitched into white paper cover and glued into printed red wrapper.

103

APTHORP HOUSE, 1760–1960. By Wendell D. Garrett. Cambridge, Mass., Adams House, Harvard University, 1960.

9¼×6¼ inches; xviii+100 pages + [18] pages of plates.
Red cloth over boards; gold-stamped cover and spine; wrapper.

104

ART ACROSS AMERICA: AN EXHIBITION TO CELEBRATE THE OPENING OF A NEW BUILDING FOR THE MUSEUM OF ART. Utica, N.Y., Munson, Williams, Proctor Institute, 1960.

Designed by Leonard Baskin.
11×8½ inches; [168] pages numbered [i] to v and 9 to 21 including 38 pages of plates.
Smythsewn and glued into printed white paper cover.

105

THE BURYING PLACE OF GOVERNOR ARNOLD: AN ACCOUNT OF THE ESTABLISHMENT, DESTRUCTION, AND RESTORATION OF THE BURYING PLACE OF BENEDICT ARNOLD, FIRST GOVERNOR OF RHODE ISLAND AND PROVIDENCE PLANTATIONS. Newport, R.I., Privately printed, 1960.

10×6¾ inches; 135+[4] pages including 60 pages of plates; frontispiece portrait.
Smythsewn and glued into printed gray paper cover.

106

CANADIAN SILVERSMITHS AND THEIR MARKS, 1667–1867. By John Emerson Langdon. Lunenburg, Vt., Privately printed, 1960.

9½×6½ inches; xvi+190 pages; illustrated.
500 copies bound in gray-green cloth over boards; silver-stamped cover and spine.

107

DANIEL WEBSTER: THE NOBLEST EFFORT OF HIS CAREER. Edited by Edward Connery Lathem. Lunenburg, Vt., The Stinehour Press, 1960.

11¼×8¾ inches; [12] pages + [4] pages of holograph facsimile (9¾×8 inches) bound in.
150 copies printed on untrimmed paper; handsewn into printed light brown paper cover.

108

THE DARK ISLAND: TWENTY POEMS. By Gabrielle Ladd.
Lunenburg, Vt., [Privately printed], 1960.

$7\frac{3}{4} \times 5\frac{3}{4}$ inches; 32 pages.
Light blue paper over boards.

109

THE ERIE CANAL: THE STORY OF THE DIGGING OF
CLINTON'S DITCH. [By Walter D. Edmonds.] Utica,
N.Y., Munson, Williams, Proctor Institute and the
Oneida Historical Society, 1960.

$5\frac{3}{4} \times 8\frac{1}{2}$ inches; [20] pages.
Saddlewire stitched into printed white paper cover.

110

THE GLADES CONGRESS OR OPERATION VELLUM VALISE.
[Minot, Mass., Privately printed], 1960.

"A pictorial record, together with minutes of the proceedings and a list
of conspirators and hosts at a gathering in honor of Mr. and Mrs. Walter
Muir Whitehill at The Glades, Minot, Mass., 13 September 1958."
9×6 inches; [24] pages including 12 pages of photographs.
150 copies handsewn into white paper cover.

111

THE GOLDEN HOUSE OF NERO: SOME ASPECTS OF
ROMAN ARCHITECTURE. By Axel Boëthius. Ann Arbor,
Mich., The University of Michigan Press, 1960 (Jerome
Lectures, Fifth Series).

$11\frac{1}{4} \times 8\frac{1}{2}$ inches; [10]+195 pages; illustrated.
Black cloth over boards; gold-stamped spine; wrapper.

112

HELMUT SIBER'S PAINTINGS OF WEATHER. Lunenburg,
Vt., Printed at The Stinehour Press, [1960].

Cover title.
$9\frac{1}{4} \times 6\frac{1}{8}$ inches; [8] pages including 2 pages of plates.
Handsewn into printed green paper cover.

113

MEDICAL HISTORY, HUMANISM AND THE STUDENT OF MEDICINE. By Henry R. Viets, M.D. Hanover, N.H., Dartmouth Publications, 1960.

8¾×6 inches; 32 pages + [5] pages of photographs; portraits.
1,000 copies Smythsewn and glued into white paper cover; glued into green paper wrapper.

114

NEW POEMS, 1960. By Witter Bynner. New York, N.Y., Alfred A. Knopf, 1960.

First edition.
8¾×5½ inches; [14]+134+[6] pages.
1,750 numbered copies bound in black and white paper and white quarter cloth over boards; wrapper.

115

ON THE VIRTUES OF CYDER AND KINDRED TOPICS. By John Adams. [Lunenburg, Vt.], For the Glades Congress, June 1960.

Cover title.
5¾×4¼ inches; [12] pages.
Handsewn white paper signature; unbound.

116

THE STORY OF MOUNT WASHINGTON. Hanover, N.H., Dartmouth Publications, 1960.

9¾×6¼ inches; [12]+303 pages + [20] leaves of plates; map on end-leaves.
Green cloth over boards; gold-stamped cover and spine.

117

VIEWS FROM THE CIRCLE: SEVENTY-FIVE YEARS OF GROTON SCHOOL. Groton, Mass., Trustees of Groton School, 1960.

9½×6¼ inches; [vi]+387+[2] pages.
Maroon cloth over boards; stamped in black, gold, and white on cover and spine.

118

AMERICA'S FIRST CENTENNIAL CELEBRATION. By David B. Little. Boston, Mass., Club of Odd Volumes, 1961.

8¼×7¼ inches; 64 pages; illustrated.
150 copies bound in decorated paper and quarter leather over boards; gold-stamped spine. Also issued in paper cover.

119

AROUND THE WORLD IN 1912 AND 1913: DIARY OF MARGARET THOMAS. Boston, Mass., Privately printed, 1961.

11¼×8¾ inches; [4]+iii+74 pages + [40] pages of plates.
Orange and gold Japanese paper and white quarter cloth over boards.

120

THE CARTERS OF REDLANDS. By B. Noland Carter. Cincinnati, Ohio, Privately printed, 1961.

9½×6½ inches; 40 pages + [9] pages of plates.
Printed light green paper and dark green quarter cloth over boards; silver-stamped spine.

121

A CASE IN POINT: A REPORT OF THE THIRD ANNUAL CONFERENCE OF THE COMMISSION ON RESEARCH AND EXPERIMENTATION OF THE COUNCIL FOR THE ADVANCEMENT OF SMALL COLLEGES. Plainfield, Vt., [Published for the Commission], 1961.

Conference held at Malone College, Canton, Ohio, 9–15 July 1961.
8×6¼ inches; 42 pages.
Saddlewire stitched and glued into printed gray paper cover.

122

CONCISE CALENDER FOR YOUNG FARMERS AND GARDENERS. With wood engravings by John Melanson. Boston, Mass., [Privately printed], 1961.

"From Thomas's *Massachusetts, Connecticut, Rhode-Island, Newhampshire and Vermont Alamanack, . . . for the Year of our Lord 1793 . . .* [with] Best wishes for a merry Christmas and a happy new year from Sinclair Hitchings. . . ."

8½×5¾ inches; [16] pages.
Handsewn into brown paper cover; wrapper.

123

DR. JOHNSON AND "THE GREAT EPISTOLICK ART." By Robert Halsband. With a facsimile of a letter to Mrs. Thrale from the original in the Hyde Collection. New York, N.Y., Columbia University Press for the Annual Dinner of the Johnsonians, 1961.

10×7½ inches; [8] pages + [4] pages of facsimiles.
150 copies distributed at the Grolier Club, 22 September 1961; handsewn into printed blue paper cover.

124

THE HUBBLE ATLAS OF GALAXIES. By Allan Sandage. Washington, D.C., Carnegie Institution of Washington, 1961 (Publication Number 618).

11½×15 inches; viii+32+50 leaves of plates.
Dark blue cloth over boards; silver-stamped cover and spine.

125

JOURNAL OF A HUNTING EXCURSION TO LOUIS LAKE, 1851. Blue Mountain Lake, N.Y., Adirondack Museum, 1961.

11¼×8¾ inches; [80] pages including 41 pages of illustrated holograph facsimile.
1,000 copies bound in light green cloth over boards; label on cover; spine printed in black and stamped in gold.

126

THE LAST FIRE-HAUNTED SPARK. By Raymond Holden with wood engravings by John Melanson. Newport, N.H., [Privately printed], 1961.

9¼×6¼ inches; [16] pages.
600 copies saddlewire stitched into light yellow paper cover.

127

A LETTER FROM JOHN TO ABIGAIL ADAMS IN 1774.
Cambridge, Mass., The Belknap Press of Harvard University Press, 1961.

Issued to commemorate the publication of the first four volumes of *The Adams Papers*.
8¼×6¼ inches; [4] pages of holograph facsimile.
Handsewn into light brown paper cover.

128

THE LIFE AND WORKS OF JOHN HAY (1838–1905).
Providence, R.I., Brown University Library, 1961.

A commemorative catalogue of the exhibition shown at the John Hay Library of Brown University in honor of the centennial of his graduation at the Commencement of 1858.
9½×6¼ inches; xii+51 pages + [4] leaves of plates.
Red paper over boards; gold-stamped spine. (4951)

129

MANCHESTER VERMONT: A PLEASANT LAND AMONG THE MOUNTAINS, 1761–1961. By Edwin L. Bigelow and Nancy H. Otis. Manchester, Vt., The Town of Manchester, 1961.

9½×6¼ inches; xiii+[3]+317 pages + [24] pages of plates.
Green cloth over boards; gold-stamped cover and spine.

130

THE MIDDLE ROAD. By Llewellyn Howland. South Dartmouth, Mass., The Concordia Company, Inc., 1961.

9½×6¼ inches; viii+134 pages; illustrated.
Light brown cloth over boards; wrapper.

131

PIRANESI. Northampton, Mass., Smith College Museum of Art, 1961.

6×9 inches; 109+[39] pages of plates.
Printed brown paper and black quarter cloth over boards; gold-stamped spine. (3907)

132

RIGHTS OF MAN. By Thomas Paine, with an introduction
by Howard Fast and illustrations by Lynd Ward. Lunenburg, Vt., Printed for Members of the Limited Editions Club
at The Stinehour Press, 1961.

12½×9½ inches; xvi+[2]+269+[3] pages.
1,500 copies numbered and signed by the artist; bound in quarter cloth
over boards; gold-stamped cover and spine; slipcase.

133

A SETH EASTMAN SKETCHBOOK, 1848–1849. Introduction by Lois Burkhalter. Austin, Tex., Published for the
Marion Koogler McNay Art Institute, San Antonio,
by the University of Texas Press, 1961.

11¼×8¾ inches; xxvi pages + 68 pages of plates.
Printed brown cloth over boards; gold-stamped spine; wrapper.

134

THE SONG OF THE EXPLORER: A POEM. By Charles Parker
Bancroft. [Lunenburg, Vt., Privately printed, 1961.]

7×4¾ inches; [20] pages.
Printed on untrimmed handmade paper; handsewn into printed green
and black paper cover; white label laid onto cover.

135

STRING TOO SHORT TO BE SAVED: MEMOIRS OF A DIS-
APPEARING NEW ENGLAND. By Donald Hall. Illustrations
by Mimi Korach. New York, N.Y., The Viking Press, 1961.

9¼×5¾ inches; [xii]+143 pages.
Decorated paper and black quarter cloth over boards; gold-stamped
spine; wrapper.

136

TRAVELS AND EXPLORATIONS. By Charles Parker
Bancroft. [Lunenburg, Vt., Privately printed for Mrs.
Elizabeth Bancroft McLean, 1961.]

7¾×7 inches; [72] pages including 68 pages of manuscript facsimile; manuscript illustrations.
Handsewn into printed green and black paper cover; printed label and cloth.

[1962]

137

DANTE'S DIVINE POEM WRITTEN DOWN FREELY INTO ENGLISH. By Clara Stillman Reed. Wilbraham, Mass., Privately printed, 1962.

9¾×6¼ inches; vi+312 pages; illustrated.
300 copies bound in blue marbled paper and blue quarter cloth over boards; gold-stamped spine.

138

DARTMOUTH LYRICS. By Richard Hovey. Introduction by Carlos Baker. Hanover, N.H., Dartmouth Publications, 1962.

Includes "Richard Hovey's Autobiography."
8¾×5¾ inches; xvi+61 pages.
Gray paper over boards.

139

THE DRAKE FAMILY OF NEW HAMPSHIRE. By Alice Smith Thompson. With an historical introduction on the family background in England by Sir Anthony Richard Wagner. Concord, N.H., New Hampshire Historical Society, 1962.

Designed by Ray Nash.
10×6½ inches; xiv+340+[2] pages + [20] leaves of plates; maps on endleaves.
550 copies (including 50 numbered from I to L) bound in dark blue cloth over boards; blind-stamped cover and gold-stamped spine; wrapper. (126215)

140

Drawings for the Iliad. By Leonard Baskin. Introduction by Marvin S. Sadik. New York, N.Y., Delphic Arts, [1962].

11 × 7½ inches; [32] pages including 24 pages of plates.
Saddlewire stitched into printed white paper cover. (106226)

141

Forty Dartmouth Poems. Selected, and with an introduction, by Richard Eberhart. Hanover, N.H., Dartmouth Publications, 1962.

9 × 6 inches; 51 pages.
300 copies handsewn into white paper cover and glued into green paper wrapper.

142

Greek Gods and Heroes. Boston, Mass., Museum of Fine Arts, 1962.

Fifth edition (revised).
Designed by Carl Zahn.
8½ × 7 inches; 105 pages; illustrated.
Smythsewn and glued into printed blue paper cover.

143

Independent Historical Societies: An Enquiry into Their Research and Publication Functions and Their Financial Future. By Walter Muir Whitehill. Boston, Mass., The Boston Athenaeum; Distributed by Harvard University Press, 1962.

9½ × 6½ inches; xviii + 593 pages.
Bound in blue cloth over boards; gold-stamped spine.

144

A Journal of the Adventures of Matthew Bunn. Chicago, Ill., The Newberry Library, 1962.

10½ × 6¼ inches; [8] + 24 pages; facsimile.
2,000 copies bound in green boards. (96230)

145

LEONARD BASKIN. Brunswick, Me., Bowdoin College
Museum of Art, 1962.

Designed by Leonard Baskin.
9½×6½ inches; [112] pages including 76 pages of plates; bibliography.
Smythsewn and glued into printed white paper cover. (106203)

146

M. AND M. KAROLIK COLLECTION OF AMERICAN WATER
COLORS AND DRAWINGS, 1800–1875. Boston, Mass.,
Museum of Fine Arts, 1962.

10×8¾ inches; Vol. I: 337 pages; illustrated (some colored). Vol. II:
352 pages; illustrated (some colored).
Each volume bound in gray paper and brown quarter cloth over boards;
gold-stamped cover; spine printed in black and stamped in gold; together in a slipcase. (106229)

147

OLD MASTER DRAWINGS FROM CHATSWORTH. [Wash-
ington, D.C., Smithsonian Institution, 1962.]

A loan exhibition from the Devonshire Collection.
10×7½ inches; 46 pages + [96] pages of plates.
Smythsewn and glued into printed light blue paper cover. (See item
412.) (96222)

148

ONE HUNDRED AND TWENTY-TWO YEARS: JOURNEY
TOWARD CONCORD. By Thomas Boylston Adams. New
York, N.Y., The Pierpont Morgan Library, 1962.

7¾×5 inches; [20] pages; illustrated.
200 copies handsewn into light brown paper cover.

149

STATE PAPERS OF VERMONT, VOLUME 11: GENERAL
PETITIONS, 1797–1799. Edited by Allen Soule. Montpelier, Vt., Secretary of State, 1962.

9¼×6¼ inches; xvii+494 pages.
Green cloth over boards; gold-stamped cover and spine.

150

SURSUM CORDA: REMARKS MADE AT THE FIFTIETH RE-
UNION OF THE CLASS OF 1912, DARTMOUTH COLLEGE,
9 JUNE 1962. [By Henry R. Viets. Lunenburg, Vt.,
Privately printed], 1962.

Cover title.
9½×6¾ inches; [4] pages; single folded leaf. (96217)

151

THREE HUNDRED YEARS OF MILTON: 1662–1962.
Milton, Mass., Milton Tercentenary Committee, 1962.

10×7 inches; 35 pages + [5] pages of maps; illustrated.
Saddlewire stitched into blue paper cover.

152

THE VANITY OF HUMAN WISHES. By Samuel Johnson.
New York, N.Y., For the Annual Dinner of the Johnsonians,
1962.

Facsimile of the original in the Hyde Collection; keepsake in commem-
oration of Dr. Johnson's 253rd birthday.
6¾×5¾ inches; [26] pages; facsimile.
Handsewn into marbled paper cover; printed white label on cover.

153

WELL DRESSED LINES STRIPPED FROM THE REELS OF
FIVE NEW ENGLANDERS. New York, N.Y., Privately
printed for The Anglers' Club of New York, 1962.

9½×6¼ inches; ix+82 pages.
500 copies bound in brown cloth over boards; printed labels on cover
and spine.

154

ACCOUTREMENT PLATES NORTH AND SOUTH 1861–
1865. An authoritative reference with comparative values
by William G. Gavin. Foreword by Stephen V. Grancsay.
Philadelphia, Pa., Riling and Lentz, 1963.

8¾×5½ inches; xvii+[3]+217+[3] pages; illustrated.
Blue cloth over boards; wrapper. (86321)

155

ANDREW WYETH: DRY BRUSH AND PENCIL DRAWINGS.
Cambridge, Mass., Fogg Art Museum; Distributed by the
New York Graphic Society, 1963.

8¾×11¼ inches; [72] pages including 34 pages of plates.
Smythsewn and glued into printed white paper cover. An edition for the
New York Graphic Society bound in white buckram over boards; spine
stamped in red.

156

ANDREW WYETH: A LOAN EXHIBITION ORGANIZED BY
THE FOGG ART MUSEUM. [Foreword by Philip Hofer; in-
troduction by Agnes Mongan.] Cambridge, Mass., Fogg
Art Museum, [1963].

8½×11 inches; [72] pages including 39 pages of plates.
Smythsewn and glued into printed white paper cover. (126218)

157

APPALOOSA: THE SPOTTED HORSE IN ART AND HISTORY.
Text by Francis Haines. Austin, Tex., University of Texas
Press, 1963.

11¼×8¾ inches; xii+103 pages; illustrated.
Brown cloth over boards; wrapper. (106231)

158

ARCHAIC CHINESE JADES: MR. AND MRS. IVAN B. HART
COLLECTION. Catalogue by Elizabeth Lyons. Edited by

Robert J. Poor with an introduction by Charles MacSherry. Northampton, Mass., Smith College Museum of Art, 1963.

8½×5½ inches; 70+[2] pages; illustrated.
Smythsewn and glued into paper cover; green paper wrapper. (116207)

159

THE BÉLA BARTÓK ARCHIVES: HISTORY AND CATALOGUE. By Victor Bator. New York, N.Y., Bartók Archives, 1963.

11×8½ inches; 39 pages + [7] leaves of plates.
Smythsewn and glued into printed white paper cover.

160

BLAKE'S GRAVE: A PROPHETIC BOOK, BEING WILLIAM BLAKE'S ILLUSTRATIONS FOR ROBERT BLAIR'S THE GRAVE, ARRANGED AS BLAKE DIRECTED. With a commentary by S. Foster Damon. Providence, R.I., Brown University Press, 1963.

14¼×11½ inches; [46] pages including 13 pages of plates.
Brown paper over boards. (16313)

161

CALLIGRAPHY AND HANDWRITING IN AMERICA, 1710–1962. Compiled by P. W. Filby. Caledonia, N.Y., Italmuse, Inc., 1963.

11×8½ inches; [86] pages including 52 pages of plates.
Perfect-bound in printed white paper cover.

162

A COLLECTION OF WOOD ENGRAVINGS BY JOHN MELANSON. Lunenburg, Vt., The Stinehour Press, [1963].

Cover title: "Wood Engravings by John Melanson." Includes engravings cut for the Press during the years 1959 to 1963.
9¾×7 inches; [18] untrimmed leaves of Hosho paper with 17 wood engravings printed from the original blocks.
Handsewn and glued into printed brown paper cover.

163

DEBTS HOPEFUL AND DESPERATE: FINANCING THE PLYMOUTH COLONY. By Ruth A. McIntyre. Plymouth, Mass., Plimoth Plantation, 1963.

9¼×6¼ inches; 86 pages; illustrated.
Blue cloth over boards; wrapper. (16334)

164

DEDICATION OF [a] WINDOW TO SARAH WESTON ANGIER [at] ST. ANDREW'S BY-THE-SEA. Hyannis Port, Mass., [Privately printed], 1963.

9×6¼ inches; [10] pages; frontispiece photograph (colored) tipped in.
Red cloth over boards; gold-stamped cover and spine. (66338)

165

DRAKE IN ENGLAND: GENEALOGICAL RESEARCHES WITH PARTICULAR REFERENCE TO THE DRAKES OF ESSEX FROM MEDIEVAL TIMES. By Sir Anthony Wagner. Concord, N.H., New Hampshire Historical Society, 1963.

Revised edition printed by The Stinehour Press in 1970. 12×8 inches; 83 pages + 2 folded leaves of genealogical tables tipped in. Smythsewn and glued into dark blue paper cover; gold-stamped cover and spine; slipcase. (See item 440.) (56342)

166

DRAWINGS FOR DANTE'S INFERNO BY RICO LEBRUN. [Translation and introduction by John Ciardi. With a note on the drawings of Lebrun by Leonard Baskin.] New York, N.Y., Kanthos Press, 1963.

Designed by Leonard Baskin.
17¼×13 inches; [96] pages including 36 pages of plates.
2,000 copies, each with 4 original lithographs printed on Strathmore cover stock; 100 numbered copies, each containing 7 original lithographs, printed on handmade Arches paper; 25 additional copies, containing artist's proofs, are *hors commerce*; bound in black cloth over boards; slipcase. (86337)

167

FATHER ABRAHAM'S SPEECH. By Benjamin Franklin. [Boston, Mass.], G. K. Hall and Company, Christmas 1963.

7×4½ inches; [2]+22+[4] pages; facsimile.
Saddlewire stitched into blue paper cover. (106318)

168

THE GROLIER CLUB ITER ITALICUM. Edited by Gabriel Austin. New York, N.Y., The Grolier Club, 1963.

9¾×6¾ inches; xxi+[3]+298 pages; illustrated.
750 copies bound in brown cloth over boards; wrapper. (16317)

169

A HISTORY OF THE NATIONAL SOCIETY OF THE COLONIAL DAMES OF AMERICA IN THE STATE OF NEW HAMPSHIRE, 1936–1963. By Grace Holbrook Blood. Portsmouth, N.H., [Printed for the Society], 1963.

9¼×6¼ inches; [2]+36+[2] pages; illustrated.
Blue cloth over boards. (116232)

170

INDIAN SCULPTURE FROM THE COLLECTION OF MR. AND MRS. EARL MORSE. Cambridge, Mass., Fogg Art Museum, Harvard University, 1963.

9×6 inches; 24+[2] pages + [38] pages of plates numbered 1 to 38.
Smythsewn and glued into printed brown and white paper cover.

171

LONG REMEMBERED: FACSIMILES OF THE FIVE VERSIONS OF THE GETTYSBURG ADDRESS IN THE HANDWRITING OF ABRAHAM LINCOLN. Notes and comments on the preparation of the address by David C. Mearns and Lloyd A. Dunlap. Washington, D.C., The Library of Congress, 1963 (Library of Congress Facsimile Number 3).

14¼×10¾ inches; [40] pages including 11 leaves of facsimile.
Smythsewn and glued into printed yellow-brown paper cover. (96330)

172

MAINE AND ITS ARTISTS, 1710–1963. Catalogue for an exhibition designed by Ian L. Robertson. Waterville, Me., Friends of Art at Colby, 1963.

12 ×9 inches; [32] pages.
Saddlewire stitched; blue wrapper. (36318)

173

OCCASIONEM COGNOSCE. A poem by Marianne Moore. Cambridge, Mass., Lowell House, Harvard College, 1963.

Printed as a Lowell House "Separatum" in honor of Eliot and Mary Perkins.
Designed by Eric Martin and Lawrence Scott.
12 ×7 inches; [4] pages.
175 copies handsewn into dark blue paper cover; blind-stamped cover with printed label.

174

OCEAN STEAM VESSELS: DRAWINGS BY SAMUEL WARD STANTON. Upper Montclair, N.J., Sold and distributed by H. Kneeland Whiting, 1963.

Contains most of the original drawings that illustrated Stanton's *American Steam Vessels* (1895).
8½ ×11 inches; 40 pages including [36] pages of plates.
Saddlewire stitched into printed blue paper cover. (56333)

175

ON TROUT STREAMS AND SALMON RIVERS. By Dana S. Lamb. Barre, Mass., Barre Publishers, 1963.

9¼ ×6¼ inches; [10]+97 pages; illustrated.
1,500 copies bound in green cloth over boards; gold-stamped cover and spine. 50 copies printed on rag paper and bound in quarter oasis niger and numbered 1 to 50.

176

OUR DEVIL TAKES A HOLIDAY: LETTERS AND SKETCHES

SENT BACK TO THE SHOP. Written and drawn by John R. Nash. Lunenburg, Vt., The Stinehour Press, 1963.

8½×5¼ inches; 27 pages.
Smythsewn and glued into white paper cover; glued into printed paper wrapper.

177

PALMER FAMILY COLLECTIONS. [Preface by Robert O. Parks.] Sarasota, Fla., Ringling Museum of Art, 1963.

9½×6½ inches; 24+[2] pages + [18] pages of plates.
1,500 copies saddlewire stitched into gold paper cover. (16301)

178

PAUL SAMPLE RETROSPECTIVE. [With a foreword by Richard Eberhart.] Hanover, N.H., Hopkins Center, Dartmouth College, 1963.

9×6 inches; [8] pages.
Saddlewire stitched into printed gray paper cover. (56341)

179

THE PICTORIAL HISTORY OF HUNTSVILLE, 1805–1865. By Victor B. Haagen. Huntsville, Ala., Victor B. Haagen, 1963.

10¼×8¼ inches; 128 pages; illustrated.
Dark blue cloth over boards; gold-stamped cover and spine; wrapper. (96323)

180

RAMON GUTHRIE KALEIDOSCOPE. Lunenburg, Vt., The Stinehour Press, 1963.

9×5¾ inches; xi+[1]+149 pages; illustrated.
Cream cloth over boards; wrapper. Another edition (Hanover, N.H., 1963) issued in 100 copies; 9⅜×6⅛ inches; bound in green quarter cloth and paper over boards; wrapper. (36308)

181

REMEMBER ME. By Rosabel N. Loveridge. [Lunenburg, Vt., Privately printed], 1963.

8½ × 5¼ inches; [10]+66+[2] pages; illustrated.
Printed paper over boards.

182

ROBERT FROST: FARM-POULTRYMAN. Edited by Edward Connery Lathem and Lawrance Thompson. Hanover, N.H., Dartmouth Publications, 1963.

8¾ × 5¾ inches; 116 pages.
Brown paper over boards; wrapper. (66325)

183

ROBERT FROST: HIS "AMERICAN SEND-OFF," 1915. [Edited by Edward Connery Lathem.] Lunenburg, Vt., The Stinehour Press, 1963.

11½ × 9 inches; [24] pages; manuscript facsimile.
325 copies saddlewire stitched into blue paper wrapper. (36355)

184

RUSSELL COWLES: SEVENTY-FIFTH ANNIVERSARY RETROSPECTIVE. Hanover, N.H., Dartmouth College, Hopkins Center, April 1963.

9 × 6 inches; [8] pages.
Saddlewire stitched into illustrated brown paper cover. (36339)

185

SIGNET. By George Santayana. [Cambridge, Mass.], The Signet Society, 1963.

8¾ × 5¾ inches; [11] pages; facsimile.
2,000 copies saddlewire stitched into printed blue paper cover. (96324)

186

THE SOMERSET CLUB COOK BOOK. [With an introduction

by Alexander W. Williams.] Boston, Mass., The Somerset Club, 1963.

9¼×6¼ inches; 113 pages; illustrated.
3,000 copies bound in blue cloth over boards. (56338)

187

THIRTY-FIVE DARTMOUTH POEMS. Selected, and with an introduction, by Richard Eberhart. Hanover, N.H., Dartmouth Publications, 1963.

9×6 inches; 44 pages.
200 copies handsewn into light brown paper cover and glued into light green wrapper. (66331)

188

THOUGHTS FROM ADAM SMITH. Compiled with an introduction and comments by Clyde E. Dankert. Hanover, N.H., Privately printed, 1963.

9¼×6¼ inches; 39 pages.
Red cloth over boards; wrapper. (116221)

189

THREE VISITORS TO EARLY PLYMOUTH: LETTERS ABOUT THE PILGRIM SETTLEMENT IN NEW ENGLAND DURING ITS FIRST SEVEN YEARS. By John Pory, Emmanuel Altham, and Isaack de Rasieres. Edited by Sydney V. James, Jr., with an introduction by Samuel Eliot Morison. Plymouth, Mass., Plimoth Plantation, 1963.

9¼×6¼ inches; xiii+[1]+84 pages; illustrated.
Green cloth over boards; wrapper. (16335)

190

TREASURES FROM THE PLANTIN-MORETUS MUSEUM. Hanover, N.H., The Hopkins Center, Dartmouth College, 1963.

9¼×6 inches; [24] pages; illustrated.
500 copies saddlewire stitched into brown paper cover. (36336)

191

VERMONT IMPRINTS, 1778–1820: A CHECKLIST OF
BOOKS, PAMPHLETS, AND BROADSIDES. Compiled by Mar-
cus A. McCorison. Worcester, Mass., American Antiquarian
Society, 1963.

10 × 6¾ inches; xxiv + 597 pages.
Green cloth over boards; blind-stamped seal on cover; gold-stamped
spine; wrapper. (126327)

[1964]

192

ANCIENT MEXICO IN MINIATURE: SCULPTURE FROM
THE COLLECTION OF FRANCES PRATT AND BUMPEI USUI.
[New York, N.Y.], American Federation of Arts, 1964.

4½ × 3½ inches; [40] pages including 12 pages of plates.
Saddlewire stitched into printed brown paper cover. (126349)

193

ARISTOTLE: POLITICS AND POETICS. Translated by Ben-
jamin Jowett and S. H. Butcher with an introduction by
Horace M. Kallen and portraits by Leonard Baskin. New
York, N.Y., The Limited Editions Club, 1964.

11 × 8¼ inches; xxi + [5] + 331 pages + [20] pages of plates.
1,500 copies bound in two cloths, white and blue, over boards; slipcase.
(46320)

194

THE BEGINNINGS OF THE THAYER SCHOOL OF ENGI-
NEERING AT DARTMOUTH COLLEGE. Edited by Edward
Connery Lathem. With an introduction by Dean Myron
Tribus. Hanover, N.H., Thayer School of Engineering, 1964.

9½ × 6¼ inches; ix + [1] + 125 pages; illustrated.
Blue cloth over boards; wrapper. Another edition issued in 100 copies;
7 × 10 inches; xiii + [1] + 125 + [5] pages; illustrated; bound in green
marbled paper and quarter cloth over boards. (106338+66402)

195

BODRUM 1963: MINORITY REPORT OF AN "EXHIBITION."
Boston, Mass., Privately printed, 1964.

9 × 6 inches; 32 pages.
Saddlewire stitched into light brown paper cover. (36416)

196

A BRIEF GUIDE TO THE PRINCIPAL COLLECTIONS OF THE
RARE BOOK DEPARTMENT. [Hanover, N.H.], Published by
the Friends of the Dartmouth Library, [1964].

Cover title.
9 × 6 inches; 43 pages.
Saddlewire stitched into paper cover. (16627)

197

BRIGHT SALMON AND BROWN TROUT. By Dana S. Lamb.
Barre, Mass., Barre Publishers, 1964.

Designed and illustrated by Shirley Errickson.
9¼ × 6¼ inches; [8]+111 pages.
1,500 copies bound in yellow cloth over boards; gold-stamped cover
and spine. 350 copies printed on rag paper and bound in quarter oasis
niger and numbered 1 to 350.

198

THE BROTHERHOOD OF CHRISTIANS AND JEWS. An ad-
dress given at the Jewish Community House of Taunton,
Massachusetts, by John M. Oesterreicher. Newark, N.J.,
Institute of Judaeo-Christian Studies, 1964.

8½ × 6¼ inches; 16 pages.
Saddlewire stitched into red paper cover. (46448)

199

BYRON THOMAS: A RETROSPECTIVE EXHIBITION.
Hanover, N.H., Dartmouth College, 1964.

6¼ × 9¼ inches; [16] pages including 5 pages of plates (some colored).
Saddlewire stitched into yellow paper cover. (86424)

200

CALLIGRAPHY AND PRINTING IN THE SIXTEENTH CEN-
TURY: [A] DIALOGUE ATTRIBUTED TO CHRISTOPHER
PLANTIN. Edited, with English translation and notes, by
Ray Nash. Foreword by Stanley Morison. Antwerp,
Belgium, The Plantin-Moretus Museum, 1964.

Includes facsimile of "La Premiere, et la seconde partie des dialogues
francais, ..."
7¼×4¾ inches; 77+[42] pages including facsimile pages numbered
[217] to 255; illustrated.
500 copies bound in printed paper and quarter cloth over boards; gold-
stamped spine; wrapper.

201

CONTEMPORARY CANADIAN ESKIMO ART: THE CHAUN-
CEY C. NASH COLLECTION. By Beekman H. Pool. Boston,
Mass., The Club of Odd Volumes, 1964.

9¾×7 inches; [14] pages + [24] pages of plates (some colored).
134 copies bound in light brown cloth over boards; colored plate laid
onto cover; acetate wrapper. Also issued Smythsewn and glued into
printed blue and white paper cover. (106303)

202

THE COUNTRY BOOK CLUB: A POEM. By Charles Shillito.
Boston, Mass., G. K. Hall and Company, 1964.

Christmas greeting including a facsimile of the London (1788) printing
of the poem.
10¾×7¾ inches; [40] pages including facsimile pages numbered [1]
to 39; title page illustrated with a vignette by Thomas Rowlandson.
Saddlewire stitched into brown paper cover. (106421)

203

EIGHTEENTH CENTURY VENETIAN DRAWINGS FROM THE
CORRER MUSEUM. Washington, D.C., Smithsonian Institution, 1964.

10×7½ inches; 58+[3] pages + [111] pages of plates.
Saddlewire stitched and glued into printed blue paper cover. (66346)

204

THE FOGG ART MUSEUM: A SURVEY OF THE COLLEC-
TIONS. Cambridge, Mass., Harvard University, 1964.

8¼×5½ inches; [73] pages including 63 pages of plates.
Smythsewn and glued into printed black and white paper cover. (96426)

205

GRAND. By Tennessee Williams. New York, N.Y., House of
Books, Ltd., 1964.

First edition.
7¾×5¼ inches; [34] pages.
300 copies signed by the author; bound in yellow cloth over boards.
(56411)

206

GREECE UNTRODDEN. By Alan J. B. Wace. Illustrations
by Elektra Megaw. Athens, Greece, [Privately printed],
1964.

8¾×5¾ inches; 116 pages.
Saddlewire stitched into printed blue paper cover. (46404)

207

HISTORICAL SITES AND HOUSES OF LANCASTER, NEW
HAMPSHIRE, 1764–1964. Lancaster, N.H., Lancaster
Bicentennial, 1964.

9¼×6¼ inches; 72 pages; illustrated.
Smythsewn and glued into brown paper cover. (46450)

208

INDIAN MINIATURES FROM THE COLLECTION OF MIL-
DRED AND W. G. ARCHER, LONDON. [With an introduc-
tion by Sherman E. Lee.] Washington, D.C., Smithsonian
Institution, 1964.

8¾×5¾ inches; [72] pages; illustrated.
Smythsewn and glued into printed white glossy paper cover. (66302)

NOTES ON

Printing & Graphic Arts

THE STINEHOUR PRESS · LUNENBURG · VERMONT

VOLUME I	PUBLISHED QUARTERLY · DECEMBER 1953	NUMBER 4

RAY NASH   ROLLO G. SILVER, *Editor*   RODERICK D. STINEHOUR

Hawthorn  ouse

BY

RODERICK D. STINEHOUR

AWTHORN HOUSE
became an imprint twenty-odd years ago when Edmund B. Thompson, printer, published a colored map of the town he had located in, Windham, Connecticut. This modest issue, 500 copies at 50 cents postpaid, was the first of a series of books and printed pieces that by their fresh vitality and honest workmanship, seemed to spring from the sources of American tradition and to express the modern spirit of freedom in a form that is familiar. The press, active for the ten-year period 1932–42, had printed more than half a hundred books when the war stopped it.

Hawthorn House was named for a flowering bush, originally called the mayflower, with historic roots in early New England. Because of this, and also because it was in bloom when Edmund Thompson, a native of New York City, set up his country shop, the name seemed best to identify the press. Thompson wrote concerning this choice: "If, to a few initiates the name of Hawthorn House suggests a New England setting, and more specifically a quiet spot

Address the editor at Simmons College, Boston 15, Massachusetts. Send subscriptions ($1 a year) to The Stinehour Press, Lunenburg, Vermont. Entered as second-class matter at the post office at Lunenburg, Vermont. Copyright, 1953, by The Stinehour Press.

SEE APPENDIX

The Relic & other poems

ROBERT HILLYER

New York, Alfred A. Knopf

1957

A Selective Bibliography
of Important Books
Pamphlets and Broadsides
Relating to
Michigan History

Bibliography and Notes by
Albert Harry Greenly

MCMLVIII
THE STINEHOUR PRESS
Lunenburg, Vermont

ENTRY 86

VIEWS
FROM THE
CIRCLE

Seventy-five years of Groton School

MCMLX

ENTRY 117

THE GROLIER CLUB
ITER ITALICUM

Edited by
Gabriel Austin

NEW YORK · MCMLXIII

ENTRY 168

✦ ✦ ✦ ✦ ✦ ✦ ✦ ✦ ✦

Preface

SEVENTY-NINE YEARS AGO a group of noble men formed the Grolier Club and stated that its general purpose was the promotion of the arts of the book. In 1884 they probably did not think of travel as a means of fulfilling that object. Indeed the Grolier began as a group of congenial New Yorkers, but such is the power of books that its membership spread gradually throughout this country and abroad. By 1949, the members, still concentrated in the East, came from all parts of the country—its great librarians, printers, collectors, dealers and others who promoted and appreciated the book. Our President at that time was Frederick B. Adams, Jr., the Director of the Pierpont Morgan Library, formerly an important man of business. Devoted to books, he had the vision of a future Grolier Club no longer beset by the vicissitudes of the recent years. He realized the purpose of a club of bookmen must be in the great benefits of personal acquaintance, of exchange of ideas and enthusiasm for books, and of the opportunities to see other collections. As more and more of these treasures were only to be seen in institutions, it was necessary for the members, like Mahomet, to go to these institutions. It was a

vii

ENTRY 168

209

JEAN CHARLOT: POSADA'S DANCE OF DEATH. With four relief engravings by José Guadalupe Posada. Title page wood engraving by Fritz Eichenberg. New York, N.Y., Pratt Graphic Art Center, 1964.

Designed by Bert Waggott.
11 ×8¾ inches; [5] pages + 4 pages of engravings numbered I to IV + engraved title page (signed by the artist).
500 copies numbered and signed by the artist (copies 1 to 25 have been reserved for the artist and copies 26 to 50 have been reserved for the Museum of Modern Art); saddlewire stitched into white paper cover and glued into printed red-purple wrapper. (76431)

210

JULES PASCIN'S CARIBBEAN SKETCHBOOK. Introduction by John Palmer Leeper. Austin, Tex., University of Texas Press, 1964.

10¼×8¾ inches; x+106 pages; illustrated.
Light brown cloth over boards; wrapper. (76405)

211

A MEMOIR OF LITTLE MOOSE: FOR MOOSES, NOT MICE. By Professor P. H. Bear [Philip Hofer. Lunenburg, Vt., Privately printed, 1964.]

8½×5¼ inches; [14] pages; illustrated.
200 copies saddlewire stitched into printed blue paper cover. (76434)

212

MEMORIALS OF THE MASSACHUSETTS SOCIETY OF THE CINCINNATI. By Bradford Adams Whittemore. Boston, Mass., Printed for the Society, 1964.

10 ×6½ inches; xliv+[2]+852 pages; illustrated.
Brown cloth over boards; wrapper. (26334)

213

A NEW GUIDE TO THE MASSACHUSETTS STATE HOUSE. By Sinclair H. Hitchings and Catherine H. Farlow. Boston,

Mass., John Hancock Mutual Life Insurance Company, 1964.

9×6 inches; 108 pages; illustrated.
Smythsewn and glued into printed blue paper cover. (76339)

214

NEW JERSEY ROADMAPS OF THE 18TH CENTURY. Princeton, N.J., Princeton University Library, 1964.

10×8 inches; [48] pages including 35 pages of plates.
Smythsewn and glued into printed green paper cover. (46433)

215

OLIVIA RODHAM. [By Robbins Milbank.] Nelson, N.H., Published by the Trustees of the Olivia Rodham Memorial Library, 1964.

8¼×5½ inches; 18 pages; illustrated.
500 copies saddlewire stitched into printed white paper cover. (26453)

216

ONE GOLDEN DAY. By Rosabel N. Loveridge. Illustrated by Jane Wentzell. Lunenburg, Vt., Privately printed, 1964.

8¾×5½ inches; [10]+64 pages.
Bound in printed yellow paper over boards. (56425)

217

ONE HUNDRED BOOKS FAMOUS IN SCIENCE. By Harrison D. Horblit. New York, N.Y., The Grolier Club, 1964.

11¼×8¼ inches; [10]+449+[5] pages; illustrated; facsimiles; bibliography.
1,000 copies bound in two cloths, blue and gray, over boards; slipcase. (106301)

218

PAINTINGS AND DRAWINGS: PETER BLUME IN RETROSPECT, 1925 TO 1964. Manchester, N.H., The Currier

Gallery of Art; Hartford, Conn., Wadsworth Atheneum, 1964.

10×7½ inches; 43+[5] pages; illustrated.
Smythsewn and glued into printed brown and white paper cover. (16434)

219

THE PORTRAYAL OF THE NEGRO IN AMERICAN PAINTING. Brunswick, Me., Bowdoin College Museum of Art, 1964.

Designed by Leonard Baskin.
10×8½ inches; [60] pages + [80] pages of plates.
Smythsewn and glued into printed white paper cover. (36443)

220

THE PRATT COLLECTION OF EGYPTIAN AMULETS. Hanover, N.H., Dartmouth Publications, 1964.

9×6 inches; 16+[1] pages including 6 pages of plates.
Handsewn into printed yellow paper cover. (16344)

221

RADICAL PERIODICALS IN AMERICA, 1890–1950; WITH A GENEALOGICAL CHART AND A CONCISE LEXICON OF THE PARTIES AND GROUPS WHICH ISSUED THEM. A bibliography with brief notes by Walter Goldwater. New Haven, Conn., Yale University Library, 1964.

10¼×7 inches; 15+[3]+5 pages.
Red cloth over boards; gold-stamped cover and spine. (16419)

222

RANDOLPH CHURCH: A HISTORY. Delivered by Arthur Pease on the Occasion of the Eightieth Anniversary of the Church. Randolph, N.H., [Privately printed], 1964.

8¾×5¾ inches; 16 pages.
250 copies handsewn into printed green paper cover. (56439)

223

RENAISSANCE BRONZES IN AMERICAN COLLECTIONS.
Northampton, Mass., Smith College Museum of Art, 1964.

Designed by Leonard Baskin.
9×6¼ inches; [73] pages including 28 pages of plates.
Smythsewn and glued into white paper cover. (26419)

224

SAMUEL ELIOT MORISON. . . . By Walter Muir Whitehill.
Cambridge, Mass., Printed for Leavitt and Peirce, April
1964.

12×9 inches; broadside; framed. (46402)

225

SANTAYANA AT THE "GAS HOUSE." By Joel Porte.
Lunenburg, Vt., [Privately printed, 1964?].

9×6 inches; [2]+18 pages; frontispiece portrait.
Saddlewire stitched into blue paper cover; silver-stamped cover.

226

A SEIDEL FOR JAKE WIRTH; RAISED BY WALTER MUIR
WHITEHILL, PETER A. WICK, RAY ALLEN BILLINGTON,
SINCLAIR HITCHINGS, FRANCIS W. HATCH, DAVID MC-
CORD, JOHN PETERSON ELDER, AND LUCIEN PRICE IN
1964. [Boston, Mass., Privately printed], 1964.

9¼×6¼ inches; [2]+45+[5] pages; illustrated.
Printed brown paper over boards. Another edition saddlewire stitched
into printed brown paper cover. (36438)

227

SEVENTY-FIFTH ANNIVERSARY OF THE PRESENTATION
BY OLIVER WENDELL HOLMES OF HIS PERSONAL MED-
ICAL LIBRARY TO THE BOSTON MEDICAL LIBRARY ON
THE 29TH OF JANUARY 1889. Boston, Mass., The Boston
Medical Library and The Harvard Medical Library, 1964.

9¾×6¼ inches; 30+[6] pages; facsimile; illustrated.
200 copies handsewn into light brown paper cover. (126334)

228

SOME DRAWINGS AND LITHOGRAPHS FOR GOETHE'S FAUST. By Eugène Delacroix. Introduction by Philip Hofer. Cambridge, Mass., Harvard College Library Department of Printing and Graphic Arts, 1964.

8¾ × 11¼ inches; [16] pages including 7 pages of plates.
Saddlewire stitched into printed black paper cover. (46440)

229

SOME FRUITS OF THE EXPEDITION: PASSAGES FROM RECENT WRITINGS. By Julian P. Boyd. Lunenburg, Vt., [Privately printed], 1964.

7½ × 5 inches; 53 pages.
Smythsewn and glued into printed green paper cover. (106452)

230

TEACHER, SCHOOL, CHILD: THE 1963 ANNIVERSARY CONFERENCES ON EDUCATION AT GODDARD COLLEGE. Edited by Wilfrid Hamlin. Plainfield, Vt., Goddard College, 1964.

9 × 6 inches; 101 + [3] pages.
Saddlewire stitched into printed cream board. (76420)

231

TEXTILES OF OAXACA. [Introduction by Gerald Williams.] Hanover, N.H., Hopkins Center, Dartmouth College; Manchester, N.H., The Currier Gallery of Art, 1964.

9 × 7½ inches; 63 pages including 15 pages of plates; bibliography.
Saddlewire stitched into printed brown paper cover. (86425)

232

THIS WAS A MAN: A BIOGRAPHY OF GENERAL WILLIAM WHIPPLE. By Dorothy Mansfield Vaughan. Lunenburg, Vt., [Privately printed], 1964.

8½ × 5½ inches; 14 + [2] pages.
500 copies handsewn into printed gray paper cover. (66406)

233

TWENTY-ONE DARTMOUTH POEMS. Selected by Richard Eberhart. Hanover, N.H., Dartmouth Publications, 1964.

9×6 inches; 28 pages.
200 copies saddlewire stitched into white paper cover and glued into light yellow wrapper. (106407)

234

A UNIFIED FIELD THEORY. By Miles V. Hayes, Ph.D. Lunenburg, Vt., [Privately printed], 1964.

9¼×6¼ inches; viii+[2]+86 pages.
500 copies bound in blue cloth (some in green cloth) over boards; wrapper. (126322)

235

WALT KUHN: AN IMAGINARY HISTORY OF THE WEST. Foreword by Fred S. Bartlett. Colorado Springs, Colo., Amon Carter Museum of Western Art and the Colorado Springs Fine Arts Center, 1964.

8½ × 10 inches; [60] pages including 34 pages of plates (some colored). Smythsewn and glued into printed white paper cover. (36425)

[1965]

236

AGHT'AMAR: CHURCH OF THE HOLY CROSS. By Sirarpie der Nersessian. Cambridge, Mass., Harvard University Press, 1965 (Harvard Armenian Texts and Studies Number 1).

12¼ × 10 inches; 60 pages + [68] pages of plates (some colored); map. Light brown cloth over boards; wrapper. (56430)

237

THE ANATOMY OF THE BRAIN AND NERVES. By Thomas

Willis. Edited by William Feindel. Montreal, Canada, McGill University Press, 1965.

Designed by Robert R. Reid.
12¾×8 inches; illustrated. Vol. I: xx+104 pages. Vol. II: xii+[12]+ 192 (i.e. 137)+[28] pages.
2,000 copies bound in vellum paper; vellum paper slipcase. (96417)

238

AN ANNOTATED LIST OF THE PUBLICATIONS OF THE REVEREND THOMAS FROGNALL DIBDIN, D.D., BASED MAINLY ON THOSE IN THE HARVARD COLLEGE LIBRARY WITH NOTES OF OTHERS. [By William A. Jackson.] Cambridge, Mass., Printed for the Houghton Library, 1965.

12¼×8¼ inches; 63 pages; illustrated.
500 copies bound in light brown cloth over boards. (76408)

239

"THE BEGGAR'S OPERA" BY HOGARTH AND BLAKE. A portfolio compiled by Wilmarth S. Lewis and Philip Hofer. Cambridge, Mass., Harvard University Press; New Haven, Conn., Yale University Press, 1965.

[Text]: 12¼×9¼ inches; 15+[17] pages. Saddlewire stitched into blue paper cover. [Portfolio]: 21×25¾ inches; 11 plates numbered I to XI.
350 sets together in a hinged box covered with brown cloth. (126412)

240

A BLAKE DICTIONARY: THE IDEAS AND SYMBOLS OF WILLIAM BLAKE. By S. Foster Damon. Providence, R.I., Brown University Press, 1965.

11¼×7¾ inches; xii+460+[3] pages + [12] pages of plates numbered I to XII.
Blue cloth over boards. (36460)

241

BRUCE ROGERS, A GENTLE MAN FROM INDIANA. By

Philip C. Duschnes. [Lunenburg, Vt., Privately printed], 1965.

Delivered at the 25th Annual Meeting of the Friends of the Brown University Libraries, 25 March 1963.
9×6¼ inches; 25 pages; facsimile.
750 copies saddlewire stitched into printed brown paper cover. (66504)

242

DANIEL WEBSTER AND A SMALL COLLEGE. By John C. Sterling. Hanover, N.H., Dartmouth Publications, 1965.

11¼×8¾ inches; [6]+62+[4] pages; illustrated.
Printed green paper and black quarter cloth over boards. (16511)

243

DR. TUCKER'S DARTMOUTH. By Robert French Leavens and Arthur Hardy Lord. Hanover, N.H., Dartmouth Publications, 1965.

9¾×6½ inches; 273+[3] pages; illustrated.
Green cloth over boards; wrapper. (96431)

244

EXETER REMEMBERED. Edited by Henry Darcy Curwen. Exeter, N.H., Phillips Exeter Academy, 1965.

9×6 inches; xv+[1]+240 pages.
Red cloth over boards; wrapper. Also issued Smythsewn and glued into printed paper cover. (116418)

245

THE FRANCIS A. COUNTWAY LIBRARY OF MEDICINE. Boston, Mass., [Harvard University], 1965 (Guides to the Harvard Libraries Series Number 9).

Cover title; at head of title: "Library Guide."
8½×6 inches; 31 pages; illustrated.
Saddlewire stitched into printed white paper cover. (See items 400 and 590.) (26543)

246

THE GREAT DESIGN: TWO LECTURES ON THE SMITHSON
BEQUEST BY JOHN QUINCY ADAMS. Edited with an introduction by Wilcomb E. Washburn. Foreword by L. H. Butterfield. Washington, D.C., Smithsonian Institution, 1965.

9¼×6¼ inches; 95+[5] pages; illustrated.
Marbled paper and blue quarter cloth over boards. (76505)

247

HILL COUNTRY NORTH. By John Williams Andrews.
Westport, Conn., The Pavilion Press; Boston, Mass., Bran-
den Press, 1965.

9¼×6 inches; [10]+58+[4] pages; illustrated.
1,000 copies bound in blue cloth over boards; wrapper. (86454)

248

"I HAVE THAT HONOR": TRIBUTES TO J. FRANK
DOBIE. By Frank H. Wardlaw. Foreword by Walter Muir
Whitehill. Paisano, Tex., and Biddeford Pool, Me., The
Congressional Press, 1965.

7¾×5¼ inches; [28] pages; illustrated.
500 copies perfect-bound in tan paper cover. (46518)

249

IMAGES OF THE DANCE: HISTORICAL TREASURES OF THE
DANCE COLLECTION, 1581–1861. By Lillian Moore. New
York, N.Y., The New York Public Library, Astor, Lenox,
and Tilden Foundations, 1965.

11¼×8¾ inches; 86 pages; illustrated (colored frontispiece laid in).
Bound in green, blue, and white decorated paper and blue quarter
cloth stamped in silver over boards. (96402)

250

INDRANI AND I. By Anne de Viri. New York, N.Y., Red
Dust, Inc., 1965.

8½×5½ inches; 127 pages.
Red paper over boards; wrapper. Also issued Smythsewn and glued into
printed light brown paper cover. (36520)

251

JAN VAN KRIMPEN: A PERSPECTIVE ON TYPE AND TYPOGRAPHY. By John Dreyfus. [New York, N.Y., Printed for Gallery 303], 1965.

Cover title. First appeared in *Printing and Graphic Arts*, VII, 4 (1959); here reprinted for the Heritage of the Graphic Arts lecture series.
9¼×6½ inches; [20] pages.
Saddlewire stitched into white paper cover. (76517)

252

LAST CAMP. By Francis J. Mathues. Lunenburg, Vt., North Country Publishing Company, 1965.

9×6 inches; 33 pages.
300 copies saddlewire stitched into printed light yellow paper cover. (66530)

253

MASSACHUSETTS SILVER IN THE FRANK L. AND LOUISE C. HARRINGTON COLLECTION. By Kathryn C. Buhler. Worcester, Mass., Barre Publishers, 1965.

10¼×8¼ inches; [2]+121+[5] pages; illustrated.
300 copies bound in light blue paper over boards. (86436)

254

MASTER PRINTS OF THE 20TH CENTURY: A TRIBUTE TO JAKOB ROSENBERG. Cambridge, Mass., Fogg Art Museum, Harvard University, 1965.

8½×5½ inches; [88] pages; illustrated.
Smythsewn and glued into printed red paper cover. (116402)

255

MISTRESS OF HERSELF. By Diana Whitehill Laing. Barre, Mass., Barre Publishers, 1965.

9¼×6 inches; 246+[2] pages; illustrated.
Maroon cloth over boards; wrapper. (46517)

256

MUSIC IN PRINTS. By Sydney Beck and Elizabeth E. Roth.
New York, N.Y., The New York Public Library, 1965.

10¼×8¼ inches; [60] leaves including 52 pages of plates.
Blue cloth over boards. (96403)

257

THE PATHFINDER. By James Fenimore Cooper. With an
introduction by Robert E. Spiller and illustrations by Richard M. Powers. Lunenburg, Vt., Printed for the Members
of The Limited Editions Club, 1965.

10×6¾ inches; xvi+474+[4] pages + [17] pages of plates.
Green and black paper and black quarter cloth over boards; slipcase.
(76407)

258

PEACE THROUGH LAW: A BASIS FOR AN EAST-WEST
SETTLEMENT IN EUROPE. By B. Carroll Reece. Edited by
the Honorable Louise Goff Reece. New Canaan, Conn.,
The Long House, Inc., 1965.

9¼×6¼ inches; 114 pages; illustrated.
Light blue cloth over boards. Also issued Smythsewn and glued into
gray paper cover. (76436)

259

THE PHOENIX-SK CLUB OF HARVARD COLLEGE. Cambridge, Mass., [Privately printed], 1965.

Includes a "History of the Club" by Samuel Eliot Morison and wood
engravings by John Melanson.
9¼×6¼ inches; 112 pages.
Blue cloth over boards; gold-stamped cover and spine; wrapper. (116437)

260

REMARKS ABOUT JACOB WIRTH, 1880–1965, FOR THE
MEMORIAL SERVICE AT THE FIRST CHURCH IN BOSTON

ON 14 DECEMBER 1965. By Walter Muir Whitehill. [Boston, Mass., Privately printed, 1965.]

Cover title.
8½×5½ inches; 7 pages.
Handsewn into light brown paper cover. (126538)

261

SHAKESPEARE AND VOLTAIRE. By Theodore Besterman. New York, N.Y., The Pierpont Morgan Library, 1965.

8½×5¾ inches; 46+[2] pages.
Smythsewn and glued into printed yellow paper cover. (16507)

262

SONNETS TO BAEDEKER. By David McCord. Illustrations by John Lavalle. [Lunenburg, Vt., Privately printed], 1965.

8½×5½ inches; [36] pages.
Smythsewn and glued into light orange paper cover. (116534)

263

THIRTY-TWO DARTMOUTH POEMS. Selected by Richard Eberhart. Hanover, N.H., Dartmouth Publications, 1965.

Illustrated with a wood engraving by David Godine.
9×6 inches; 38 pages.
200 copies handsewn into light brown paper cover and glued into light brown wrapper. (96520)

264

A TRADITION OF CONSCIENCE: PROPOSALS FOR JOURNALISM. By Joseph Pulitzer, Jr. Foreword by Marquis W. Childs. With five etchings by Leonard Baskin. St. Louis, Mo., [Privately printed], 1965.

12¾×9¼ inches; [4]+69+[5] pages; bibliography.
250 copies bound in paper and blue quarter leather over boards; slipcase. (76308)

265

2,000 YEARS OF CALLIGRAPHY. A THREE-PART EXHI-
BITION ORGANIZED BY THE BALTIMORE MUSEUM OF
ART, THE PEABODY INSTITUTE LIBRARY, AND THE
WALTERS ART GALLERY: A COMPREHENSIVE CATA-
LOGUE. Baltimore, Md., The Walters Art Gallery, 1965.

11¼×8¾ inches; 201+[3] pages; illustrated.
Printed red paper and white quarter cloth over boards. (36519)

266

THE VOICE OF THE WHALEMAN WITH AN ACCOUNT OF
THE NICHOLSON WHALING COLLECTION. By Stuart C.
Sherman. Providence, R.I., Providence Public Library,
1965.

10¼×7¼ inches; 219 pages; illustrated.
Tan cloth and green quarter cloth over boards; wrapper. (26442)

267

WHEREOF WE ARE MADE: EARLY RECOLLECTIONS.
By Robert Cutler. Lunenburg, Vt., Privately printed, 1965.

9¼×6¼ inches; 64 pages.
Blue cloth over boards. (86532)

268

WOOD-SMOKE AND WATER CRESS. By Dana S. Lamb.
Barre, Mass., Barre Publishers, 1965.

9¼×6 inches; 89+[3] pages.
1,300 copies bound in brown cloth over boards. 200 copies bound in
paper and tan quarter leather over boards; slipcase. (46510)

269

ANCESTORS AND DESCENDANTS OF HAVILAH BURRITT HINMAN OF STRATFORD, NEW HAMPSHIRE. . . . Compiled by Gertrude B. Wright. Hanover, N.H., Privately printed, 1966.

9¼×6¼ inches; xvii+[1]+262+[2] pages; illustrated.
200 copies bound in green cloth over boards; wrapper. (76304)

270

THE ANIMAL HOTEL. By Jean Garrigue. New York, N.Y., Eakins Press, 1966.

Designed by Edith McKeon.
9¾×6 inches; 94+[2] pages.
Green cloth over boards; wrapper. (16642)

271

ART AND EDUCATION: A SYMPOSIUM HELD IN THE WIGGIN GALLERY, BOSTON PUBLIC LIBRARY. Boston, Mass., Boston Public Library, 1966.

Includes "On Being a Noticer" by David McCord; "Art in a Library" by David Bain Little; and "A New Audience for Our Public Collections" by Sinclair H. Hitchings.
8¾×5¾ inches; 47 pages.
1,000 copies bound in gold paper over boards. (56613)

272

A BACKWARD GLANCE: COMMENCEMENT IN 1916. By Robert Cutler. Lunenburg, Vt., Privately printed, 1966.

9×6 inches; 39 pages.
Saddlewire stitched into printed gray paper cover. (106654)

273

BOOKS IN PRINT: THE STINEHOUR PRESS. Lunenburg, Vt., The Stinehour Press, 1966.

Cover title.
5¼×3½ inches; [8] pages.
Saddlewire stitched into printed blue paper cover; return order card inserted.

274

CANADIAN SILVERSMITHS, 1700–1900. By John E Langdon. Toronto, Ont., Privately printed, 1966.

11¼×8¾ inches; xx+249+[3] pages; illustrated.
1,000 copies bound in blue cloth over boards; wrapper. (26522)

275

CANTUS FIRMUS. By Johannes Alexander Gaertner. Lunenburgiae, Vermontensium, Apud Typographicum Stinehourianum, 1966.

7¼×5 inches; xxx pages.
Smythsewn and glued into white paper cover reinforced with boards. (86538)

276

A CENTURY OF AMERICAN STILL-LIFE PAINTING, 1813–1913. Selected by William H. Gerdts. New York, N.Y., The American Federation of Arts, 1966.

11 ×8½ inches; [24] pages; illustrated.
Saddlewire stitched into gold paper cover. (86630)

277

CHARLES M. RUSSELL: PAINTINGS, DRAWINGS, AND SCULPTURE IN THE AMON G. CARTER COLLECTION. A descriptive catalogue by Frederic G. Renner. Foreword by Ruth Carter Johnson. Austin, Tex., Published for the Amon Carter Museum of Western Art, Fort Worth, by the University of Texas Press, 1966.

11¾ × 11¼ inches; xvi+148 pages + [35] pages of colored plates (additional colored plate in limited edition); map; bibliography.
Dark blue cloth over boards; gold-stamped spine; wrapper. (16601)

278

COIN AND TEMPLE: A STUDY OF THE ARCHITECTURAL REPRESENTATION ON ANCIENT JEWISH COINS. By Alice Muehsam. Leeds, England, Leeds University Oriental Society, 1966 (Near Eastern Researches Number 1).

$11\frac{1}{4} \times 8\frac{3}{4}$ inches; ix+[1]+70 pages + xi leaves of plates.
Smythsewn and glued into brown paper over boards. (106431)

279

COLONIAL ARCHITECTURE OF ANTIGUA GUATEMALA.
By Sidney David Markman. Philadelphia, Pa., Printed for
the American Philosophical Society, 1966 (Memoirs of the
American Philosophical Society Volume 64).

$11\frac{1}{4} \times 8\frac{3}{4}$ inches; xviii+[2]+355+[3] pages; illustrated.
2,000 copies bound in yellow cloth over boards; wrapper. (56438)

280

DIRECTOR'S CHOICE: JAFFE-FRIEDE GALLERY. Hanover, N.H., Hopkins Center, Dartmouth College, 1966.
$11\frac{1}{4} \times 8\frac{1}{2}$ inches; [8] pages.
Saddlewire stitched into brown paper cover. (56620)

281

EXCERPTS FROM THE DUSTY RIDGE LETTERS. By Leslie
Somers Watt. Edited by Donald Watt, Jr., and Teddy
Watt. Decorations by Wendy Watson. Lunenburg, Vt., The
Stinehour Press, 1966.
Designed by Aldren A. Watson.
$8 \times 4\frac{3}{4}$ inches; 50 pages.
150 copies: some bound in orange paper over boards; some Smythsewn
and glued into orange paper cover. (66639)

282

FITZ HUGH LANE: THE FIRST MAJOR EXHIBITION.
[Introduction by John Wilmerding. Lincoln, Mass., De
Cordova Museum; Waterville, Me., Colby College Art
Museum, 1966.]
$6 \times 9\frac{1}{4}$ inches; [32] pages including 9 pages of plates.
Saddlewire stitched into printed white paper cover. (26602)

283

FOUNDERS OF THE COSMOS CLUB OF WASHINGTON, 1878.

ROBERT FROST:
Farm-Poultryman

The story of Robert Frost's career
as a breeder and fancier of hens
& the texts of eleven long-forgotten
prose contributions by the poet, which appeared
in two New England poultry journals
in 1903-05, during his years of farming
at Derry, New Hampshire

Edited by

EDWARD CONNERY LATHEM
& LAWRANCE THOMPSON

Dartmouth Publications

HANOVER · NEW HAMPSHIRE · 1963

The Universal Chicken Feed

MR. CALL remained a seeker for truth to the end of his days in the hen business. (This is not an obituary. Mr. Call still lives, only not on the proceeds of his hens, or the expectation thereof.) In the fat months, when the hens laid, he staid at home and sawed wood, as the saying is; but in the lean months he went visiting. And because he was a pretty good sort of fellow, people always indulged his curiosity about their methods, and told him all they knew, especially with regard to feeding; but he never seemed to find out what he was after, for before long he was back again if possible more curious than ever.

"What are you feeding?" was his stock question, and though there was a discouraging sameness to the replies he got, he persevered with a devotion worthy of a loftier cause. He felt that there was something his hens lacked that once found would make them lay every day in the year. That something eluded him. Often he thought he had it. Once he grasped at sunflower seeds; he had heard of them before, but had clean forgotten them. Again, India wheat came to him as a revelation. He thought that an evening mash might be

93

---

minutes over low heat stirring with a wooden spoon. Cool and chill. ¶ Make the Cream Sauce. ¶ Shape the fish mixture into cutlet-shaped patties ¼ inch thick. Dip into the eggs beaten with 2 tablespoons of water and then into fine bread crumbs. ¶ Fry in deep fat (375° F.), turning each "cutlet" once. When golden brown, drain on paper toweling and place on a heated platter. Cover with Cream Sauce. ¶ *8 servings*

FROGS' LEGS PROVENÇALE

12 pairs frogs' legs	6 tablespoons butter
milk	2 tablespoons olive oil
flour	2 cloves garlic, minced
salt and pepper	2 teaspoons chopped parsley
	½ lemon

Wash the frogs' legs in water to which a little vinegar has been added. Pat dry with a towel and soak in milk for 15 minutes. ¶ Dredge the legs in flour seasoned with salt and pepper. Fry in a mixture of 2 tablespoons of butter and 2 tablespoons of olive oil, heated until sizzling. When golden brown, transfer the legs to a very hot platter. ¶ Put the remaining butter and the garlic in the same skillet and heat until the butter is brown and foamy. ¶ Sprinkle the legs with parsley and lemon juice and pour the foaming butter over everything. Serve immediately. ¶ *2 to 3 servings*

56

MEATS

BEEF CLUB STYLE

1 tablespoon diced pepper	1 cup Quick Demi-glace Sauce
1 tablespoon chopped onion	(page 102)
4 tablespoons butter	4 large mushroom caps
	2 individual sirloin *or*
	tenderloin steaks

Sauté the pepper and onion in 2 tablespoons of butter just until tender. Combine with the Demi-glace Sauce or leftover brown gravy. Simmer while preparing the rest of the recipe. ¶ Sauté the mushroom caps in butter. ¶ Charcoal broil, grill, or pan broil the steaks. Pour the sauce over the steaks and top with mushroom caps. ¶ *2 servings*

BEEFSTEAK DES GOURMETS

4 shallots	1 teaspoon chopped tarragon
butter	4-pound Porterhouse steak
1 tablespoon chopped parsley	salt and pepper
2 teaspoons chopped chives	Potatoes Rissolées (page 93)

Mince the shallots and sauté in 2 tablespoons of butter until soft. Mash to a pulp and spread on a steak platter. ¶ Chop the herbs.

57

A Seidel For

Jake Wirth

Das Kaiserfass.

Jacob Wirth Co.

German Restaurant

ENTRY 226

FRITZ HEUSER IN ASGARD

July 1 1949

WAD

W. A. Dwiggins

A Seidel for Jake Wirth

raised by Walter Muir Whitehill, Peter A. Wick,
Ray Allen Billington, Sinclair Hitchings, Francis
W. Hatch, David McCord, John Petersen Elder,
and Lucien Price in 1964

INTRODUCTION

to the Anatomy of the Brain and Nerves with
a Note on Pordage's English Translation and
a Bibliographic Survey of *Cerebri Anatome*

Printed for *McGill University Press* by *The Stinehour Press,*
Lunenburg, Vermont

A Bibliographic Survey of
Cerebri Anatome

H. R. DENHAM
Chief Cataloguer, Wellcome Historical Medical Library

INTRODUCTION
The London Editions   The Latin Collected Editions
The Amsterdam Editions   The English Collected Editions

LIST OF EDITIONS
Separate Editions of *Cerebri Anatome*
Collected Editions Containing *Cerebri Anatome*
IN LATIN   IN ENGLISH
Another Work Containing *Cerebri Anatome*

INTRODUCTION

THOMAS WILLIS began his career as a medical writer
in 1659 with *Diatribae Duae Medico-Philosophicae,*[*] a collection of three essays—on fermentation, fevers, and urines.
The next five years were dedicated to the intensive research
into the structure of the brain and nervous system from which,
in 1664, emerged his *Cerebri Anatome.* In the meantime five
editions of the *Diatribae* had appeared, the first three in London, the last two at the Hague and Amsterdam. Thus, although
it was *Cerebri Anatome* which established Willis as one of the
leading medical figures of his time, the earlier work had already
served to make his name known outside his own academic circle

[*] The title-page of the first edition of the *Diatribae* bears the date 1659, but Professor J. F. Fulton (*A Bibliography of Two Oxford Physiologists*, Oxford, 1935, p.13 *f*)
drew attention to the fact that John Aubrey's copy in the Bodleian Library contains
inscriptions dated 1658. However, this may have been an advance copy which
Aubrey was able to obtain from the publisher Allestry before the date of general
publication.

67

Jackson saw that without such enthusiasm many of these
books would not have been preserved, and the attitudes and
traditions of collecting would be very different today. So he
continued to gather Dibdinian editions and information, if only
as an office of piety, and the result is this, his last completed
work. He had seen and approved the title-page and general design of the book, and the text was in the hands of the com-
positor at the time of his death on October 18, 1964.

The virtues of the book, then, are Jackson's. He had directed
that a set of proofs be sent for comment to Nicolas Barker, the
bibliographer of the Roxburghe Club, and to Barker we are in-
debted for a careful reading and a number of excellent sugges-
tions, including the insertion of no. 58a. The faults must be laid
to Jackson's two colleagues, who have seen the book through its
proof stages without the benefit, never more profoundly missed,
of the author's final judgment.

W. H. BOND
JAMES E. WALSH

8

Preface

THE occasion of the publication of
this list—it makes no pretense of
being a bibliography—is that for
some years Mr. Philip Hofer and
the writer have intended to present
to Harvard the more important of
their annotated or association reference books and at that time to
publish a list of them. Recently
Mr. Hofer, finding his reference shelves crowded, decided to
present his Dibdins—it cannot be said that they were frequently
consulted—and the writer did the same. It was then determined
that a separate list would be more appropriate, particularly as
Harvard already had a distinguished Dibdin collection to which
these more recent gifts would be added.

The Harvard collection is now at least as strong as any known
to the writer, but it is not complete, and therefore it has been
thought proper to add notes of all those separate publications
that have been found elsewhere, excluding only the advertise-
ments, syllabi, tickets, etc., for his various lectures; the Roxburghe Club notices, etc., that he probably wrote; the printed
material relating to the libel suit brought against him by a Mr.
Sleigh in 1838, of which copies are in the British Museum; and
his more miscellaneous contributions to periodicals that he did

9

By George Crossette. Washington, D.C., Cosmos Club, 1966.

9¼×6¼ inches; 176 pages; illustrated.
Light brown cloth over boards. (126405)

284

GOOD READING FOR YOUTH. Concord, N.H., New Hampshire State Library, 1966.

Compiled under the direction of the Children's Services Division of the American Library Association. Annotated by Siri Andrews.
9×6 inches; 72 pages.
Smythsewn and glued into printed white paper cover. (36623)

295

A GUIDE TO THE HILL-STEAD MUSEUM. With an introduction and notes on the principal paintings. Farmington, Conn., Trustees of the Hill-Stead Museum, 1966.

6×8 inches; [32] pages including 14 leaves of plates.
Smythsewn and glued into gray-blue paper cover. (46612)

286

"HOPPY" ON HIS EARLY DARTMOUTH YEARS: SOME INFORMAL REMINISCENCES OF ERNEST MARTIN HOPKINS. Tape-recorded and edited by Edward Connery Lathem. Hanover, N.H., Dartmouth College, 1966.

5×7½ inches; 32 pages numbered [i] to vi+7 to 32; frontispiece.
1,150 copies bound in black cloth over boards; wrapper. Also issued Smythsewn and glued into printed paper cover. (126601)

287

THE HOWLAND FOUNDATION, INC., AND THE VIRGULAK INSTITUTE FOR THE PREVENTION OF NARCOTICS ADDICTION. [Norwalk, Conn., Privately printed], 1966.

Cover title.
10×8 inches; 13 pages.
Saddlewire stitched into cream paper cover. (86646)

288

INTERVIEWS WITH ROBERT FROST. Edited by Edward Connery Lathem. New York, N.Y., Holt, Rinehart and Winston, 1966.

9¼×6¼ inches; xiii+[1]+295+[3] pages.
Black cloth over boards; wrapper. (86530)

289

ITALIAN ARCHITECTURAL DRAWINGS LENT BY THE ROYAL INSTITUTE OF BRITISH ARCHITECTS, LONDON. Introduction by John Harris. Washington, D. C., The Smithsonian Institution, 1966.

7½ × 10 inches; [64] pages including 34 pages of plates.
Smythsewn and glued into printed light brown paper cover. (96615)

290

ITALIAN DRAWINGS IN THE ART MUSEUM [of] PRINCETON UNIVERSITY: 106 SELECTED EXAMPLES. [Princeton, N.J.], The Art Museum of Princeton University, 1966.

7½ × 10 inches; 64 pages + [110] pages of plates.
Smythsewn and glued into printed white paper cover. (96535)

291

JAPANESE TWENTIETH CENTURY PRINTS FROM THE COLLECTION OF C. ADRIAN RÜBEL. Cambridge, Mass., Fogg Art Museum, Harvard University, 1966.

8¼×5½ inches; [74] pages including 50 pages of plates.
Smythsewn and glued into printed white paper cover. (26620)

292

JUST FRAGMENTS. By Carl A. Weyerhaeuser. Milton, Mass., [Privately printed], 1966.

8¼×5¼ inches; 142 pages.
Gray paper and red quarter cloth over boards; gold-stamped spine. (16615)

293

LETTERS TO CHILDREN. By Beatrix Potter [with illustrations by the author]. Foreword by Philip Hofer. Cambridge, Mass., Harvard College Library Department of Printing and Graphic Arts; New York, N.Y., Walker and Company, 1966.

7¾×5 inches; 48 pages.
3,500 copies bound in blue cloth over boards. (66628)

294

LUCY CRAWFORD'S HISTORY OF THE WHITE MOUNTAINS. Edited and with an introduction by Stearns Morse. Hanover, N.H., Dartmouth Publications, 1966.

7¾×5¼ inches; xxvi+279 pages; frontispiece portrait; maps on endleaves.
Maroon cloth over boards; gold-stamped cover and spine. (46537)

295

LYRIC VERSE: A PRINTER'S CHOICE. Compiled and printed by David Godine. Lunenburg, Vt., Privately printed, 1966.

Senior Fellowship project, Dartmouth College.
10×6½ inches; [4]+75+[7] pages.
500 copies: 40 copies printed on heavy Fabriano paper; 30 copies printed on light Fabriano; 150 copies printed on Curtis Rag paper; 280 copies printed on Curtis Tweedweave paper. The copies on Fabriano are numbered and signed by the printer and are bound in marbled paper and blue quarter goatskin over boards. (56618)

296

THE MAKING OF BOOKS IN THE RENAISSANCE AS TOLD BY THE ARCHIVES OF THE PLANTIN-MORETUS MUSEUM. By Leon Voet. New York, N.Y., American Friends of the Plantin-Moretus Museum, 1966.

First appeared in *Printing and Graphic Arts*, X, 2 (1966).
9½×6¼ inches; 30 pages numbered [33] to 62; illustrated; facsimile; map.
Handsewn into brown paper cover and glued into yellow paper wrapper. (96617)

297

MASTERPIECES FROM MONTREAL: SELECTED PAINTINGS
FROM THE COLLECTIONS OF THE MONTREAL MUSEUM
OF FINE ARTS. [Introduction by David G. Carter. Mon-
treal, Quebec, Montreal Museum of Fine Arts, 1966.]

11 × 8½ inches; 39 pages + 102 pages of plates.
Smythsewn and glued into printed blue and white paper cover. (106505)

298

MESSAGE FROM THE INTERIOR. [Photographs] by Walker
Evans. [Afterword by John Szarkowski.] New York, N.Y.,
The Eakins Press, 1966.

14½ × 14¼ inches; [28] pages including 12 pages of plates.
Bound in gray cloth over boards; printed label laid onto cover; spine
stamped in white. (36630)

299

MORE SUNSHINE THAN SHADOW: A DOCTOR'S LIFE.
By Roy J. Heffernan, M.D. Doonaree [Milton, Mass.],
Privately printed, 1966.

9¼ × 6¼ inches; 78 pages.
Cream paper and green quarter cloth over boards. (116650)

300

MY LOVE. By Rosabel N. Loveridge. Lunenburg, Vt.,
Privately printed, 1966.

8¾ × 5½ inches; [8] + 67 pages; illustrated.
Printed paper over boards. (66525)

301

THE NATIONAL SOCIETY OF THE COLONIAL DAMES OF
AMERICA IN THE STATE OF NEW HAMPSHIRE. [Concord,
N.H.], The National Society . . . in New Hampshire, [1966].

Cover title; at head of title: "Constitution and Bylaws."
9 × 6 inches; 18 pages.
Saddlewire stitched into printed blue paper cover.

302

OBSERVATION TOWER. By David McCord. [Boston, Mass.,
Club of Odd Volumes], 1966.

11¾×7 inches; [3]-page folded leaflet. (36637)

303

THE ODD TALES OF IRENE ORGEL. New York, N.Y.,
The Eakins Press, 1966.

Designed by Edith McKeon.
9½×6 inches; 114+[6] pages.
Bound in gold cloth over boards; wrapper. (96603)

304

THE PROVIDENT INSTITUTION FOR SAVINGS IN THE
TOWN OF BOSTON, 1816–1966. A Historical Sketch by
Walter Muir Whitehill. Boston, Mass., The Provident In-
stitution for Savings, 1966.

9×6¼ inches; 122 pages; illustrated; maps; portraits.
Smythsewn and glued into blue and white paper cover. (16630)

305

READY FOR THE HA HA AND OTHER SATIRES. By Jane
Mayhall. New York, N.Y., Eakins Press, 1966.

Designed by Edith McKeon.
9½×6 inches; 102 pages.
Blue cloth over boards; wrapper. (26609)

306

REPORT ON THE NEW ENGLAND EDUCATION DATA
SYSTEMS. Cambridge, Mass., The New England Education
Data Systems, 1966.

9¼×8 inches; 44 pages; illustrated.
Smythsewn and glued into printed green paper cover.

307

ROBERT FROST AND THE LAWRENCE, MASSACHUSETTS, "HIGH SCHOOL BULLETIN": THE BEGINNINGS OF A LITERARY CAREER. By Edward Connery Lathem and Lawrance Thompson. New York, N.Y., The Grolier Club, 1966.

12 ×9¾ inches; 94+[2] pages.
1,200 copies bound in paper and blue quarter cloth over boards. (26540)

308

SELECTED PROSE OF ROBERT FROST. Edited by Hyde Cox and Edward Connery Lathem. New York, N.Y., Holt, Rinehart, Winston, 1966.

8½×5¾ inches; 119 pages.
Bound in two cloths, white and blue, over boards; wrapper. (106515)

309

SKETCHES BY CONSTABLE FROM THE VICTORIA AND ALBERT MUSEUM. [Washington, D.C.], Circulated by the Smithsonian Institution, 1966 (Smithsonian Publication Number 4610).

Designed by Crimilda Pontes.
7½×10 inches; 32 pages + [48] pages of plates.
Smythsewn and glued into printed light green paper cover. (36518)

310

STORIES FROM THE SECOND GRADE. Lunenburg, Vt., Lunenburg Village School, 1966.

8½×5⅝ inches; 20 pages.
Saddlewire stitched into cream paper cover. (56637)

311

TO WIN THE HUNT. By Jane McIlvaine. Illustrated by Nelson McClary. Barre, Mass., Barre Publications, 1966.

At head of title: "A Virginia Foxhunter in Ireland."
8¾×6¼ inches; 100 pages.
Printed green paper and white quarter cloth over boards; silver-stamped spine. (16632)

312

25 DARTMOUTH POEMS. With "Notes on Poetry" and a postscript by Richard Eberhart. [Hanover, N.H., Dartmouth College, 1966.]

9×6 inches; 37 pages.
Handsewn and glued into printed red wrapper. (86676)

313

TWICE-TOLD TALES. By Nathaniel Hawthorne. Selected and introduced by Wallace Stegner. Illustrated by Valenti Angelo. New York, N.Y., Limited Editions Club, 1966.

Designed by Lewis F. White.
11×7¾ inches; xv+[1]+411+[3] pages.
1,500 copies bound in light blue cloth over boards; slipcase. (26638)

[1967]

314

AMERICAN STILL-LIFE PAINTING, 1913–1967. Selected by William H. Gerdts. New York, N.Y., The American Federation of the Arts, 1967.

11×8½ inches; [20] pages; illustrated.
Saddlewire stitched into green paper cover. (86726)

315

THE BAGATELLES FROM PASSY. By Benjamin Franklin. New York, N.Y., Eakins Press, 1967.

Designed by Edith McKeon.
7×4¼ inches; 188+[2] pages; facsimile.
Blue and white cloth over boards. (66708)

316

BOOKS WORTH RE-READING. [Introductory note by Sanford B. Ferguson.] Hanover, N.H., Dartmouth College Committee on Freshman Reading, 1967.

Results of a survey of the Dartmouth faculty and administrators.
9 ×6 inches; [8] pages.
Saddlewire stitched in printed yellow paper cover. (86710)

317

CANADIAN BOOKS—LIVRES CANADIENS: CURRENT DESIGN AND PRODUCTION. Hanover, N.H., Dartmouth College Library, 1967.

8½ ×5½ inches; 20 pages.
300 copies saddlewire stitched into printed gray paper cover. (26713)

318

A CHRONICLE OF THE DIVISION OF LABORATORIES AND RESEARCH, NEW YORK STATE DEPARTMENT OF HEALTH, THE FIRST FIFTY YEARS, 1914–1964. By Anna M. Sexton. Lunenburg, Vt., The Stinehour Press, 1967.

9¼ ×6¼ inches; xx+252 pages; illustrated.
Green cloth over boards; wrapper. (86606)

319

THE CHURCH AND SOCIAL MORALITY. By Charles McCollough. Hanover, N.H., Dartmouth College, The William Jewett Tucker Foundation, 1967.

The Richard Fletcher Memorial Prize Essay for 1967.
9 ×6 inches; 12 pages.
Saddlewire stitched into red paper cover. (86706)

320

THE COUNTRY MOUSE AND THE TOWN MOUSE. Illustrated by Wendy Watson. Lunenburg, Vt., The Stinehour Press, Christmas 1967.

Stinehour Press keepsake; designed by Edith McKeon.
6 ×4 inches; [32] pages.
Blue-green cloth over boards. (106735)

321

Echoes of Forty-five Flawless Years. By Mary Parmly Kones Sachs. Hanover, N.H., Privately printed, 1967.

9×5¾ inches; xi+[1]+182+[2] pages.
500 copies bound in red paper over boards. (96628)

322

Elizabeth Newt. By Harold Fleming. New York, N.Y., Red Dust, Inc., 1967.

8½×5½ inches; 147 pages.
Blue paper over boards; wrapper. Also issued Smythsewn and glued into printed cream paper cover. (96623)

323

The Etchings of Canaletto. By Jacob Kainen. Washington, D.C., The Smithsonian Press, 1967.

Designed by Crimilda Pontes.
7¾×10¼ inches; [64] pages including 39 pages of plates.
Light blue cloth over boards; gold-stamped cover and spine; wrapper. (86623)

324

Fables of a Jewish Aesop. Translated from the fox fables of Berechiah ka-Nakdan by Moses Hadas. Illustrated with woodcuts by Fritz Kredel. New York, N.Y., Columbia University Press, 1967.

8¾×5¼ inches; xi+[8]+233+[3] pages.
Light brown cloth over boards; wrapper. (66631)

325

Festival Designs by Inigo Jones: An Exhibition of Drawings for Scenery and Costumes for the Court Masques of James I and Charles I. Introduction and catalogue by Roy Strong; foreword by Thomas S.

Wragg. [Washington, D.C., International Exhibitions Foundation, 1967.]

From the Devonshire Collection, Chatsworth.
8½ × 10 inches; [148] pages including 97 pages of plates (some colored).
Smythsewn and glued into printed paper cover. (116645)

326

GERMAN EXPRESSIONISM AND ABSTRACT ART: THE
HARVARD COLLECTIONS. By Charles L. Kuhn. Cambridge, Mass., Busch-Reisinger Museum; Distributed by the
Harvard University Press, 1967.

Supplement to the *Catalogue of Twentieth Century German Art at Harvard*
(1957).
10 × 7½ inches; [66] pages including 30 pages of plates.
Smythsewn and glued into orange paper cover. (36730)

327

THE GLORY AND THE DREAM: ABRAHAM LINCOLN
AFTER GETTYSBURG. By Michael A. Musmanno. New
Canaan, Conn., The Long House, Inc., 1967.

9¼ × 6¼ inches; 62 + [2] pages.
Blue cloth over boards; wrapper. (86745)

328

HAROLD WAVE WHICKER, 1895–1955: A BRIEF SELECTION FROM HIS WORK AS AUTHOR AND ARTIST. Lunenburg, Vt., Privately published, 1967.

9¼ × 6 inches; 143 + [3] pages; illustrated.
500 copies bound in gray paper and blue quarter cloth over boards.
(86632)

329

THE HOUGHTON LIBRARY, 1942–1967: A SELECTION
OF BOOKS AND MANUSCRIPTS IN HARVARD COLLECTIONS. Introduction by W. H. Bond. Cambridge, Mass.,
Harvard College Library, 1967.

Issued with "A Selection of Color Reproductions" (10¼×14¼ inches; [10] leaves including 9 leaves of plates) in a gray paper portfolio. 14¾×10¾ inches; xiv+[2]+255+[1] pages; illustrated. Black cloth over boards. (36611)

330

IN TOUCH WITH SPACE AND OTHER POEMS. By Chilson H. Leonard. Exeter, N.H., Privately published by the Phillips Exeter Academy Press, 1967.

9×6 inches; 69 pages.
Smythsewn and glued into green paper cover. (46726)

331

THE LEDYARD CANOE CLUB AT DARTMOUTH. A history by Thomas Falcon. Hanover, N.H., Privately printed, 1967.

9¾×6¼ inches; xi+[1]+54+[2] pages; illustrated.
500 copies bound in printed glossy white paper over boards. (126633)

332

LETTERS FROM SANDY. Lunenburg, Vt., Privately printed, 1967.

9¼×6¼ inches; [80] pages; illustrated.
Gray cloth over boards. (86717)

333

A MEMOIR OF THE LATE WASHINGTON PLATT. By L. Wethered Barrall. Peterborough, N.H., Published privately by the Richard R. Smith Co., 1967.

7¾×5¼ inches; 30 pages; frontispiece portrait.
125 copies bound in blue cloth over boards; gold-stamped spine. (86677)

334

NINETEEN DARTMOUTH POEMS. Selected by Richard Eberhart. Hanover, N.H., Dartmouth Publications, 1967.

9×6 inches; 31 pages.
200 copies handsewn into beige paper cover and glued into beige wrapper. (126709)

335

NOT FAR FROM THE RIVER. By Dana S. Lamb. Barre, Mass., Barre Publishers, 1967.

9¼ × 6¼ inches; 101 pages.
1,500 copies (200 of which have been printed on Curtis Rag paper and bound by hand) bound in brown cloth over boards; gold-stamped spine; acetate wrapper; slipcase. (56728)

336

REBA PAEFF MIRSKY: MAY 25, 1902 – NOVEMBER 22, 1966. [Lunenburg, Vt., Privately printed], 1967.

Designed by Reynard Biemiller.
10 × 6¾ inches; [30] pages including 9 pages of holograph music score in facsimile; frontispiece portrait.
1,000 copies bound in blue marbled paper and white quarter paper over boards; gold-stamped cover and spine. (36710)

337

THE ST. JOHNSBURY ATHENAEUM AND ART GALLERY: A CATALOGUE OF THE COLLECTION. St. Johnsbury, Vt., [Published by the Athenaeum and Art Gallery, 1967].

9¼ × 6 inches; [26] pages including 6 pages of plates (some colored).
Saddlewire stitched into white printed paper cover. (36709)

338

ST. MARK'S SCHOOL: A CENTENNIAL HISTORY. By Edward Tuck Hall. Southboro, Mass., Printed for the Alumni Association, 1967.

9½ × 6¼ inches; xiii + [1] + 290 pages; illustrated.
Blue cloth over boards; wrapper. (16729)

339

SARAH ORNE JEWETT LETTERS. Enlarged and revised edition with an introduction and notes by Richard Cary. Waterville, Me., Colby College Press, 1967.

9½ × 6¼ inches; viii + 186 + [2] pages; illustrated.
Green cloth over boards; wrapper. (36723)

340

SASANIAN SILVER: LATE ANTIQUE AND EARLY MEDI-
EVAL ARTS OF LUXURY FROM IRAN. Ann Arbor, Mich.,
The University of Michigan Museum of Art, 1967.

10 × 7½ inches; 158 pages including 70 pages of plates.
Smythsewn and glued into decorated yellow and white boards. (36727)

341

THE SCULPTURE OF GASTON LACHAISE. With an essay by
Hilton Kramer and appreciations by Hart Crane, E. E.
Cummings, Marsden Hartley, Lincoln Kirstein, A. Hyatt
Mayor, and Henry McBride. New York, N.Y., Eakins Press,
1967.

Designed by Edith McKeon.
11¼ × 8¾ inches; 49 pages; 84 leaves of plates.
Brown cloth over boards; wrapper. (26738)

342

A SYSTEM OF ARCHITECTURAL ORNAMENT ACCORDING
WITH A PHILOSOPHY OF MAN'S POWERS. By Louis H.
Sullivan, together with drawings for the Farmers' and Mer-
chants' Union Bank of Columbus, Wisconsin, and a note by
Ada Louise Huxtable. New York, N.Y., Eakins Press, 1967.

Designed by Edith McKeon.
10¼ × 8¾ inches; [80] leaves including 33 pages of plates.
Red cloth over boards; wrapper. Also issued Smythsewn and glued into
red boards; wrapper. (16716)

343

THIRTY-ONE SONNETS. By Richard Eberhart. New York,
N.Y., Eakins Press, 1967.

Designed by Edith McKeon.
6½ × 5¼ inches; [44] pages.
Red cloth over boards; wrapper. (96641)

344

A Toe-Hold on the Dark: Poems. By David Erland Charles Forslund (1938–1967). Colorado Springs, Colo., The Colorado College, 1967.

9 × 6 inches; 52 pages.
Saddlewire stitched into printed dark red paper cover. (56827)

345

The Writings of Thomas Jefferson. Selected and edited by Saul K. Padover. Illustrated with lithographs by Lynd Ward. New York, N.Y., Limited Editions Club, 1967.

11 × 7¼ inches; x+[2]+362+[4] pages.
1,500 copies bound in marbled paper and blue quarter cloth over boards. (106630)

346

A Tribute to the Book by Henry Stevens of Vermont. Lunenburg, Vt., The Stinehour Press, 1967.

Designed by Roderick D. Stinehour.
24 × 18 inches; broadside (folded to 12 by 9 inches) printed in red and black. Included in *Homage to the Book: Sixteen Designers.* Foreword by Frederick B. Adams, Jr.; New York, N.Y., West Virginia Pulp and Paper Company (1968). (16705)

⌈1968⌉

347

Additions and Corrections to Vermont Imprints 1778–1820. [By Marcus A. McCorison. Worcester, Mass.], American Antiquarian Society, [1968].

Cover title.
9¾ × 6½ inches; 33+[3] pages.
Saddlewire stitched into printed green paper cover. (36441)

348

Adventures: Rhymes and Designs. By Vachel Lindsay. With an essay by Robert F. Sayre. New York, N.Y., Eakins Press, 1968.

Designed by Edith McKeon.
9½×6¼ inches; 287 pages.
Green cloth over boards; wrapper. (46827)

349

AMERICAN PAINTINGS OF THE 19TH CENTURY FROM THE COLLECTION OF MR. AND MRS. LAURANCE ROCKE-FELLER. Hanover, N.H., Beaumont-May Gallery, Hopkins Center, 1968.

4¾×6¼ inches; [14] pages including frontispiece illustration.
Saddlewire stitched into brown paper cover. (96813)

350

THE APPARATUS OF SCIENCE AT HARVARD, 1765–1800. By David P. Wheatland. Cambridge, Mass., Harvard University, 1968.

Designed by Edith McKeon and Roderick Stinehour.
11¼×8¾ inches; xi+[1]+203 pages; illustrated.
Red cloth over boards. (36722)

351

A BIBLIOGRAPHY OF WORD FORMATION IN THE GER-MANIC LANGUAGES. By Richard J. Seymour. Durham, N.C., Duke University Press, 1968.

9½×6¼ inches; xv+[1]+158 pages.
Gray cloth over boards; wrapper. (36728)

352

THE BITCH-GODDESS SUCCESS: VARIATIONS ON AN AMERICAN THEME. By Alexis de Tocqueville, Washington Allston, Henry David Thoreau, Walt Whitman, William James, Louis H. Sullivan, Charles Ives, Vachel Lindsay,

Maxwell E. Perkins, W. H. Auden, John F. Kennedy, George F. Kennan. New York, N.Y., The Eakins Press, 1968.

Designed by Edith McKeon.
6½×4¼ inches; 105+[3] pages.
Brown cloth over boards; wrapper. (96715)

353

COLLECTIVE BARGAINING IN THE PUBLIC SECTOR: THE PUBLIC SERVICE FACES A NEW ERA IN PERSONNEL ADMINISTRATION. Hanover, N.H., Dartmouth College Public Affairs Center, 1968 (Fifth Annual Orvil E. Dryfoos Conference on Public Affairs).

9×6 inches; 98 pages.
Smythsewn and glued into printed gray paper cover. (46905)

354

DARTMOUTH OUTING CLUB TRAIL GUIDE, 1968 EDITION. Hanover, N.H., Dartmouth Outing Club, 1968.

6¼×3½ inches; 110+[2] pages; illustrated; maps.
Smythsewn and glued into gray paper cover. (126719)

355

THE DRAWINGS OF HYMAN BLOOM. Introduction by Marvin S. Sadik. Storrs, Conn., University of Connecticut Museum of Art, 1968.

Designed by Leonard Baskin.
11×8½ inches; [80] pages including 44 pages of plates.
4,000 copies Smythsewn and glued into printed white paper cover. (56847)

356

FIFTY DARTMOUTH POEMS. Selected and with an introduction by Richard Eberhart. Hanover, N.H., Dartmouth Publications, 1968.

9×6 inches; 52 pages.
200 copies handsewn into blue paper cover and glued into blue wrapper. (36910)

357

THE FIRST NINETY YEARS OF THE PROVIDENCE PUBLIC LIBRARY, 1878–1968. By Stuart C. Sherman. Providence, R.I., Privately printed, 1968.

8½×5½ inches; 35 pages; illustrated.
500 copies Smythsewn and bound in brown paper cover and glued into orange wrapper. (66846)

358

THE FRENCH BRONZE, 1500 TO 1800. Foreword by F. J. B. Watson. New York, N.Y., M. Knoedler and Co., 1968.

Designed by Leonard Baskin.
11×8½ inches; [22] pages; illustrated; bibliography.
3,000 copies Smythsewn and glued into printed white paper cover. (86806)

359

GIVERS AND TAKERS: POEMS. By Jane Mayhall. New York, N.Y., The Eakins Press, 1968.

5½×4¼ inches; 47 pages.
Smythsewn and glued into printed blue paper cover. (66847)

360

GODS AND HEROES: BAROQUE IMAGES OF ANTIQUITY. Introduction by Eunice Williams. New York, N.Y., Wildenstein, 1968.

A loan exhibition from North American collections for the benefit of the archeological exploration of Sardis. Appeared in a slightly different format in 1969.
10¼×7¾ inches; 24 pages + [56] pages of plates.
Smythsewn and glued into dark yellow paper cover. (36829)

361

HARD FLAMES. By Francis J. Mathues. Lunenburg, Vt., The North Country Publishing Company, 1968.

Cover design by John Steinberger.
9×6 inches; 33 pages.
300 copies saddlewire stitched into gray paper cover. (56811)

362

THE HEALTH OF THE ESKIMOS: A BIBLIOGRAPHY, 1857–1967. Compiled by Robert Fortuine. Hanover, N.H., Dartmouth College Libraries, 1968.

9 × 6 inches; 87 pages.
Smythsewn and glued into printed white paper cover. (36840)

363

I LIKE PEOPLE AND PLACES. By Dorothy Hunt Smith. Princeton, N.J., At the Sign of Al Kalbu al Kabir al Aswad, 1968.

8¾ × 5¾ inches; 65 + [3] pages; illustrated.
Printed paper and brown quarter cloth over boards. (66826)

364

JAKOB-CREUTZFELDT DISEASE. By Walter R. Kirschbaum, M.D. New York, N.Y., American Elsevier Publishing Company, Inc., 1968.

9½ × 6¼ inches; 251 pages; illustrated.
Gray cloth over boards; wrapper. (96732)

365

THE JUNGLE BOOKS. By Rudyard Kipling. Illustrated by David Gentleman. Introduction by Bonamy Dobrée. Lunenburg, Vt., Printed for Members of The Limited Editions Club, 1968.

Designed by John Dreyfus.
10½ × 7¼ inches; xiii + [5] + 383 + [1] pages + [16] pages of colored plates.
1,500 copies signed by the illustrator; bound in marbled paper and green quarter cloth over boards; gold-stamped spine; slipcase covered in green paper. (26839)

366

A LAND CALLED CRETE: A SYMPOSIUM IN MEMORY OF HARRIET BOYD HAWES, 1871–1945. Northampton,

Mass., Smith College, 1968 (Smith College Studies in History XLV).

9 × 7 inches; 153 pages; illustrated.
Smythsewn and glued into white paper cover. (36858)

367

THE LIFE AND MORALS OF JESUS OF NAZARETH. Extracted textually from the Gospels of Matthew, Mark, Luke, and John by Thomas Jefferson. New York, N.Y., The Eakins Press, [1968].

Designed by Edith McKeon.
5½ × 4½ inches; 152 pages.
Blue cloth over boards; spine stamped in black and gold; wrapper. (36830)

368

THE LIVELY ANATOMY OF GOD. By Nancy Willard. New York, N.Y., Eakins Press, 1968.

Designed by Edith McKeon.
9½ × 6 inches; 95 pages.
Red cloth over boards; wrapper. (126726)

369

LODGE OF ST. ANDREW, APRIL 29 – MAY 2, 1968. Boston, Mass., Published by the Lodge, 1968.

10¼ × 7¼ inches; 32+[4] pages; illustrated.
50 copies bound in light green paper and dark green quarter leather over boards. (96830)

370

MAP OF SAN LORENZO: AN OLMEC SITE IN VERACRUZ, MEXICO. By Michael D. Coe. New Haven, Conn., Yale University Department of Anthropology, [1968].

12 × 9 inches; 15 pages + site map (in pocket); bibliography.
Saddlewire stitched into blue-green paper cover. (36828)

371

A New Library at Exeter. [Exeter, N.H.], Trustees of the Phillips Exeter Academy, 1968.

8¼×6¾ inches; 14+[2] pages including 2 pages of illustrations laid in. Saddlewire stitched into printed gray and brown paper cover. (26809)

372

Opportunities for Research in the John Carter Brown Library. Providence, R.I., Brown University, 1968.

7½×5 inches; 88 pages; illustrated. Saddlewire stitched and glued into printed white paper cover. (116743)

373

Ovid: Acis, Galatea, and Polyphemus (Metamorphoses XIII 750–897). Edited with introduction, notes, and vocabulary by David D. Coffin. Exeter, N.H., Phillips Exeter Academy Press, 1968.

9×6 inches; 24 pages. Saddlewire stitched into printed yellow-brown paper cover. (96706)

374

The Paintings of Charles Hawthorne. Introduction by Marvin S. Sadik. Storrs, Conn., The University of Connecticut Museum of Art, 1968.

Designed by Leonard Baskin.
11×8½ inches; [88] pages including 50 pages of plates; colored frontispiece.
Smythsewn and glued into printed off-white paper cover. (76824)

375

Philip Hofer as Author and Publisher. Introductory by Ray Nash. Cambridge, Mass., Harvard College Library Department of Printing and Graphic Arts, 1968.

10¼×7¼ inches; 64+[2] pages; illustrated; bibliography.
500 copies bound in printed gray paper and red quarter cloth over boards. (106721)

376

A Philosophy of Language Instruction. By John A. Rassias. With an introduction by C. Phillip Bosserman. Hanover, N.H., Dartmouth College, 1968.

9 × 6 inches; 36 pages.
Saddlewire stitched into light brown paper cover. (86838)

377

A Poem "On the Demolition of Dartmouth College." By Philip Freneau. As it originally appeared in the year 1790, now published with an introductory note by Edward Connery Lathem. Hanover, N.H., Hanover Historical Society, 1968.

7¾ × 5 inches; [16] pages.
Handsewn signature of untrimmed handmade paper; no cover. (106656)

378

Poems. By Elizabeth Hamlin. Lunenburg, Vt., Privately printed, 1968.

9 × 6 inches; 33 + [3] pages.
Saddlewire stitched into light blue paper wrapper. (46843)

379

The Popular Leaders of the American Revolution. By Merrill Jensen. Schenectady, N.Y., The Friends of the Union College Library, 1968 (Publication Number 2).

8¼ × 5½ inches; 23 pages.
250 copies handsewn into brown paper cover and glued into printed green wrapper. (56808)

380

Roy Lyman Butterfield, 1882–1968; Ethel Place Butterfield, 1884–1940. Remarks by their Sons. Hartwick, N.Y., [Privately printed], 1968.

8½ × 5½ inches; [14] pages; illustrated.
Handsewn into blue paper cover. (76823)

381

THE SPEE CLUB OF HARVARD UNIVERSITY. Cambridge,
Mass., Privately published, 1968.

9¼×6¼ inches; [2]+75+[3] pages; illustrated.
Red cloth over boards. (86711)

382

TO REMEMBER BARBARA FOSTER VIETOR. New Haven,
Conn., Privately published, [1968].

8½×11 inches; [36] pages including 24 pages of facsimiles; illustrated.
Saddlewire stitched into printed paper cover. (116738)

383

TWO POEMS. By Emily Dickinson. [Illustrations and letter-
ing by Marie Angel.] Cambridge, Mass., Walker and Company in association with the Department of Printing and
Graphic Arts, Harvard College Library, 1968.

5×5 inches; [8] pages.
9,500 copies handsewn into printed cream paper cover. (46803)

384

UNTO THE GENERATIONS: THE ROOTS OF TRUE AMER-
ICANISM. By Daniel L. Marsh. New Canaan, Conn., The
Long House, Inc., 1968.

9¼×6¼ inches; 173 pages.
Blue cloth over boards; wrapper. (26833)

385

VARUJAN BOGHOSIAN: ARTIST IN RESIDENCE. Hanover,
N.H., Dartmouth College, 1968.

8⅛×8 inches; [8] leaves including 8 pages of plates.
Double leaves bound oriental fashion and glued into brown paper cover
and gold paper wrapper. (66819)

386

VENETIAN BRONZES FROM THE COLLECTIONS OF THE
CORRER MUSEUM, VENICE. Introduction and notes by
Professor Giovanni Mariacher. Washington, D.C., Smith-
sonian Institution, [1968].

Designed by Crimilda Pontes.
10×7 inches; [52] pages including 35 pages of plates.
Smythsewn and glued into printed black glossy paper cover. (86818)

387

VENICE AND THE DEFENSE OF REPUBLICAN LIBERTY:
RENAISSANCE VALUES IN THE AGE OF THE COUNTER-
REFORMATION. By William J. Bouwsma. Berkeley and Los
Angeles, Calif., University of California Press, 1968.

9×6 inches; xv+[1]+670 pages + [16] pages of plates; frontispiece;
illustrated endleaves; bibliography.
Bound in red cloth and black quarter buckram over boards; gold-
stamped spine. (116635)

388

VIEWS OF FLORENCE AND TUSCANY BY GIUSEPPE ZOC-
CHI, 1711–1767: SEVENTY-SEVEN DRAWINGS FROM THE
COLLECTION OF THE PIERPONT MORGAN LIBRARY. By
Elaine Evans Dee. [Washington, D.C.], International Ex-
hibitions Foundation, 1968.

8½×10 inches; [34] pages + [77] pages of plates numbered 1 to 77.
Smythsewn and glued into printed white paper cover. (86837)

389

WALT WHITMAN'S BLUE BOOK: THE 1860–61 LEAVES
OF GRASS CONTAINING HIS MANUSCRIPT ADDITIONS
AND REVISIONS. [Textual analysis by Arthur Golden.]
New York, N.Y., New York Public Library, 1968.

8¾×5¾ inches; Vol. I: [7]+456+[6] pages with [8] additional leaves
tipped in; illustrated; facsimile. Vol. II: lxv+[3]+428 pages.
Blue cloth over boards; together in slipcase. (26521)

390

WILLIAM BARTRAM: BOTANICAL AND ZOOLOGICAL DRAWINGS, 1756–1788. Edited with an introduction and commentary by Joseph Ewan. Philadelphia, Pa., The American Philosophical Society, 1968 (Memoirs of the American Philosophical Society, Vol. 74).

Reproduced from the Fothergill Album in the British Museum (Natural History).
16 × 11¾ inches; x + [2] + 180 pages including [59] colored plates numbered 1 to 59 + colored frontispiece.
Green cloth over boards; gold-stamped cover and spine. (106823)

391

YOUR SON, CALVIN COOLIDGE: A SELECTION OF LETTERS FROM CALVIN COOLIDGE TO HIS FATHER. Edited by Edward Connery Lathem with an introduction by John Coolidge. Montpelier, Vt., Vermont Historical Society, 1968.

9½ × 6½ inches; xi + [1] + 243 pages including 5 pages of facsimiles.
Smythsewn and glued into blue buckram over boards; gold-stamped spine; wrapper. (86741)

⌈1969⌉

392

AMERICAN PENMANSHIP, 1800–1850: A HISTORY OF WRITING AND A BIBLIOGRAPHY OF COPYBOOKS FROM JENKINS TO SPENCER. By Ray Nash. Worcester, Mass., American Antiquarian Society, 1969.

9½ × 6¼ inches; xii + 303 + [3] pages.
Black cloth over boards. (106508)

393

THE BEDSIDE COMPANION. By Robert Cutler. Lunenburg, Vt., Privately printed, 1969.

9 × 6 inches; xiii + [1] + 73 pages.
Smythsewn and glued into blue paper cover. (16931)

394

CLASSROOM MANAGEMENT. By Judith M. Smith and Donald E. P. Smith. New York, N.Y., Learning Research Association, Inc., 1969.

9¼×6 inches; 61 pages; illustrated.
Smythsewn and glued into printed black and orange paper cover. (106910)

395

A DARTMOUTH READER. Edited by Frances Brown. Hanover, N.H., Dartmouth Publications, 1969.

9½×6¼ inches; 339+[5] pages.
Green cloth over boards; wrapper. (86922)

396

EDUCATION IN THE GRAPHIC ARTS: A SYMPOSIUM HELD IN THE WIGGIN GALLERY, BOSTON PUBLIC LIBRARY. Boston, Mass., Boston Public Library, 1969.

Includes "The Undergraduate and the Graphic Arts" by Ray Nash; "The Education of a Graphic Artist" by Fritz Eichenberg; and "Graphic Arts Education: A Museum Program" by Frederick Walkey.
8¾×5¾ inches; [2]+43+[2] pages.
1,000 copies bound in green paper over boards. (56756)

397

FAIRY TALES FOR COMPUTERS. By E. M. Forster, Franz Kafka, Theodor Herzl, Samuel Butler, Paul Valéry, Hans Christian Andersen. New York, N.Y., Eakins Press, 1969.

Designed by Edith McKeon Abbott.
5½×4¼ inches; x+163+[3] pages.
Smythsewn and glued into blue paper cover. (66909)

398

THE FIFTEEN DECISIVE BATTLES OF THE WORLD. By Sir Edward S. Creasy. With an introduction by Harrison

W. Baldwin and illustrations by Joseph Domjan. New York, N.Y., For the Members of the Limited Editions Club, 1969.

12½×9½ inches; x+211 pages + [15] pages of colored plates.
1,500 copies numbered and signed by the artist; bound in blue decorated cloth over boards; gold-stamped label on spine; slipcase. (66814)

399
FIVE ADDLED ETCHERS. By Leonard Baskin. Hanover, N.H., Dartmouth Publications, 1969 (The First Hamilton B. Mitchell Lecture on Printing and Graphic Arts).

Designed by Ray Nash.
12½×9½ inches; 52+[3] pages including 15 pages of plates + 1 extra plate tipped in.
Printed yellow paper over boards; printed in red and black on cover and spine; wrapper. (46817)

400
THE FRANCIS A. COUNTWAY LIBRARY OF MEDICINE. Boston, Mass., [Harvard University Libraries], 1969 (Guides to the Harvard Libraries Series Number 9).

Revised edition.
Cover title; at head of title: "Library Guide."
8½×6 inches; 33 pages; illustrated.
Saddlewire stitched into printed white paper cover. (See items 245 and 590.) (76931)

401
FROM THE BOSPORUS TO SAMARKAND: FLAT-WOVEN RUGS. By Anthony N. Landreau and W. R. Pickering. Washington, D.C., The Textile Museum, 1969.

Designed by Crimilda Pontes.
11×8 inches; 112 pages including [93] pages of plates (some colored).
Smythsewn and glued into printed white paper cover. (26943)

402
GREETINGS TO DARTMOUTH: BICENTENNIAL CONVOCA-

tion and Commencement, June 15, 1969. Hanover, N.H., Dartmouth College, 1969.

9 ×6 inches; 61 pages.
Smythsewn and glued into printed yellow paper cover. (66935)

403

It's Better than Working: Confessions of a Rare Book Dealer. By Philip C. Duschnes. New York, N.Y., Philip C. Duschnes, 1969.

"Two chapters from an unfinished autobiography."
9 ×6 inches; [8] pages; illustrated.
750 copies handsewn into light green paper cover. (86933)

404

Just Now for Instance: A Retrospective Selection of Ninety Poems. By Julian M. Drachman. Foreword by Mark Van Doren. Drawings by Lawrence Scott. Lunenburg, Vt., Privately published, 1969.

$9\frac{1}{2}$ ×$6\frac{1}{4}$ inches; [2]+148 pages.
1,000 copies bound in blue paper and red quarter cloth over boards. (16935)

405

Lenox: Massachusetts Shire Town. By David H. Wood. Drawings by Vaughn Gray. Lenox, Mass., Published by the Town, 1969.

$9\frac{1}{2}$ ×$6\frac{1}{4}$ inches; xiv+219 pages.
Red cloth over boards; wrapper. (76818)

406

Man, Land: Williams College Center for Environmental Studies, The First Two Years. By William Carney. Williamstown, Mass., Williams College, 1969.

6 ×9 inches; 58+[2] pages; illustrated.
Smythsewn and glued into printed paper cover. (116921)

407

MARTIN JOHNSON HEADE. By Theodore E. Stebbins, Jr. College Park, Md., University of Maryland Art Gallery, 1969.

Designed by Leonard Baskin.
8½×10¼ inches; [120] pages including 66 leaves of plates.
Smythsewn and glued into printed white paper cover. (56916)

408

NATURE AND LOVE POEMS. By Ruth Herschberger. New York, N.Y., The Eakins Press, 1969.

Designed by Edith McKeon Abbott.
5×6 inches; 54 pages.
Light green cloth over boards; cover and spine stamped in green and gold; wrapper. (106817)

409

NEW HAMPSHIRE FIGHTS THE CIVIL WAR. By Mather Cleveland, M.D. New London, N.H., [Privately printed], 1969.

12¼×7¼ inches; 230 pages including [24] pages of photographs; bibliography; maps on endleaves.
Blue buckram over boards; gold-stamped cover and spine; wrapper. (86815)

410

NICCOLÒ MACHIAVELLI: THE FIRST DECENNALE. Florence, Italy, Villa I Tatti: The Harvard University Center for Italian Renaissance Studies; Distributed by Harvard University Press, 1969.

Includes facsimile of the first edition (February 1506).
8½×5½ inches; [34] pages including 23 pages of facsimile.
Smythsewn and glued into light red-brown paper cover. (56909)

411

THE NOTEBOOK OF JOHN SMIBERT. With essays by Sir David Evans, John Kerslake, and Andrew Oliver; and with notes relating to Smibert's American portraits by Andrew Oliver. Boston, Mass., Massachusetts Historical Society, 1969.

Includes facsimile from the notebook in the Public Record Office, London.
10 ×6¾ inches; vi+131 pages; facsimile; maps.
Red-brown cloth over boards; gold-stamped cover and spine. (76817)

412

OLD MASTER DRAWINGS FROM CHATSWORTH. Introduction and catalogue by James Byam Shaw; foreword by Thomas S. Wragg. Washington, D.C., International Exhibitions Foundation, 1969.

A loan exhibition from the Devonshire Collection.
10 ×7½ inches; 50 pages + [110] pages of plates.
Smythsewn and glued into printed orange paper cover. (See item 147.) (56956)

413

PEN AND BRUSH: THE AUTHOR AS ARTIST. By Lola L. Szladits and Harvey Simmonds. New York, N.Y., The New York Public Library, 1969.

10¼ ×7¾ inches; 59 pages; illustrated.
2,000 copies Smythsewn and glued into printed brown paper cover. (66903)

414

PIERRE REVERDY: SELECTED POEMS. [Translated] by Kenneth Rexroth. New York, N.Y., New Directions, 1969.

8¼ ×5½ inches; xiii+[1]+78+[4] pages.
150 copies signed by the translator; bound in brown cloth over boards; slipcase. (106835)

415

POEMS OF THE PAST. By Marcus Selden Goldman. Lunenburg, Vt., Privately printed, 1969.

9½ ×6¼ inches; xvii+[1]+109 pages.
Brown paper over boards. (36914)

416

PRINT COLLECTING TODAY: A SYMPOSIUM HELD IN
THE WIGGIN GALLERY, BOSTON PUBLIC LIBRARY.
Boston, Mass., Boston Public Library, 1969.

Includes "A Collector's View of Print Collecting Today" by Arthur
Vershbow; "Prints as a Public Resource" by Sinclair Hitchings; and
"The Pleasure of Learning, Looking, the Excitement of Buying" by
R. E. Lewis.
$8\frac{3}{4} \times 5\frac{3}{4}$ inches; 41+[3] pages.
1,500 copies bound in decorated orange paper over boards. (36947)

417

PRINTING IN DELAWARE, 1761–1800: A CHECKLIST.
By Evald Rink. Wilmington, Del., Eleutherian Mills Historical Library, 1969.

$9\frac{1}{2} \times 6\frac{1}{4}$ inches; 214+[2] pages; illustrated.
Blue cloth over boards. (36933)

418

REFLECTIONS ON A LONG LIFE: ELIZABETH KELLOGG,
1870–1967. Edited with an introduction by Dorothy Good-
win Blodgett. Lunenburg, Vt., Privately printed, 1969.

9×6 inches; 67 pages; frontispiece portrait.
Smythsewn and glued into printed light red board. (106950)

419

SAVANNAH REVISITED: A PICTORIAL HISTORY. By Mills
Lane. Athens, Ga., The University of Georgia Press, 1969.

$10\frac{3}{4} \times 12\frac{1}{4}$ inches; 96 pages including 84 pages of plates.
Blue cloth over boards; gold-stamped spine. (See items 612 and 868.)
(66920)

420

SIXTY DARTMOUTH POEMS. Selected and with a foreword
by Richard Eberhart. Hanover, N.H., Dartmouth Publications, 1969.

9×6 inches; 65 pages.
200 copies handsewn into light blue paper cover and glued into printed
light blue wrapper. (116901)

421

SOCIAL HISTORY OF THE CLUB OF ODD VOLUMES, 1887–1967. By Alexander Whiteside Williams. Boston, Mass., [Printed for the Club], 1969.

9×5¾ inches; xi+[1]+75+[5] pages, with two announcements laid in. 161 copies bound in printed paper and black quarter cloth over boards; slipcase. (26849)

422

A SOCIETY'S CHIEF JOYS: AN INTRODUCTION TO THE COLLECTIONS OF THE AMERICAN ANTIQUARIAN SOCIETY. With a foreword by Walter Muir Whitehill. Worcester, Mass., American Antiquarian Society, 1969.

10¾×7¾ inches; 30+[121] pages including 41 pages of plates; illustrated; portraits (some colored).
Light green cloth over boards; printed label laid onto cover; gold-stamped spine. (126844)

423

STUDIES IN HONOR OF SAMUEL MONTEFIORE WAXMAN. Edited by Herbert H. Golden. Boston, Mass., Boston University Press, 1969.

Designed by David Ford.
9½×6¼ inches; ix+[1]+263 pages; illustrated.
Blue cloth over boards; slipcase. (86814)

424

20TH CENTURY REFLECTIONS: DARTMOUTH ALUMNI COLLEGE LECTURES, 1968. Hanover, N.H., Dartmouth College, 1969.

9¼×6 inches; [4]+267+[3] pages.
Smythsewn and glued into glossy black paper cover. (66924)

425

THE UNDERGRADUATE AND THE GRAPHIC ARTS. By Ray Nash. [Lunenburg, Vt., Privately printed], 1969.

Cover title. Printed as a keepsake for Roderick D. Stinehour's lecture in the Heritage of the Graphic Arts Series, 1969. First appeared in *Education in the Graphic Arts* (1969).
8×5½ inches; [20] pages.
200 copies handsewn into white paper cover and glued into printed blue wrapper. (106902)

426

A UNIVERSITY COLLECTS: GEORGIA MUSEUM OF ART, THE UNIVERSITY OF GEORGIA. Selected by Stuart P. Feld. Athens, Ga., Georgia Museum of Art, 1969.

Designed by Leonard Baskin.
11×8½ inches; [30] pages + [44] pages of plates.
Smythsewn and glued into printed white paper cover. (66931)

427

VESSEL OF SADNESS. By William Woodruff. Gainesville, Fla., Kallman Publishing Co., 1969.

9¼×6¼ inches; 152 pages; illustrated; maps on endleaves.
Black cloth over boards. Also issued Smythsewn and glued into printed paper cover. (56911)

428

THE WEBSTER COTTAGE AND THOSE WHO LIVED THERE. By Francis Lane Childs. Hanover, N.H., Hanover Historical Society, 1969.

9×6 inches; 40 pages + [8] pages of plates.
2,000 copies saddlewire stitched into printed white paper cover. (46904)

⌈1970⌉

429

AMERICAN SILVERSMITHS IN BRITISH NORTH AMERICA, 1776–1800. By John E. Langdon. Toronto, Ont., Privately published, 1970.

10×6½ inches; 82 pages; bibliography.
350 copies bound in light gray cloth and black quarter cloth over boards; gold-stamped spine; slipcase. (116940)

Daniel Webster
and a Small College

BY JOHN C. STERLING

HANOVER · NEW HAMPSHIRE
Dartmouth Publications
MCMLXV

Daniel Webster—The Early Years

ON a summer afternoon in 1790, a frail, black-eyed boy, barefooted and dressed in a tow shirt and coarse cassimere trousers, stepped out of his father's tavern at Salisbury Lower Village, in the upper valley of the Merrimack River. Across the highway was the general store kept by his schoolteacher, William Hoyt, filled with tempting things to eat and wear. There his glance fell on a novelty,—a large cotton handkerchief, crudely printed on both sides,— and, having already a passion for literature, he bought it with the coins which were jingling in his pocket. What he saw was the text of the Federal Constitution, which had recently been ratified by the states and was being circulated in this quaint fashion. Then and there he sat down under a spreading elm and read it through.*

Webster was then eight and a half years old.

His father Ebenezer Webster was of the fourth generation of Websters that had lived in New England—mostly in New Hampshire. Ebenezer had fought against the Indians with the famous Rogers Rangers. Later, he served under General Jeffrey Amherst in Canada, returning as captain. Still later, he joined the Continental army. For a while he served directly under General Washington around Boston. Without any schooling, he had taught himself to read and to write. He became a leading citizen and a respected judge. His first wife died, leaving Ebenezer with three small children. He soon remarried, this time to a thirty-seven-year-old spinster. Daniel, on January 18, 1782, became the fourth child of that second marriage. By this time Ebenezer had built a frame house in Salisbury Lower Village, where the Pemigewasset and the Winnepesaukee Rivers flow together to make the Merrimack, near Frank-

* *Daniel*, 1930. [Footnote references to sources are abbreviated and refer to the chronological "List of Works Consulted" on page 57. Thus "*Daniel*, 1930" refers to *Daniel Webster* by Claude Moore Fuess, published in Boston by Little, Brown in 1930.]

1

---

9 HANS BURGKMAIR
1473–1531, German
Musicians in Emperor Maximilian's Triumphal Procession
WOODCUT

THIS particular wind band of Maximilian's musical entourage consists of two *Krummhorns*, two *Pommers*, and a *Posaune* (trombone) playing the upper, middle, and bass parts respectively. The *Krummhorn* was a kind of oboe curved roughly in the shape of an oxhorn. Its special feature was the concealed reed encased in a wooden cap so that it was out of reach of the player's lips. (The embouchure of the instrument on the extreme right is purely a matter of artistic license.) Apparently the *Krummhorn* went out of fashion in the early seventeenth century; the last composition for it appeared in a German publication of 1617. The *Pommers* are simply the larger members of the shawm family. Pictured here are two tenors, readily distinguished by their perforated wooden barrel, or *fontanelle*, a slide-on device at the lower end of the instrument which serves to protect the brass key governing the lowest tone.

Posaune, the German word for trombone, may have been derived from *Bůsine* which was the name for the instrument in the days of Maximilian I when it began an independent existence. However, the Italian *trombone* is more descriptive of its origin since the word stands for large *tromba*, or trumpet. Made more flexible and versatile by the addition of a slide, the trombone played a prominent part (an ideal bass) in ceremonial bands of princes, as well as in church and civic music.

THE VOICE
OF THE WHALEMAN

WITH AN ACCOUNT OF THE
NICHOLSON WHALING COLLECTION

BY STUART C. SHERMAN

PROVIDENCE PUBLIC LIBRARY
PROVIDENCE
1965

ENTRY 266

ACKNOWLEDGMENTS

A SCHOLARLY BOOK is rarely the sole work of an author. Its conception and writing may be his but the book is a synthesis of ideas contributed by many. This book is no exception.

It is a special privilege to acknowledge here my indebtedness to Mr. Lawrence C. Wroth, Librarian Emeritus of the John Carter Brown Library, who taught me the fundamentals of Bibliography and the real meaning of the word 'standard'.

The members of the Nicholson Whaling Collection Advisory Group offered advice and criticism which contributed significantly to the book. I am grateful for their interest. The group consists of Professor Benjamin C. Clough, Professor Robert W. Kenny and Mr. Paul C. Nicholson, Jr., each of whom are trustees of the Providence Public Library; Mr. W. Easton Louttit, Jr., trustee emeritus; Mr. Charles F. Batchelder of Milton, Massachusetts; Mr. Gale Blosser of Millbrae, California; Mr. M. V. Brewington, Assistant Director and Curator of Maritime History at the Peabody Museum of Salem; and Mr. Henry Beetle Hough, Editor and Publisher of *The Vineyard Gazette*.

Mr. Batchelder, a noted whaling collector and bibliographer, was outstandingly helpful. He was candid in his criticism of the manuscript and was always generous in sharing his own fund of knowledge of the literature of whaling. This is a better book because of his interest.

Mr. Philip B. Simonds, President of the Board of Trustees of

5

ENTRY 266

---

ing him and gnashing his teeth, and he said: "Art thou he whom the king delighteth to honor? Can the Ethiopian change his skin? Nay, but by the sayings of thy mouth hast thou stumbled, and by the wickedness thou hast forged against me. Upon thyself shall thy wickedness be poured, for I did dwell secure with thee."

The parable: He seeketh not peace for his soul who forgeth evil against his neighbor and speaketh against him in frowardness. When one letteth out water, it is the beginning of strife; his one verdict is death. Who slandereth his neighbor in secret, him will I cut off.

86

Hen & Mistress

YEARN NOT FOR THE DAINTIES
OF HIM THAT PERSUADES THEE
BY THE SMOOTHNESS OF HIS LIPS.

A HEN scattered her food and gathered it between her feet; she separated ears and cut them off; she opened her feet out to uncover the dust with her claw and the chaff blown out of the granary. Often she labored in vain, for she did not find enough to satisfy her. Her mistress looked upon her and saw that her heart was persuaded to give her soul livelihood by her toil; her mercies were warmed and she said to her: "Lo, I have swaddled thee and brought thee up, and therefore do I take pity upon thee for that thy corn is scattered and dispersed—the leavings of the hail—and thy soul falls short in seeking it. The seeds are rotten under their clods; therefore art thou

156

meager and wonderfully reduced—as one that gathereth ears in the valley of Rephaim—and thou crouchest in a troubled vale. Better for thee half a homer, aye, a homer of wheat, as thou sittest at the gate of hope, than that thou

shouldst grieve all the day. Lo, I put before thee all my grain, my threshing and the corn of my floor, worth a hundred pieces of silver, current money with the merchant. Go not to glean in another field. Lo, thou hast uncovered the dust and covered it again; what hast thou gathered this day, where is thy labor? Thou art wearied but hast not found that for which thou hast toiled; before thy bread cometh sighing." As the mistress spoke thus in her ears, she was despised in her eyes, and she said to her: "If thou wouldst give me each month thy granary full of wheat threshed and ground, I would regard it as bread of idleness. Better for me to endure poverty, to defile my horn in the dust than that some cruel one drive me from the granary. Whoso rests his hope upon another, the increase of his house shall depart. Better for me to go forth

157

ENTRY 324

THE
HOUGHTON
LIBRARY

1942-1967

A Selection of Books and Manuscripts
in Harvard Collections

CAMBRIDGE
The Harvard College Library
MCMLXVII

I Like People & Places

I Like

People & Places

BY Dorothy Hunt Smith

AT THE SIGN OF *Al Kalbu al Kabir al Aswad*

PRINCETON · NEW JERSEY · 1968

430

ARABIC AND PERSIAN POEMS IN ENGLISH. By Omar S. Pound. New York, N.Y., New Directions Publishing Corp., 1970.

9¼×6¼ inches; 80 pages; bibliographical note.
Green cloth over boards; wrapper. (17047)

431

THE BICK COLLECTION OF ITALIAN RELIGIOUS DRAWINGS. Sarasota, Fla., The John and Mable Ringling Museum of Art, 1970.

9×7 inches; [80] pages including 28 pages of plates.
Smythsewn and glued into printed white paper cover. (97051)

432

THE BLATHWAYT ATLAS: A COLLECTION OF FORTY-EIGHT MANUSCRIPT AND PRINTED MAPS OF THE SEVENTEENTH CENTURY RELATING TO THE BRITISH OVERSEAS EMPIRE IN THAT ERA, BROUGHT TOGETHER ABOUT 1683 FOR THE USE OF THE LORDS OF TRADE AND PLANTATIONS BY WILLIAM BLATHWAYT, SECRETARY. A facsimile reproduction edited by Jeannette D. Black. Providence, R.I., Brown University Press, 1970 (A Brown University Bicentennial Publication).

Volume I: The Maps. 23×14 inches; [8] pages handsewn in a single signature. With a "Manuscript List of Maps" 23×14 inches; [4] pages of holograph facsimile in one unsewn signature; and 48 maps in facsimile (some colored), each 23×28 inches (folded to 23×14 inches).
Together in a hinged box, 25×15¼×2 inches, covered in rust-red buckram printed in red and stamped in gold on the cover and spine. (106831)

433

BUCK FEVER AND OTHER DIVERSIONS. By Harold Willard Gleason. [Lunenburg, Vt., Privately printed, 1970.]

8¾×5¾ inches; 41 pages.
Smythsewn and glued into printed yellow paper over boards. (107001)

434

CATALOGUE OF THE HARVARD COLLEGE CHAPTER OF ΦBK, ALPHA OF MASSACHUSETTS. With the constitution, an annotated list of orators and poets, and with an essay on the orations and poems by David T. W. McCord. Cambridge, Mass., Printed for the Chapter, 1970.

9¼×6¼ inches; ix+393 pages.
Crimson cloth over boards; gold-stamped cover and spine; wrapper. (36513)

435

THE CENTENNIAL OF THE P[OCUMTUCK] V[ALLEY] M[EMORIAL] A[SSOCIATION] AND DEDICATION OF THE HERITAGE FOUNDATION LIBRARY. Deerfield, Mass., [Deerfield Academy], 1970.

8½×5½ inches; 27 pages; illustrated.
Smythsewn and glued into blue-green paper cover; printed white label laid onto cover. (37029)

436

THE COMPLETE POOR RICHARD ALMANACS PUBLISHED BY BENJAMIN FRANKLIN. Reproduced in facsimile with an introduction by Whitfield J. Bell, Jr. Barre, Mass., Imprint Society, 1970.

Designed by Klaus Gemming.
8¾×5½ inches; Vol. I: (1733–1747), xxv+[7]+360 pages; frontispiece. Vol. II: (1748–1758), [8]+420+[4] pages; frontispiece.
Bound in brown cloth over boards; slipcase. (87013)

437

A COPY OF PLEASANT VERSES ADDRESSED TO SIR JOSHUA REYNOLDS AND CO. . . . CONTAINING A DELICATE IRONY DIRECTED AT DR. SAMUEL JOHNSON. By Thomas Barnard. Prepared for the press by Frederick W. Hilles. Lunenburg, Vt., Printed for the Johnsonians, 1970.

A keepsake to celebrate Dr. Johnson's 261st birthday.
9×6 inches; 8 pages + [4] pages of holograph facsimile (12¾×7¾ inches) in a pocket.
263 copies saddlewire stitched into printed light brown paper cover. (67002)

438

DARTMOUTH DRAWINGS. By George T. Plowman.
With an introduction by his son E. Grosvenor Plowman.
Hanover, N.H., Dartmouth College Library, 1970.

Cover title.
12½×7½ inches; [14] leaves including 7 leaves of plates.
1,000 copies handsewn into green paper cover. (37005)

439

DAVID CLAYPOOL JOHNSTON: AMERICAN GRAPHIC HUMORIST, 1798–1865. By Malcolm Johnson. [Lunenburg, Vt., Printed at The Stinehour Press], 1970.

9¼×7¼ inches; 47 pages; illustrated.
1,800 copies bound in printed white paper over boards. Also issued saddlewire stitched into printed white paper cover. (17046)

440

DRAKE IN ENGLAND. By Sir Anthony Wagner. Concord, N.H., New Hampshire Historical Society, 1970.

Revised edition.
12¼×8¼ inches; 119 pages + 2 leaves of genealogical tables tipped in; maps.
Dark blue cloth over boards; gold-stamped cover and spine. (See item 165.) (116815)

441

FABLES BY THE LATE MR. JOHN GAY. In one volume complete with wood engravings by Gillian Lewis Tyler. Barre, Mass., Imprint Society, 1970.

10¾×7½ inches; xix+[1]+234+[6] pages.
1,950 copies bound in printed brown paper and red quarter cloth over boards; slipcase. (66943)

442

FRAGMENTS AFTER. By Carl A. Weyerhaeuser. Milton, Mass., [Privately printed], 1970.

8½ × 5¼ inches; 153 pages.
Blue paper and red cloth over boards; gold-stamped spine. (47019)

443

GEORGIA O'KEEFFE. By Lloyd Goodrich and Doris Bry. New York, N.Y., Published for the Whitney Museum of American Art by Praeger Publishers, 1970.

11¼ × 8¾ inches; 195 pages including 121 pages of plates numbered 1 to 121 (some colored); bibliography.
White cloth over boards. Also issued Smythsewn and glued into printed white board. Black and white plates printed by The Meriden Gravure Company; color engravings by Publicity Engravers, Inc., and printed at the Press of A. Colish. (37046)

444

THE HISTORY OF PRINTING IN AMERICA; WITH A BIOGRAPHY OF PRINTERS AND AN ACCOUNT OF NEWSPAPERS. By Isaiah Thomas, LL.D. Edited by Marcus A. McCorison from the second edition. Barre, Mass., Imprint Society, 1970.

Includes an original leaf from the first edition (1810).
10 × 6¾ inches; xxi + 650 pages; frontispiece portrait.
1,950 numbered copies bound in light blue cloth over boards; gold-stamped spine; slipcase. (96939)

445

HORTUS BOTANICUS: THE BOTANIC GARDEN AND THE BOOK: FIFTY BOOKS FROM THE STERLING MORTON LIBRARY. Compiled by Ian MacPhail; introductory essay by Joseph Ewan. Lisle, Ill., The Morton Arboretum, 1970.

Designed by Suzette Morton Davidson.
8¼ × 6¼ inches; 119 pages including 41 pages of plates (some colored).
2,000 copies Smythsewn and glued into printed light blue paper cover. (97126)

446

ILLINGWORTH ON TARGET. By Draper Hill with an introduction by Malcolm Muggeridge. Boston, Mass., Boston Public Library, 1970.

7×9 inches; 45 pages including 18 pages of plates.
1,000 copies saddlewire stitched into printed cream paper cover. (87009)

447

ILLUSTRATIONS TO THE DIVINE COMEDY OF DANTE BY LEONARD BASKIN. Introduction by Dale Roylance. New Haven, Conn., Yale University, 1970.

Designed by Leonard Baskin. Includes plates selected from the Grossman edition (1969).
13×8¾ inches; [32] pages including 22 pages of plates.
Saddlewire stitched into printed brown paper cover. (57001)

448

LATIN: A COURSE FOR SCHOOLS AND COLLEGES. By John A. Anderson and Frank J. Groten, Jr. Pottstown, Pa., The Hill School, 1970.

9¼×6¼ inches; 357+[3] pages; map on endleaves.
Blue cloth over boards. (56932)

449

LEONARD BASKIN: THE GRAPHIC WORK, 1950–1970. New York, N.Y., The Far Gallery, 1970.

Designed by Leonard Baskin.
11×8½ inches; [104] pages including 72 pages of plates (some colored); frontispiece portrait.
Smythsewn and glued into printed white paper cover. (17008)

450

LETTERS FROM THE THIRD GRADE. Compiled by Freeman Keith. [Lunenburg, Vt., The Stinehour Press], 1970.

5×8 inches; [48] pages.
Saddlewire stitched into printed white paper cover. (67047)

451

LIBROS VIRUMQUE CANO GAUDEAMUS: THE GIFTS OF JOHN NICHOLAS BROWN TO THE JOHN CARTER BROWN LIBRARY FROM 1924 TO 1969. Providence, R.I., The Associates of the John Carter Brown Library, [1970].

10½×7 inches; [4]+80+[4] pages; frontispiece portrait.
Bound in printed red-yellow paper and red quarter cloth over boards; gold-stamped spine. Also issued Smythsewn and glued into printed red-gold paper cover. (86942)

452

LIVINGDYING: POEMS OF CID CORMAN. Title page illustration by Shiryū Morita. New York, N.Y., New Directions Publishing Corporation, 1970.

8¼×5¾ inches; [64] pages.
Black linen over boards. Also issued Smythsewn and glued into printed black and white glossy paper cover. (96942)

453

THE LONG POINT COMPANY. Recollections by Edward Harris. Further recollections by Junius S. Morgan. New York, N.Y., Privately published, 1970.

9×5¾ inches; 45+[3] pages.
Brown paper and brown quarter cloth over boards. (86940)

454

MYFANWY THOMAS REMEMBERS ROBERT FROST. [Amherst, Mass.], The Friends of the Amherst College Library, 1970.

Cover title.
6¾×5 inches; [4] pages French fold.
400 copies unbound; French fold.

455

THE NOTORIOUS JUMPING FROG AND OTHER STORIES.

By Mark Twain. Selected and introduced by Edward Wagenknecht. Illustrated by Joseph Low. New York, N.Y., Limited Editions Club, 1970.

11¼×7 inches; xiv+[4]+301+[3] pages.
1,500 copies bound in three cloths, brown, red, and blue, over boards; slipcase. (66912)

456

P. P. RUBENS: THE LEOPARDS. By Julius S. Held. [Lunenburg, Vt., Privately printed], 1970.

Designed by Anna H. Audette.
9½×12 inches; 15 pages + [10] pages of plates numbered I to x.
Saddlewire stitched into printed white paper cover; acetate wrapper. (57028)

457

PAINTINGS BY EDWIN SCOTT. An appreciation . . . by M. Henri Focillon. Biographical notes by Donald McClelland. Washington, D.C., The Smithsonian Institution, 1970.

Designed by Crimilda Pontes.
10×8 inches; 55 pages including 30 pages of plates.
Smythsewn and glued into printed white paper cover. (57023)

458

A PENCIL IN PENN: SKETCHES OF PITTSBURGH AND SURROUNDING AREAS. Drawings by Edward Brown Lee with text by Edward Brown Lee, Jr. Pittsburgh, Pa., [Privately printed], 1970.

8½×8¼ inches; 122 pages including [48] pages of plates (some colored).
Bound in blue cloth over boards; silver-stamped spine; wrapper. (37051)

459

THE PHILLIPS EXETER ACADEMY: A PICTORIAL HISTORY. Edited by Edward C. Echols. Exeter, N.H., The Phillips Exeter Academy Press, 1970.

11¼×8¾ inches; viii+109 pages; facsimiles; colored frontispiece portrait.
Bound in red-brown cloth over boards; silver-stamped spine; wrapper. (26829)

460

THE PROTEAN CENTURY, 1870–1970. New York, N.Y., M. Knoedler and Co., 1970.

10¼×8¼ inches; [106] pages including 63 pages of plates.
Gray paper over boards. Also issued Smythsewn and glued into gray paper cover. (116925)

461

RALPH J. CONDON AND THE CONDON MEDAL. By Frank C. Foster. Waterville, Me., Colby College, 1970.

9×6 inches; 18+[2] pages; frontispiece portrait.
500 copies saddlewire stitched into printed cream paper cover. (27028)

462

REFLECTIONS. By Rigel Osborn Belt. [Lunenburg, Vt.], Printed at The Stinehour Press, [1970].

9½×6¼ inches; 46+[2] pages.
Red-orange paper and brown quarter cloth over boards; gold-stamped cover and spine. (37022)

463

RENAISSANCE BOOKS OF SCIENCE FROM THE COLLECTION OF ALBERT E. LOWNES. Compiled by David R. Godine. Hanover, N.H., Dartmouth College, 1970.

9¾×6¼ inches; 123 pages including 33 pages of plates.
1,000 copies: some bound in red cloth over boards, gold stamped spine, illustration laid onto cover; others issued Smythsewn and glued into printed white paper cover. (37021)

464

ST. BOTOLPH CLUB: ITS BIRTH AND EARLY CLUB HIS-

TORY. By Joseph Henry Curtis. [Boston, Mass., Privately printed, 1970.]

8½ × 5½ inches; [20] pages.
Saddlewire stitched into gold-brown paper cover. (17022)

465

SAMPLER FROM THE CLASS OF 1926 MEMORIAL COLLECTION OF ILLUSTRATED BOOKS PUBLISHED IN NEW ENGLAND 1769–1869. Hanover, N.H., Dartmouth College Library, 1970.

11¼ × 8¾ inches; [36] pages; illustrated.
2,000 copies bound in light blue-green paper over boards. (37006)

466

SELECTED PROSE OF JOHN WESLEY POWELL. Edited and introduced by George Crossette. Boston, Mass., David R. Godine, 1970.

10 × 6½ inches; 122 pages including 14 pages of plates; frontispiece portrait.
1,500 copies bound in light green cloth over boards; label laid onto spine. (47015)

467

SEVENTY DARTMOUTH POEMS. Selected and with a preface and an essay on "War Poetry" by Richard Eberhart. Hanover, N.H., Dartmouth Publications, 1970.

9 × 6 inches; 87 pages.
200 copies handsewn into beige board and glued into printed beige wrapper. (107002)

468

TEN LITTLE RABBITS: A COUNTING BOOK WITH MINO THE MAGICIAN. By Maurice Sendak. Philadelphia, Pa., The Philip H. and A. S. W. Rosenbach Foundation, 1970.

3½ × 2¾ inches; [29] pages; illustrated (some colored).
Saddlewire stitched and glued into blue marbled paper cover; illustration laid onto cover. (57008)

469

A Tribute to Professor I. I. Rabi on the Occasion of His Retirement from Columbia University. New York, N.Y., Columbia University Department of Physics, 1970.

9×6 inches; 119 pages; illustrated; portrait; tables.
Smythsewn and glued into blue paper cover. (17032)

470

Vermont Clock and Watchmakers, Silversmiths and Jewelers, 1778–1878. By Lilian Baker Carlisle. Burlington, Vt., Privately published, 1970.

11¼×9 inches; xi+[1]+313 pages; illustrated.
1,000 copies bound in red cloth over boards; wrapper. (96929)

[1971]

471

Blind in the Hamptons? By Francis J. Mathues. Lancaster, N.H., The North Country Publishing Company, 1971.

9×6 inches; 25 pages.
300 copies saddlewire stitched into printed blue paper cover. (127003)

472

Boswell, Johnson, and the Petition of James Wilson. [Foreword by W. H. Bond.] Cambridge, Mass., Printed for the Houghton Library, 1971.

Keepsake printed for The Johnsonians.
11×8¾ inches; [8]+22 pages; facsimile.
150 copies printed for The Johnsonians and 500 copies for general circulation; saddlewire stitched into light green paper cover. (47140)

473

The British Look at America During the Age of Samuel Johnson. An exhibition with an address by Her-

man W. Liebert. Providence, R.I., The Associates of the
John Carter Brown Library, 1971.

10½×7½ inches; vi+55 pages.
Smythsewn and glued into light brown paper cover. (87130)

474

BROOKLINE SAVINGS BANK AND ITS COMMUNITY, 1871–
1971. By Bertram K. Little. With a foreword by H. S.
Payson Rome and an introduction by Walter Muir Whitehill. Brookline, Mass., Brookline Savings Bank, 1971.

9¼×6¼ inches; 69 pages; illustrated; portraits.
Blue cloth over boards; gold-stamped spine; wrapper. Also issued Smythsewn and glued into blue paper cover. (107130)

475

A CHRISTMAS CAROL. By Charles Dickens. Introduction
and notes by Philip Collins. New York, N.Y., New York
Public Library, 1971 (Levy Memorial Publication Fund
Publication Number 3).

The public reading version; a facsimile of the author's prompt copy.
6×9¼ inches; xxvi+206+[2] pages; facsimile.
Red cloth over boards; gold-stamped spine; wrapper. (67121)

476

COLBY IN THE SIXTIES: A TEN-YEAR REPORT FROM
THE PRESIDENT. By Robert E. L. Strider. Waterville, Me.,
Colby College, 1971.

9×6 inches; 55 pages.
Smythsewn and glued into light blue paper cover. (37104)

477

COLLECTOR'S GUIDE TO THE NATIONAL GEOGRAPHIC
MAGAZINE. By Edwin C. Buxbaum. Wilmington, Del.,
[Privately printed], 1971.

11¼×8¼ inches; viii+390 pages; illustrated.
Blue cloth over boards; gold-stamped leather label on spine; slipcase.
(47013)

478

CONFERENCE ON CHAVÍN. Elizabeth P. Benson, Editor. Washington, D.C., Dumbarton Oaks Research Library and Collection, [1971].

9¾×6¾ inches; vii+[3]+124 pages; illustrated (some colored); bibliography.
Dark blue cloth over boards; gold-stamped cover and spine. (47130)

479

A COPY OF A LETTER OF ROGER WILLIAMS TELLING OF THE BURNING OF PROVIDENCE AND OF HIS CONFERENCE WITH INDIANS DURING KING PHILIP'S WAR IN 1676. Transcribed with an introduction and notes by Bradford F. Swan. Providence, R.I., Published by His Excellency, Philip B. Simonds, Governor, and the Council of the Society of Colonial Wars, 1971 (Publication Number 50).

9¼×6¼ inches; [16] pages.
Handsewn into cream paper cover. (67104)

480

CUT OF NOON. By Frederick Nicklaus. New York, N.Y., David Lewis, 1971.

Designed by Edward Aho.
9¾×6 inches; [10]+53 pages.
1,000 copies bound in white cloth over boards; wrapper. (127007)

481

DESCENT AND RETURN: THE ORPHIC THEME IN MODERN LITERATURE. By Walter A. Strauss. Cambridge, Mass., Harvard University Press, 1971.

9¼×6¼ inches; viii+[4]+287 pages.
Smythsewn and glued into blue cloth over boards; silver-stamped spine. (67037)

482

DÜRER AND AMERICA. By Wolfgang Stechow. Washington, D.C., National Gallery of Art, 1971.

11 ×8¾ inches; xv pages including [2] pages of plates.
Saddlewire stitched into printed white paper cover. (37163)

483

DÜRER IN AMERICA: HIS GRAPHIC WORK. Charles W. Talbot, Editor. Notes by Gaillard F. Ravenel and Jay A. Levenson. Washington, D.C., National Gallery of Art, 1971.

Designed by Crimilda Pontes.
11 ×8½ inches; 362 pages including 200 pages of plates (some colored).
Smythsewn and glued into printed white paper cover. (117020)

484

EDWARD LEAR IN GREECE: A LOAN EXHIBITION FROM THE GENNADIUS LIBRARY, ATHENS. [Washington, D.C.], International Exhibitions Foundation, 1971.

8½ ×10 inches; 87 pages including 71 pages of plates.
Smythsewn and glued into printed white paper cover. (27118)

485

THE EIGHTEENTH CENTURY IN ITALY. By Jacob Bean and Felice Stampfle. New York, N.Y., The Metropolitan Museum of Art and The Pierpont Morgan Library, Distributed by the New York Graphic Society, 1971 (Drawings from New York Collections Vol. III).

10½ ×8 inches; 443 pages including 300 pages of plates numbered 1 to 300.
Gray cloth over boards; cover and spine printed in blue and stamped in gold; printed wrapper. Also issued Smythsewn and glued into printed paper cover. (56926)

486

THE EXAMINATION AND TRYAL OF OLD FATHER CHRISTMAS. Preface by O. B. Hardison, Jr. Boston, Mass., G. K. Hall and Co., Christmas 1971.

Facsimile of the London edition of 1687 (i.e. 1686) in the Folger Shakespeare Library.
6½ ×4 inches; 11 +63 pages; illustrated; facsimile.
Smythsewn and glued into printed maroon paper cover. (107129)

487

AN EXHIBITION OF WORKS OF ART DONATED TO THE VENICE COMMITTEE TO BE SOLD FOR THE RESTORATION OF THE SCUOLA DEI CARMINI. [Foreword by Agnes Mongan.] Cambridge, Mass., Fogg Art Museum, 1971.

At head of title: "Venice Committee—Boston Chapter."
11 × 8½ inches; 40 pages; illustrated.
Saddlewire stitched into printed white paper cover. (27126)

488

FIFTY-SIX DARTMOUTH POEMS. Selected and with a note on "Protest" and an afterword on "Seals, Terns, Time" by Richard Eberhart. Hanover, N.H., Privately printed, 1971.

9 × 6 inches; 75 pages.
200 copies handsewn into blue-gray paper cover and glued into printed blue-gray wrapper illustrated with a woodcut by Christopher Keith. (127126)

489

THE FIRST HUNDRED YEARS OF THE THAYER SCHOOL OF ENGINEERING AT DARTMOUTH COLLEGE. By William Phelps Kimball. With a foreword by Dean David Vincent Raggone. Hanover, N.H., The University Press of New England, 1971.

9½ × 6¼ inches; [2]+xii+148 pages; illustrated.
Green cloth over boards; wrapper. 100 copies specially bound in green quarter cloth and marbled paper over boards; wrapper. (67109)

490

GREEN HIGHLANDERS AND PINK LADIES. By Dana S. Lamb. Barre, Mass., Barre Publishers, 1971.

Designed by Klaus Gemming.
9¼ × 6¼ inches; 92 pages.
1,500 numbered copies bound in green cloth over boards; gold-stamped spine; slipcase. (67134)

491

A GUIDE TO THE MICROFILM EDITION OF THE PAPERS OF ELEAZAR WHEELOCK, TOGETHER WITH THE EARLY ARCHIVES OF DARTMOUTH COLLEGE AND MOOR'S INDIAN CHARITY SCHOOL AND RECORDS OF THE TOWN OF HANOVER, NEW HAMPSHIRE, THROUGH THE YEAR 1779. [Introduction by Edward Connery Lathem. Hanover, N.H., Dartmouth College Library], 1971.

9½×6¼ inches; x+279 pages.
Green buckram over boards; gold-stamped spine; wrapper. (17139)

492

HENRY JAMES IN NORTHAMPTON: VISIONS AND REVISIONS. By Dean Flower. Northampton, Mass., Friends of the Smith College Library, 1971.

Designed at The Gehenna Press.
10×7½ inches; 24+[6] pages including 12 pages of plates; portraits.
2,000 copies Smythsewn and glued into red-brown paper cover. (77140)

493

INGRES IN ROME: A LOAN EXHIBITION FROM THE MUSÉE INGRES, MONTAUBAN, AND AMERICAN COLLECTIONS. Introduction and catalogue by Hans Naef. [Washington, D.C., International Exhibitions Foundation], 1971.

8½×11 inches; xiv+138 pages including 128 pages of plates.
Smythsewn and glued into printed blue and white paper cover. (97008)

494

ITALIAN DRAWINGS: SELECTIONS FROM THE COLLECTION OF ESTHER S. AND MALCOLM W. BICK. [Edited by Franklin W. Robinson and John T. Paoletti.] Hanover, N.H., Dartmouth College, 1971.

9½×6 inches; [118] pages including 46 pages of plates numbered 1 to 46.
Smythsewn and glued into printed gray paper cover. (17111)

495

LAWRENCE COUNSELMAN WROTH, 1884–1970: THE
MEMORIAL MINUTES READ BEFORE THE FACULTY OF
BROWN UNIVERSITY, 9 FEBRUARY 1971, AND A HAND-
LIST OF HIS WRITINGS IN THE JOHN CARTER BROWN
LIBRARY OF BROWN UNIVERSITY. Providence, R.I.,
Brown University, 1971.

8½ × 5½ inches; [16] pages.
Smythsewn and glued into cream paper cover. (27115)

496

LEARNING DISABILITIES AND THE EDUCATIONALLY-
HANDICAPPED CHILD. By Conrad A. Loehner, M.D.
Upland, Calif., Phalarope Publishing Co., 1971.

9¼ × 6¼ inches; 183 pages.
Black cloth over boards; acetate wrapper. (17163)

497

A LETTER OF CHARLES DARWIN ABOUT PREPARATIONS
FOR THE VOYAGE OF THE BEAGLE, 1831. Philadelphia,
Pa., Friends of the Library [of the] American Philosophical
Society, 1971.

11 × 8½ inches; [12] pages including 4 pages of holograph facsimile.
Saddlewire stitched into printed blue paper cover. (27173)

498

MICROFILM EDITION OF THE PAPERS OF DANIEL WEB-
STER: GUIDE AND INDEX TO THE MICROFILM. Charles
M. Wiltse, Editor. Ann Arbor, Mich., University Micro-
films; Hanover, N.H., Dartmouth College Library, 1971.

10 × 6½ inches; 175 pages.
Blue cloth over boards; wrapper. (97038)

499

THE NEW SOUTH: WRITINGS AND SPEECHES OF HENRY

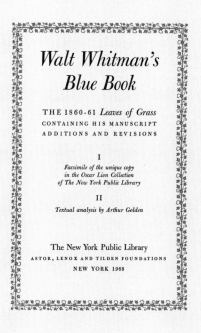

Walt Whitman's Blue Book

THE 1860-61 *Leaves of Grass*
CONTAINING HIS MANUSCRIPT
ADDITIONS AND REVISIONS

I

*Facsimile of the unique copy
in the Oscar Lion Collection
of The New York Public Library*

II

Textual analysis by Arthur Golden

The New York Public Library

ASTOR, LENOX AND TILDEN FOUNDATIONS

NEW YORK 1968

ENTRY 389

63.8 See, the many-cylinder'd steam printing-press—See, the electric telegraph (stretching across the continent, from the Western Sea to Manhattan,) [—] ⟨¶⟩ See, the strong and quick locomotive, as it departs, panting, blowing the steam-whistle; (1867: 'See, the many-cylinder'd steam printing-press—See, the electric telegraph, stretching across the Continent, from the Western Sea to Manhattan;' was followed by the new line 'See, through Atlantica's depths, pulses American, Europe reaching—pulses of Europe, duly return'd;'. The other part of 1860, 63.8, followed as a separate line: 'See, the strong and quick ...'.)

PAGE 22

63.10 See, mechanics, busy at their benches, with tools—
    See from among them, superior Presidents, emerge, dressed in working dresses; (1860R: 'drest')
  1 See, mechanics, busy at their benches, with tools—See from among them, (¶) superior [judges, philosophs,] Presidents, emerge, dressed in working dresses;

'judges, philosophs,' which might have been rejected during this or the next revision, are dropped here.

  2 See, ... tools—(¶) See from among them, [¶]ᵉ superior Presidents, ...

64.1 O Camerado close! (RR)
  1 O my comrade! ⟨O closer and closer!⟩
  2 [O my comrade!] O closer and closer!
  3 [O closer and closer!] ⟨O Camerado close!⟩

Before the final reading WW drew a cancelling stroke through 'O my comrade!' that passed through the previous one and through 'O' of 'O closer and closer!'. Another stroke then rejected the rest.

64.2 O ... only[;]⟨.⟩ (RR)

Before block-cancelling 64.3–6, which was also rejected in

ENTRY 389

AMERICAN
PENMANSHIP
1800–1850

A History of Writing and
a Bibliography of Copybooks from
Jenkins to Spencer

RAY NASH

American Antiquarian Society
WORCESTER · 1969

ENTRY 392

Gilbert Wood, an itinerant master   53

Heading of a manuscript advertisement by Gilbert Wood

Like Gilbert Wood, other peripatetic writing masters fairly often had another string to their bow. It might be cutting silhouettes, as in the case of James Guild who also painted likenesses on ivory. Earlier in the year of French's sojourn in Hanover as recorded, the local paper carried a display advertisement as follows:

Penmanship and Mezzotinto Painting. W. C. Spaulding Teacher of Penmanship and Mezzotinto Painting, having been solicited by his friends to offer his services to the Ladies and Gentlemen of Hanover, will open a Writing School at Burnham's Hotel on Monday, June 1st.

No matter how cramped, illegible or deformed, the present handwriting may be, the first principles of this system will at once eradicate all stiffness, give a free and easy command of the pen, (which all will agree must be acquired before any one can become a finished penman,) and leave the writer with a neat, bold, expeditious and mercantile style of writing, suitable for all every day purposes.

He interrupts the penmanship discourse to say a few words about Mezzotinto painting, and continues:

ENTRY 392

FIVE ADDLED ETCHERS 🙶 BY LEONARD BASKIN

Vellert

Here then is a 'little master' who painted glass but who was sufficiently driven to engrave some twenty odd plates—and rather odd they are. Not absolutely weird, or frenzied or frantically compulsive—but yet not quite wholly sane and 'healthy.' There is an unsettling quality in these plates. Is it the sly archaizing, the sudden stiffening in the mellifluous field? Vellert is a Gothic mannerist. The figures may disport themselves in their serpentine ways, but they are ill at ease, sensing somehow that their gestures hardly conform to their character. The air is sodden and heavy in these prints. They are disquieting.

In dealing with the totality of an artist's work, art historians are at the greatest pains to establish a chronology for the paintings, sculpture, or prints. They deeply investigate style and changes however subtle in that style, subjects related to specific, datable historical events, the sudden appearance of a new influence and sources and various clever and imaginative devices. There is much straining and more disquisition to support and justify a particular dating. Vellert is, I may say, unique in that he gives in unequivocating fashion, the day, month, and year, in all of his prints save three, two have the year and one is undated and unsigned, wherefore I suspect the print as not being by Vellert. What impelled him to consistently add the ephemeral day and month? If his production were prodigal and works poured from him as they do from Picasso, who, when the inspired heat is upon him, does completely date each work—but Vellert's graphic oeuvre is twenty-one prints. They form in their totality a thin fardel of obscurity; obscure to all but those who pick deeply into the wondrous enormity of *graphica* bequeathed

36

XI Vellert. Vision of St. Bernard.

1887   SOCIAL HISTORY   1967

THE CLUB OF ODD VOLUMES

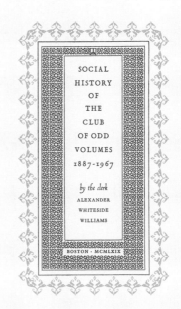

SOCIAL
HISTORY
OF
THE
CLUB
OF ODD
VOLUMES
1887-1967

by the clerk
ALEXANDER
WHITESIDE
WILLIAMS

BOSTON · MCMLXIX

The Philosopher and the Pheasants

THE Sage, awak'd at early day,
Through the deep forest took his way;
Drawn by the music of the groves,
Along the winding gloom he roves;
From tree to tree, the warbling throats
Prolong the sweet alternate notes.
But where he past, he terror threw,
The song broke short, the warblers flew;
The thrushes chatter'd with affright,
And nightingales abhorr'd his sight;
All animals before him ran,
To shun the hateful sight of man.

Whence is this dread of ev'ry creature?
Fly they our figure or our nature?

As thus he walk'd in musing thought,
His ear imperfect accents caught;
With cautious step he nearer drew,

· 43 ·

LIBROS
VIRUMQUE CANO
GAUDEAMUS

THE GIFTS OF
JOHN NICHOLAS BROWN
TO THE
JOHN CARTER BROWN LIBRARY
FROM 1924 TO 1969

A Tribute on his seventieth birthday
21 February 1970

The Associates of
the John Carter Brown Library
PROVIDENCE RHODE ISLAND

ENTRY 451

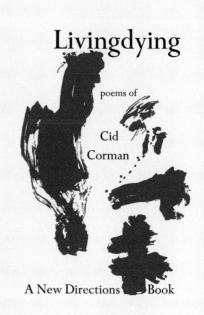

Livingdying

poems of

Cid
Corman

A New Directions Book

ENTRY 452

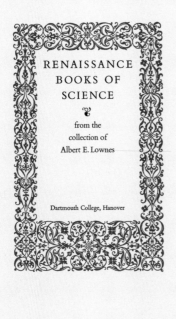

RENAISSANCE
BOOKS OF
SCIENCE

from the
collection of
Albert E. Lownes

Dartmouth College, Hanover

ENTRY 463

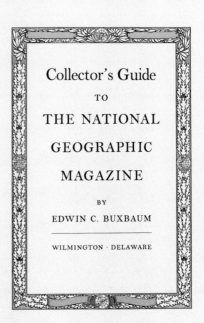

Collector's Guide
TO
THE NATIONAL
GEOGRAPHIC
MAGAZINE

BY
EDWIN C. BUXBAUM

WILMINGTON · DELAWARE

ENTRY 477

GRADY. [Introduction by Mills Lane.] Savannah, Ga., The Beehive Press, 1971.

9¼×6¼ inches; xxvii+151+[5] pages.
Gray cloth over boards; wrapper. (67050)

500

NICHOLAS II: LAST TSAR OF ALL THE RUSSIAS. By Kitsos Washburn. Washington, D.C., [Privately printed], 1971.

9¾×6¼ inches; [8] pages.
Handsewn into white paper cover. (87117)

501

OBITER SCRIPTA. By F. Lyman Windolph. Lancaster, Pa., [Privately printed], 1971.

9¼×6¼ inches; 55 pages.
Bound in printed green paper and green quarter cloth over boards; gold-stamped cover and spine. (17104)

502

THE PAINTINGS IN THE STUDIOLO OF ISABELLA D'ESTE AT MANTUA. By Egon Verheyen. New York, N.Y., Published by New York University Press for the College Art Association of America, 1971 (Monographs on Archaeology and the Fine Arts sponsored by The Archaeological Institute of America and The College Art Association of America, No. 23).

11¼×9 inches; xii+[1]+106 pages including 45 pages of plates numbered 1 to 45; bibliography.
Maroon cloth over boards. (107015)

503

THE POETRY OF ROBERT FROST. Edited by Edward Connery Lathem. Barre, Mass., Imprint Society, 1971.

Designed by Rudolph Ruzicka.
9½×6½ inches; Vol. I: xlix+[3]+270+[2] pages; frontispiece relief

portrait by Ruzicka tipped in. Vol. II: [8]+[435] pages numbered 273 to 607+[5] pages; frontispiece; bibliographical and textual notes. Decorated gray paper and gray quarter cloth over boards; slipcase. (37016)

504

ROBERT SALMON: PAINTER OF SHIP AND SHORE. By John Wilmerding. With an introduction by Charles D. Childs. Salem, Mass., Peabody Museum; Boston, Mass., Boston Public Library, 1971.

11¼×8¾ inches; 123 pages; illustrated.
Blue cloth over boards; wrapper. (26903)

505

LA SCALA: 400 YEARS OF STAGE DESIGN FROM THE MUSEO TEATRALE ALLA SCALA, MILAN. Catalogue and introduction by Mario Monteverdi. [Washington, D.C., International Exhibitions Foundation], 1971.

8½×10 inches; 91 pages including 59 pages of plates.
Smythsewn and glued into printed paper cover. (77121)

506

SELECTIONS FROM THE COLLECTION OF FREDDY AND REGINA T. HOMBURGER: A LOAN EXHIBITION. Cambridge, Mass., Fogg Art Museum, Harvard University, 1971.

8½×5½ inches; ix+190 pages including 82 pages of plates.
Smythsewn and glued into printed brown paper cover. (17149)

507

THE SICK-THINKING FAMILY AND ITS TREATMENT. By Conrad A. Loehner, M.D. Upland, Calif., Phalarope Publishing Co., 1971.

9¼×6¼ inches; 180 pages.
Black cloth over boards. (47057)

508

SIMON GIFFIN AND HIS DESCENDANTS. A genealogy compiled by Florence Giffin Martin and Mary Alsted Strange with Anne Borden Harding on Nova Scotia families. [New York, N.Y.], Published privately, 1971.

9½×6½ inches; x+328+[16] pages of plates; illustrated; maps on endleaves.
Red cloth over boards; spine printed in black and stamped in gold; wrapper. (127037)

509

SIXTEENTH CENTURY ARCHITECTURAL BOOKS FROM ITALY AND FRANCE. [Introduction by Peter A. Wick.] Cambridge, Mass., Harvard College Library Department of Printing and Graphic Arts, 1971.

11×8½ inches; [50] pages including 12 pages of plates.
Saddlewire stitched into printed white paper cover. (27114)

510

SPECIMEN DAYS. By Walt Whitman. Introduction by Alfred Kazin. Boston, Mass., David Godine Publisher, 1971.

Designed, researched, and edited by Lance Hidy.
12×8½ inches; xxiv+[2]+197 pages; illustrated.
1,250 copies bound in printed red cloth over boards; wrapper; slipcase.
5,000 additional copies issued in hardcover and paper. (106920)

511

STANDING STILL WHILE TRAFFIC MOVED ABOUT ME. A book of poems by Robert Hutchinson. New York, N.Y., The Eakins Press, 1971 (Hand and Leaf Book Number 3).

7¼×5¾ inches; 78 pages.
Red cloth over boards; gold-stamped spine; wrapper. Also issued Smyth-sewn and glued into printed red and green paper cover. (67102)

512

STORIES, FABLES, AND OTHER DIVERSIONS. By Howard Nemerov. Boston, Mass., David Godine, 1971.

Title page designed by John Benson.
9½×6¼ inches; [2]+121+[5] pages.
3,000 copies bound in red cloth over boards; wrapper. (27127)

513

THOMAS JEFFERSON'S FLOWER GARDEN AT MONTI-CELLO. By Edwin M. Betts and Hazlehurst Bolton Perkins. Charlottesville, Va., University Press of Virginia, 1971.

Second edition; designed by Edward G. Foss.
8¾×5½ inches; xi+60 pages; illustrated (some colored); bibliography.
Smythsewn and glued into printed white paper cover. (127009)

514

TOWNSHEND HERITAGE: A GENEALOGICAL, BIOGRAPH-ICAL HISTORY OF THE TOWNSHEND FAMILY AND OF THEIR OLD HOMESTEAD. . . . By Doris B. Townshend. New Haven, Conn., New Haven Colony Historical Society, 1971.

9½×6½ inches; xv+380 pages + [23] leaves of plates.
Red cloth over boards; gold-stamped spine. (37144)

515

TWO MEMENTOES FROM THE POE-INGRAM COLLECTION. [With notes by Irby B. Cauthen, Jr.] Charlottesville, Va., Bibliographical Society of the University of Virginia, 1971.

Cover title; anniversary keepsake for members, 1946–1971. Includes facsimile of Stéphane Mallarmé's first version of "Au Tombeau d'Edgar Poe" and a bookplate designed by Edouard Manet.
11¼×9¾ inch single folded leaf + [2] leaves of facsimile; together in a brown paper folder (12 × 10¼ inches).
1,500 copies (1,000 numbered and signed by Cauthen for members of the Society). (57134)

516

WAVERLEY; OR, 'TIS SIXTY YEARS SINCE. By Sir Walter
Scott. With an introductory essay by Andrew Lang and
illustrations by Robert Ball. Lunenburg, Vt., Printed for
Members of The Limited Editions Club, 1971.

10¼×7 inches; xxvi+[2]+446+[3] pages + [8] pages of plates.
1,500 copies numbered and signed by the artist; bound in brown imita-
tion leather; gold-stamped covers and spine; slipcase.

⌈1972⌉

517

A. LASSELL RIPLEY: PAINTINGS. Text by Edward Weeks.
Boston, Mass., Guild of Boston Artists; Barre, Mass., Barre
Publishers, 1972.

Designed by Charles A. Mahoney.
8¾ × 10¼ inches; [86] pages including 50 pages of plates (some colored)
numbered 1 to 50.
1,500 copies bound in orange cloth and black quarter cloth over boards;
gold-stamped cover and spine. 50 numbered copies in slipcase covered
with black paper and colored illustration laid on. (77229)

518

AN ADDRESS DELIVERED BEFORE AN INFORMAL GATH-
ERING AT STRATTON MOUNTAIN, VERMONT, OF PEOPLE
INTERESTED IN THE CREATIVE ARTS. . . . [By Norman J.
Bernstein.] Londonderry, Vt., Emerson Guild of Creative
Arts, 1972.

Cover title.
9×4 inches; [8] pages.
Saddlewire stitched; unbound. (47229)

519

AN ADDRESS DELIVERED BEFORE AN ORGANIZATIONAL
MEETING AT THE PUBLIC LIBRARY IN CHICOPEE, MAS-
SACHUSETTS, OF PEOPLE INTERESTED IN ESTABLISHING

A Repository for Memorabilia of Edward Bellamy.... [By Vernon Reyman.] Londonderry, Vt., Emerson Guild of Creative Arts, 1972.

Cover title.
9×4 inches; [8] pages.
Saddlewire stitched; unbound. (87225)

520

The American Audience for Art: Symposia Held in the Wiggin Gallery, Boston Public Library. Boston, Mass., Boston Public Library, 1972.

Includes "A New Scale of Taste and Judgment" by Charles D. Childs; "Magazines, Galleries, Museums, and Collectors" by Mario Micossi; "When Museums Behave Less Like Institutions" by John Arthur; "Four Views of the American Audience" by Samuel Grafton, Robert Hallock, Sinclair Hitchings, John Wilson.
8½×4½ inches; 57 pages.
1,500 copies bound in printed yellow paper over boards. (87134)

521

Barnabas Downs: A Brief and Remarkable Narrative.... Yarmouthport, Mass., Parnassas Imprints, 1972.

Facsimile of the edition (1786) in the John Carter Brown Library.
7½×4¼ inches; [8]+iv+16 pages; facsimile.
1,000 copies saddlewire stitched into red-brown paper cover. (17224)

522

The Best of the Anglers' Club Bulletin, 1920–1972. Selected with a preface and notes by A. Ross Jones. Introduction by Sparse Grey Hackle. New York, N.Y., The Anglers' Club, 1972.

10¼×7¼ inches; xiv+168 pages.
1,000 copies bound in green cloth over boards; slipcase. (87211)

523

Boswell's Verses on The Club. Written by James M.

Osborn in celebration of Dr. Johnson's two hundred and seventy-third birthday. Lunenburg, Vt., Printed for the Johnsonians, 1972.

"Items C1752 and M330 in Mrs. Marion Pottle's unpublished *Catalogue of the Boswell Papers.*"
11¼×8¼ inches; [8] pages + 2 pages of holograph facsimile folded in cover pocket.
263 copies saddlewire stitched into red-brown paper cover with label on cover. (67258)

524

CALVIN COOLIDGE SAYS: DISPATCHES WRITTEN BY FORMER PRESIDENT COOLIDGE AND SYNDICATED TO NEWSPAPERS IN 1930–1931. Now presented with an introduction by Edward Connery Lathem. Plymouth, Vt., Calvin Coolidge Memorial Foundation, 1972.

6×5½ inches; 394 pages; illustrated.
Blue cloth over boards; silver-stamped spine; wrapper. Also issued Smythsewn and glued into printed white paper cover. (27271)

525

CHRONOLOGICAL TABLES OF AMERICAN NEWSPAPERS, 1690–1820: BEING A TABULAR GUIDE TO HOLDINGS OF NEWSPAPERS PUBLISHED IN AMERICA THROUGH THE YEAR 1820. Compiled by Edward Connery Lathem. Barre, Mass., American Antiquarian Society and Barre Publishers, 1972.

11×8 inches; x+131 pages.
Red cloth over boards; wrapper. (37149)

526

A COMMENTARY ON THE DRESDEN CODEX: A MAYA HIEROGLYPHIC BOOK. By J. Eric S. Thompson. Philadelphia, Pa., American Philosophical Society, 1972 (Memoirs of the American Philosophical Society, Vol. 93).

11¼×15¼ inches; [12]+156+[4] pages including 25 pages of plates.
Brown linen; gold-stamped cover and spine; wrapper. (96961)

527

THE CULT OF THE FELINE: A CONFERENCE IN PRE-COLUMBIAN ICONOGRAPHY. Elizabeth P. Benson, Editor. Washington, D.C., Dumbarton Oaks Research Library and Collections and Trustees for Harvard University, 1972.

9¾ × 7 inches; vii+[3]+166 pages; illustrated.
Green cloth over boards. (77131)

528

DEATH IN VENICE. By Thomas Mann. Translated by Kenneth Burke with an introduction by Erich Heller. Illustrated with wood engravings by Felix Hoffmann. New York, N.Y., Printed for the Members of The Limited Editions Club, 1972.

Designed by Max Caflisch.
10¾ × 7¾ inches; 106+[4] double pages.
1,500 copies numbered and signed by the illustrator; bound in the oriental style; case covered with marbled paper and red quarter leather; gold-stamped spine; slipcase. (77147)

529

THE DEVIL'S DICTIONARY. By Ambrose Bierce. Introduction by Louis Kronenberger. Woodcut illustrations by Fritz Kredel. New York, N.Y., Limited Editions Club, 1972.

Designed by Eugene M. Ettenberg.
11¼ × 7 inches; xii+239+[3] pages.
1,500 copies bound in black cloth and red quarter leather over boards; slipcase. (27111)

530

DUTCH GENRE DRAWINGS OF THE SEVENTEENTH CENTURY: A LOAN EXHIBITION FROM DUTCH MUSEUMS, FOUNDATIONS, AND PRIVATE COLLECTIONS. Introduction by K. G. Boon; catalogue by Peter Schatborn. [Washington, D.C.], International Exhibitions Foundation, 1972.

10 × 7½ inches; 65 pages + 85 pages of plates; bibliography.
Smythsewn and glued into printed green paper cover. (57209)

531

EARLY AMERICAN BOOKBINDINGS FROM THE COLLECTION OF MICHAEL PAPANTONIO. New York, N.Y., The Pierpont Morgan Library, 1972.

10½×7½ inches; x+89 pages including 61 pages of plates.
Smythsewn and glued into printed off-white paper cover. (77222)

532

THE EDO CULTURE IN JAPANESE PRINTS. Introduction and some essays by George Lee; additional essays by Yasuko Betchaku, Mary G. Neill, Lucie Weinstein. New Haven, Conn., Yale University Art Gallery, 1972.

11¼×8¾ inches; 46 pages including 13 pages of plates.
Saddlewire stitched into printed brown paper cover. (67209)

533

ENGLISH DRAWINGS AND WATERCOLORS, 1550–1850, IN THE COLLECTION OF MR. AND MRS. PAUL MELLON. Introduction by Graham Reynolds. New York, N.Y., The Pierpont Morgan Library and Harper and Row Publishers, 1972.

11¼×8½ inches; xxi+107 pages + 150 pages of plates (some colored).
Bound in blue-gray cloth over boards; gold-stamped spine; wrapper.
Also issued (by The Pierpont Morgan Library and the Royal Academy of Arts, London) Smythsewn and glued into printed gray paper cover. (17162)

534

THE EUROPEAN TRAVELLER IN AMERICA. [Introduction by Howard H. Peckham. Boston, Mass., G. K. Hall and Co.], Christmas 1972.

Facsimile of the (1785) edition of Hartford, Conn.
7¾×5 inches; [7]+40 pages.
Smythsewn and glued into light blue paper cover. (87251)

535

FATHER RAVALLI'S MISSIONS. By Harold Allen. Chicago, Ill., The Good Lion (The School of the Art Institute of Chicago), 1972.

11¾×9 inches; 31 pages + 51 pages of plates; map; bibliography.
Smythsewn into wrapper. (107124)

536

FITTED TO THE BURDEN: SELECTED SPEECHES OF
HOMER DANIELS BABBIDGE, JR. Edited by William T.
O'Hara. Storrs, Conn., the University of Connecticut
Alumni Association, 1972.

9½×6¼ inches; 181 pages; frontispiece portrait.
White cloth and brown cloth over boards; gold-stamped spine. (47238)

537

FOOTSTEPS OF THE PAST: A STORY OF NINE VIRGINIA
FAMILIES. By Grace Stuart Jones Richardson. Introduction
by Burke Davis. Lunenburg, Vt., Privately printed, 1972.

10¼×7 inches; ix+[3]+103+[13] pages; illustrated; bibliography.
Bound in light blue linen and dark blue quarter buckram over boards.
(117146)

538

FRAGMENTS FINAL? By Carl A. Weyerhaeuser. Milton,
Mass., [Privately printed], 1972.

8¼×5¼ inches; 68 pages.
Gray paper and red cloth over boards; gold-stamped spine. (57242)

539

FREDERICK GARRISON HALL: ETCHINGS, BOOKPLATES,
DESIGNS. By Elton Wayland Hall. With a biographical
sketch by Ariel Hall and a personal memoir by Henry P.
Rossiter. Boston, Mass., Boston Public Library, 1972.

11½×8¾ inches; 130 pages including 52 pages of plates; portrait.
500 copies numbered and signed by the author; bound in rust-red cloth
over boards; gold-stamped spine. (47231)

540

FRUEH ON THE THEATRE. Theatrical caricatures 1906–
1962 compiled with an introduction by Maxwell Silverman

and with a preface by Brendan Gill. New York, N.Y., The New York Public Library, 1972.

11¼×8¾ inches; vii+108 pages including 104 pages of plates. Printed light brown paper over boards. Also issued Smythsewn and glued into printed paper cover. (127151)

541

GEORGE WASHINGTON ON THE DEFENSE OF BOSTON. Boston, Mass., The Associates of the Boston Public Library, 1972.

Transcription of a holograph letter dated from Cambridge, 4 April 1776.
12¼×8¼ inches; [8] pages; facsimile.
Handsewn into printed white paper cover. (97235)

542

GERMAN MASTER DRAWINGS OF THE NINETEENTH CENTURY. Cambridge, Mass., Busch-Reisinger Museum, Harvard University, 1972.

Designed by Malcolm Grear.
9½×8½ inches; [208] pages including 92 pages of plates.
Smythsewn and glued into printed blue paper cover.

543

THE GIRL FROM IPANEMA. By Charles Edward Eaton. Lunenburg, Vt., Distributed by North Country Publishing Company, 1972.

9¼×6¼ inches; [8]+193+[3] pages.
Green cloth over boards. (77144)

544

GREEK AND ROMAN PORTRAITS, 470 BC–AD 500. [Revision by Cornelius C. Vermeule and Mary B. Comstock.] Boston, Mass., Museum of Fine Arts, 1972 (Picture Book series, unnumbered).

Designed by Carl F. Zahn and Barbara Hawley.
First issued in 1959.
8½×7 inches; [82] pages including 62 pages of plates.
Glued into paper cover; printed on front and spine. (17223)

545

A HANDBOOK FOR THE NEW HAMPSHIRE GENERAL
COURT. Edited by Laurence I. Radway. Hanover,
N.H., The Public Affairs Center, Dartmouth College,
1972.

9×6 inches; 86 pages.
Smythsewn and glued into printed green paper cover. (107220)

546

A HISTORY OF GEORGIA FROM ITS FIRST DISCOVERY
BY EUROPEANS TO THE ADOPTION OF THE PRESENT
CONSTITUTION IN MDCCXCVIII. By William Bacon
Stevens. [Introduction by E. Merton Coulter.] Savannah,
Ga., The Beehive Press, 1972.

9×6 inches; Vol. I: [2]+xxxvii+[3]+503+[1] pages; Vol. II: 524+
[2] pages; facsimile.
Dark blue cloth over boards; gold-stamped spine; slipcase. (107115)

547

ILLUMINATED MANUSCRIPTS IN THE DARTMOUTH COL-
LEGE LIBRARY. Edited by Robert L. McGrath. Hanover,
N.H., Dartmouth College Library, 1972.

11×8½ inches; 35 pages including 16 pages of plates.
500 copies Smythsewn and glued into printed red paper cover. (127117)

548

JANUARY INVENTORY. By Rollo Silver. [New York, N.Y.,
The Typophiles, 1972] (Monograph Number 97).

7¾×5½ inches; [8] pages.
600 copies (200 lacking colophon) saddlewire stitched into white paper
and glued into printed paper cover. (27273)

549

JEWS IN BERKSHIRE COUNTY. By Pink Horwitt in collaboration with Bertha Skole. Williamstown, Mass., D O R
Company, 1972.

9×5½ inches; viii+74 pages.
Blue cloth over boards; gold-stamped spine; wrapper. (67257)

550

JOHN DONNE (1572–1631): A CATALOGUE OF THE AN-NIVERSARY EXHIBITIONS OF FIRST AND EARLY EDITIONS OF HIS WORKS HELD AT THE GROLIER CLUB. Compiled by Robert S. Pirie. New York, N.Y., The Grolier Club, 1972.

9¼×6¼ inches; xv+41 pages; illustrated; portrait.
500 numbered copies and 150 additional copies bound in decorated paper over boards. Also issued Smythsewn and glued into decorated paper cover. (77228)

551

JOURNAL OF SAMUEL R. OLIVER, NOVEMBER 22, 1835 – APRIL 21, 1836. With an introduction by Andrew Oliver. Hanover, N.H., Dartmouth College Library, 1972.

8½×5½ inches; [48] pages.
Handsewn into printed light brown paper cover. (57249)

552

JOURNEY WITH JOY: LETTERS FROM DATUS C. SMITH, JR., EDITED BY HIS WIFE. Princeton, N.J., Published privately at the Sign of Al Kalbu al Kabir al Aswad.

8¾×5¾ inches; 140+[2] pages; illustrated.
Decorated paper and brown quarter cloth over boards. (117118)

553

JOYCE'S ULYSSES NOTESHEETS IN THE BRITISH MUSEUM. Edited by Phillip F. Herring. Charlottesville, Va., Published for the Bibliographical Society of the University of Virginia by the University Press of Virginia, 1972.

10¼×7¾ inches; viii+[6]+345 pages + [2] leaves of colored plates; frontispiece portrait; bibliography.
Brown cloth over boards; gold-stamped spine; wrapper. (67115)

554

LIST OF PAINTINGS IN THE STERLING AND FRANCINE

CLARK ART INSTITUTE. Williamstown, Mass., Sterling and Francine Clark Art Institute, 1972.

9½×7½ inches; 144 pages; illustrated.
Smythsewn and glued into printed gray paper cover. (37245)

555

MEMOIRS, OR A QUICK GLANCE AT MY VARIOUS TRAV-ELS AND MY SOJOURN IN THE CREEK NATION. By Louis Le Clerc Milfort. Translated and edited by Ben C. McCary. Savannah, Ga., The Beehive Press, 1972.

First issued in 1959 at Kennesaw, Ga., in an edition of 900 copies.
10×6½ inches; 145 pages; map; bibliography.
Brown cloth over boards; gold-stamped spine; wrapper. (107106)

556

THE MOST DELIGHTFUL COUNTRY OF THE UNIVERSE: PROMOTIONAL LITERATURE OF THE COLONY OF GEOR-GIA, 1717–1734. Introduction by Trevor R. Reese. Savannah, Ga., The Beehive Press, 1972.

10¼×7¼ inches; xxi+[1]+217+[3] pages; bibliography.
Rust-red linen over boards; gold-stamped spine; wrapper. (97142)

557

THE NARRATIVE OF ALVAR NÚÑEZ CABEZA DE VACA. Translated by Fanny Bandelier. Introduction by John Francis Bannon. Illustrations by Michael McCurdy. With Oviedo's Version of the Lost Joint Report Presented to the Audiencia of Santo Domingo translated by Gerald Theisen. Barre, Mass., Imprint Society, 1972.

8½×6 inches; xxxi+271 pages; portrait.
1,950 copies signed by the artist; bound in printed yellow paper and red quarter leather over boards; gold-stamped spine. (107127)

558

NEW TOWNS IN-TOWN: WHY A FEDERAL PROGRAM FAILED. By Martha Derthick with a foreword by Joseph

A. Califano, Jr. Washington, D.C., The Urban Institute, 1972.

9×6 inches; xv+103 pages.
Smythsewn and glued into printed brown and white paper cover.
(127110)

559
OLD MASTER DRAWINGS FROM CHRIST CHURCH, OX-
FORD: A LOAN EXHIBITION. Introduction and catalogue
by James Byam Shaw. [Washington, D.C.], International
Exhibitions Foundation, 1972.

10×7½ inches; 70 pages + 110 pages of plates.
Smythsewn and glued into printed gray paper cover. (57223)

560
ON MUSEUM OBJECTS, TRUTH, AND EDUCATION. Re-
flections of the Secretary of the Smithsonian Institution
upon the One Hundred and Twenty-fifth Anniversary of
Its Founding, with an Account of the Celebration and a
Selection of Letters Congratulatory on the Event. By S. Dil-
lon Ripley. Washington, D.C., Smithsonian Institution
Press, 1972.

10×7 inches; 31 pages.
Saddlewire stitched into blue paper cover. (67206)

561
THE PANCHATANTRA. Translated from the Sanskrit by
Arthur W. Ryder. Illustrated by Y. G. Srimati. New York,
N.Y., Printed for the Members of The Limited Editions
Club, 1972.

Designed by Robert L. Dothard.
10¾×7½ inches; xvii+366 pages + [12] pages of colored plates.
1,500 copies bound in red cloth over boards; gold-stamped spine; tied
in a box. (47210)

562

RECONSTRUCTION IN GEORGIA: ECONOMIC, SOCIAL, POLITICAL, 1865–1872. By C. Mildred Thompson. Savannah, Ga., The Beehive Press, 1972.

9×4 inches; [8]+397+[3] pages.
Blue paper over boards; wrapper. (77132)

563

SELECTED POEMS. By F. Lyman Windolph. Lancaster, Pa., [Privately printed], 1972.

7½×5½ inches; xi+35 pages.
100 numbered copies bound in red cloth over boards; gold-stamped spine. (97223)

564

SELECTED POEMS. By Mary Wedemeyer McCarthy. New York, N.Y., [Privately printed], 1972.

8¾×5¾ inches; 75 pages.
Bound in dark blue cloth over boards; gold-stamped spine. (37223)

565

A SELECTION OF TWELVE MINIATURES FROM THE DA COSTA HOURS: PIERPONT MORGAN LIBRARY MANU-SCRIPT 399. [New York, N.Y.], The Pierpont Morgan Library, [1972].

13 7½×5½ inch cards, 12 with colored illustrations and 1 with text; together in a yellow-brown paper folder. (37250)

566

SLAVE LIFE IN GEORGIA: A NARRATIVE OF THE LIFE, SUFFERINGS, AND ESCAPE OF JOHN BROWN, A FUGITIVE SLAVE. Edited by F. N. Boney. Savannah, Ga., The Bee-hive Press, 1972.

4¾×7½ inches; xxi+[1]+216+[2] pages; frontispiece portrait.
Dark brown buckram over boards; gold-stamped spine; wrapper. Also issued in yellow buckram over boards; wrapper. (127118)

567

SÕRMUS. By Aleksis Rannit. [New Haven, Conn.], Eesti
Kirjanike Kooperatiiv, 1972.

9×7¾ inches; 43+[2] pages.
Smythsewn and glued into printed white paper cover; glassine wrapper.
(67111)

568

TOULOUSE-LAUTREC: BOOK COVERS AND BROCHURES.
Cambridge, Mass., Harvard College Library Department
of Printing and Graphic Arts, 1972.

7¾×5½ inches; 26 pages + 63 pages of plates; bibliography.
Smythsewn and glued into printed white paper cover. (117225)

569

VIOLIN ICONOGRAPHY OF ANTONIO STRADIVARI, 1644–
1737: TREATISES ON THE LIFE AND WORK OF THE
"PATRIARCH" OF VIOLINMAKERS; INVENTORY OF 700
KNOWN OR RECORDED STRADIVARI STRING INSTRU-
MENTS; INDEX OF 3,500 NAMES OF PAST OR PRESENT
STRADIVARI OWNERS; PHOTOGRAPHS OF 400 STRADI-
VARI INSTRUMENTS WITH 1,500 VIEWS. By Herbert K.
Goodkind. Larchmont, N.Y., Published by the author,
1972.

11½×9 inches; 780 pages; illustrated (some colored).
4,000 copies bound in brown cloth over boards; color portrait laid onto
cover; gold-stamped spine; slipcase. (47230)

570

THE VISIONS OF MARY. By Edward Tyler with wood
engravings by Gillian Tyler [Lunenburg, Vt., Privately
printed], 1972.

9¼×7 inches; [26] pages.
350 copies bound in beige paper over boards. (27258)

571

WILLIAM BLAKE: THE PICKERING MANUSCRIPT. Introduction by Charles Ryskamp. New York, N.Y., The Pierpont Morgan Library, 1972.

8½×5¾ inches; [6]+21 pages; facsimile.
Handsewn into printed yellow-green paper cover. (67210)

[1973]

572

AN ACCOUNT OF THE NEWLY INVENTED PENNSYLVANIA
FIRE-PLACE. By Benjamin Franklin. [Boston, Mass., G. K.
Hall and Co.], Christmas 1973.

8¼×5¼ inches; [8]+37+[2] pages; facsimile.
Saddlewire stitched into paper cover. (97303)

573

ADMINISTRATIVE FEEDBACK: MONITORING SUBORDI-
NATES' BEHAVIOR. By Herbert Kaufman with the
collaboration of Michael Couzens. Washington, D.C.,
The Brookings Institution, 1973.

8¾×5½ inches; viii+[2]+83 pages.
Blue cloth over boards; gold-stamped spine; wrapper. Also issued Smythsewn and glued into printed light brown paper cover. (17315)

574

AMBROSE SMALL PRODUCTIONS: AN EXHIBITION OF
PAINTINGS AND DRAWINGS BY ANNA BAKER. London,
Ont., Nancy Poole Studios, Inc., 1973.

"Based on an imaginary series of productions by the legendary Ambrose
Small."
7×8½ inches; [8] pages including 7 pages of plates.
Saddlewire stitched into dark yellow paper cover. (17332)

575

AMERICAN SILVER COLLECTED BY PHILIP H. HAMMER-

SLOUGH. Vol. IV. By Philip H. Hammerslough and Rita F. Feigenbaum. Hartford, Conn., Privately printed, 1973.

10¼×8 inches; v+142 pages; illustrated.
Gray paper and gray quarter cloth over boards; labels on cover; spine printed in black and stamped in gold. (57317)

576

THE ART OF THE PLAYING CARD: THE CARY COLLECTION. New Haven, Conn., Yale University Library, 1973.

10×6¾ inches; [48] pages; illustrated (some colored).
Perfect-bound in white paper cover and glued into light brown paper wrapper; colored illustration laid onto cover. (107249)

577

ART OF THE PRINTED BOOK, 1455–1955: MASTER-PIECES OF TYPOGRAPHY THROUGH FIVE CENTURIES FROM THE COLLECTIONS OF THE PIERPONT MORGAN LIBRARY, NEW YORK. With an essay by Joseph Blumenthal. New York, N.Y., Pierpont Morgan Library; Boston, Mass., David R. Godine, 1973.

Typography by Joseph Blumenthal.
12½×9¼ inches; xiv+192 pages including 126 pages of plates; bibliography.
Black quarter buckram and brown buckram over boards; gold-stamped cover and spine; wrapper. Also issued Smythsewn and glued into printed paper cover. (127213) Another edition was printed for The Bodley Head, Ltd. (London) in association with The Pierpont Morgan Library. (F87317)

578

ARTES LIBERALES: A SELECTION OF ADDRESSES BY JAMES I. ARMSTRONG. Middlebury, Vt., Middlebury College, 1973.

9¼×6¼ inches; 39 pages; frontispiece portrait.
Smythsewn and glued into printed light yellow paper cover. (87374)

579

BEAUTY AND THE BEAST. A Manuscript by Richard Doyle. [Foreword by Charles Ryskamp.] New York, N.Y., The Pierpont Morgan Library, 1973.

10 ×7 inches; [21] pages; facsimile; illustrated.
Smythsewn and glued into printed light yellow paper cover. (67319)

580

BOSTON PRINTS AND PRINTMAKERS, 1670–1775. [Foreword by Walter Muir Whitehill and Sinclair Hitchings.] Boston, Mass., The Colonial Society of Massachusetts; Distributed by the University Press of Virginia, 1973.

Proceedings from a conference held by the Colonial Society of Massachusetts, 1971.
9½ ×6¾ inches; xxv+294 pages; illustrated.
Blue cloth over boards; gold-stamped spine; wrapper. (37339)

581

CALVIN COOLIDGE: CARTOONS OF HIS PRESIDENTIAL YEARS FEATURING THE WORK OF . . . JAY N. "DING" DARLING, AUGUST 1923 – MARCH 1929. Edited by Edward Connery Lathem. Plymouth, Vt., The Calvin Coolidge Memorial Foundation, 1973.

10 ×8¼ inches; [27] leaves; illustrated.
Printed white paper over boards. Also issued saddlewire stitched into printed white paper cover. (67308)

582

A CATALOGUE OF THE BRYANT SPANISH COLLECTION. Introduction by William J. Bryant. Hanover, N.H., Dartmouth College Library, 1973.

11 ×8½ inches; viii+144 pages; illustrated; map.
Smythsewn and glued into printed cream paper cover. (17228)

583

THE CLAMOROUS MALCONTENTS: CRITICISMS AND DE-

FENSES OF THE COLONY OF GEORGIA, 1741–1743. Introduction by Trevor R. Reese. Savannah, Ga., The Beehive Press, 1973.

10¼×7¼ inches; xvi+349 pages; bibliography.
Tan cloth over boards; gold-stamped spine; wrapper. (127232)

584

COINAGE OF THE AMERICAS. Edited by Theodore V. Buttrey, Jr. New York, N.Y., The American Numismatic Society, 1973.

8½×7 inches; v+139 pages; illustrated.
Perfect-bound in printed blue paper cover. (107222)

585

A CULINARY COLLECTION: RECIPES FROM MEMBERS OF THE BOARD OF TRUSTEES AND STAFF OF THE METROPOLITAN MUSEUM OF ART. Compiled by Linda Gillies, Anita Miller, Pamela Patterson; edited by Linda Gillies. New York, N.Y., Metropolitan Museum of Art, 1973.

Designed by Peter Oldenburg.
9×7¼ inches; 173 pages; illustrated.
20,000 copies spiral bound with printed white paper covers. (67333)

586

DRAWINGS FROM THE COLLECTION OF LORE AND RUDOLF HEINEMANN. Catalogue by Felice Stampfle and Cara D. Denison with an introduction by James Byam Shaw. New York, N.Y., The Pierpont Morgan Library, 1973.

11×8 inches; 189 pages including 120 pages of plates.
Smythsewn and glued into printed dark blue paper cover. (127253)

587

ERNEST ANGELL. [New York, N.Y., The Century Association], 1973.

Cover title; remarks delivered at a memorial gathering.
7¾×5¼ inches; [20] pages.
Saddlewire stitched into brown paper cover. (57334)

588

FIELD GUIDE. By Robert Hass. Foreword by Stanley
Kunitz. New Haven, Conn., Yale University Press, 1973
(Yale Series of Younger Poets, Vol. 68).

5¼×8 inches; xvii+73 pages.
Perfect-bound in printed white paper cover. (127203)

589

FOUR PORTRAITS FROM MEMORY. By F. Lyman
Windolph. Lancaster, Pa., [Privately printed], 1973.

7½×5½ inches; xii+23 pages.
250 numbered copies bound in green cloth over boards; gold-stamped
spine. (107357)

590

THE FRANCIS A. COUNTWAY LIBRARY OF MEDICINE.
[Boston, Mass., Harvard University, 1973.]

Second revised edition.
Cover title; at head of title: "A Descriptive Handbook."
8½×8½ inches; 28 pages + [12] pages of plates.
Saddlewire stitched into printed white paper cover. (See items 245 and
400.) (97306)

591

GATHERINGS IN HONOR OF DOROTHY E. MINER. Edited
by Ursula E. McCracken, Lilian M. C. Randall, Richard
H. Randall, Jr. Baltimore, Md., The Walters Art Gallery,
[1973].

11¼×8¾ inches; xviii+353 pages; illustrated; bibliography.
Blue cloth over boards; gold-stamped cover and spine. (47303)

592

GIVERS AND TAKERS 2. Poems by Jane Mayhall. New
York, N.Y., The Eakins Press, 1973.

4×5½ inches; 78 pages.
Smythsewn and glued into printed red and black paper cover. (77205)

593

THE HERBARIUM OF SMITH COLLEGE. By C. John Buck.
An illustrated memoir with drawings by Pamela See and
photographs by Janet Borden. Foreword by Elliot Offner.
Northampton, Mass., Smith College, 1973.

Designed by Elliot Offner.
11 × 7¼ inches; [20] pages including 6 pages of plates.
Saddlewire stitched into printed cream paper cover. (87373)

594

IN REMEMBRANCE OF THINGS PAST: FOSTER AND JANET
DULLES. Lunenburg, Vt., Privately printed, 1973.

10¾ × 7¾ inches; 15 pages; illustrated.
Saddlewire stitched into printed white paper cover. (77351)

595

INDIAN SUMMER. By Roy and Susan O'Connor. [Lunen-
burg, Vt., Privately printed], 1973.

9½ × 6¼ inches; 50 pages.
Printed on Rives paper and bound in gold-stamped red leather over
boards. Also issued Smythsewn and glued into white paper cover; glued
into red paper wrapper. (117310)

596

INGRES' SCULPTURAL STYLE: A GROUP OF UNKNOWN
PAINTINGS. By Phyllis Hattis. Cambridge, Mass., Fogg Art
Museum, Harvard University, 1973.

Designed by Malcolm Grear Designers.
8½ × 9½ inches; 83 pages including [11] pages of plates.
Smythsewn and glued into printed white paper cover. (127231)

597

KARL KNATHS: FIVE DECADES OF PAINTING. Introduction by Charles Edward Eaton; catalogue by Isabel Patterson Eaton. [Washington, D.C.], International Exhibitions Foundation, 1973.

11×8½ inches; [10]+151 pages including [43] pages of plates (some colored); colored frontispiece portrait; bibliography.
Smythsewn and glued into printed blue paper cover. (47330)

598

LAY THIS LAUREL. An album on the Saint-Gaudens Memorial on Boston Common Honoring Black and White Men Together Who Served the Union Cause with Robert Gould Shaw and Died with Him July 18, 1863. With photographs by Richard Benson and an essay by Lincoln Kirstein. New York, N.Y., The Eakins Press, 1973.

9¼×8¾ inches; [84] pages including 20 pages of plates; bibliography.
Black cloth over boards; gold-stamped spine; wrapper. (37363)

599

MAX SALVADORI: A LIST OF PUBLICATIONS. [Northampton, Mass., Smith College, 1973.]
9×6 inches; [6] pages.
Saddlewire stitched into printed blue paper cover. (57312)

600

MEDIEVAL GREEK BOOKHANDS: EXAMPLES SELECTED FROM GREEK MANUSCRIPTS IN OXFORD LIBRARIES. By Nigel Wilson. Cambridge, Mass., Mediaeval Academy of America, 1973 (Publication Number 81).

Vol. I (Text): 11×8½ inches; 38 pages.
Smythsewn and glued into light blue paper cover. (127243)

601

MESOAMERICAN WRITING SYSTEMS. Elizabeth P. Benson, Editor. Washington, D.C., Dumbarton Oaks Research Library and Collections for the Trustees of Harvard University, 1973.

Proceedings of a conference at Dumbarton Oaks, 1971.
9¾×7 inches; vii+226 pages; bibliography.
White cloth over boards. (117235)

602

A MICROFICHE INVENTORY OF THE PAPERS OF GREN-
VILLE CLARK. With a biographical introduction . . . by
J. Garry Clifford. [Hanover, N.H.], Dartmouth College
Library, [1973].

4¾×6¼ inches; 15 pages saddlewire stitched into white paper folder;
15 microfiche in pocket. (107351)

603

MILTIE IS A HACKIE. A libretto by Edwin Denby. Movie
stills by Rudy Burckhardt. Edited by Kenward Elmslie.
Calais, Vt., Z Press, 1973.

11 ×7 inches; 59 pages including 30 pages of plates.
400 numbered copies perfect-bound in printed gray glossy paper cover.
(67345)

604

THE MURAL PAINTING OF TEOTIHUACÁN. By Arthur G.
Miller with drawings by G. Felipe Dávalos and an appen-
dix by Edwin R. Littmann. Washington, D.C., Trustees of
Harvard University [for] Dumbarton Oaks, 1973.

12 ×9 inches; 193 pages including 131 pages of plates (some colored).
Red cloth over boards; wrapper. (27228)

605

NINETEENTH-CENTURY FOLK PAINTING: OUR SPIRITED
NATIONAL HERITAGE: WORKS FROM THE COLLECTION
OF MR. AND MRS. PETER TILLOU. Selection and catalogue by Peter H. Tillou. Storrs, Conn., The William Ben-
ton Museum of Art, The University of Connecticut, 1973.

10 ×8½ inches; 209+[2] pages including [147] pages of plates (some
colored); bibliography.
Smythsewn and glued into printed light brown paper cover. (117236)

606

OF WHAT USE ARE OLD BOOKS? A Talk by Phyllis Goodhart Gordan. [Bryn Mawr, Pa.], Privately printed by Her Friends, April 1973.

10½ × 7½ inches; 27 + [2] pages including 9 pages of plates.
Saddlewire stitched into printed cream paper cover. (87262)

607

ONE HUNDRED MASTER DRAWINGS FROM NEW ENGLAND PRIVATE COLLECTIONS. By Franklin W. Robinson. Hanover, N.H., Trustees of Dartmouth College; Distributed by the University Press of New England, 1973.

10 × 8 inches; 219 pages including [104] pages of plates.
Smythsewn and glued into printed light brown paper cover. (127248)

608

PHILIP HOFER. [Hanover, N.H.], Friends of the Dartmouth College Library, [1973].

At head of title: "Collector's Showcase."
6 × 4½ inches; [8] panels accordion-folded; illustrated; portrait. (57304)

609

THE RAMBLER IN GEORGIA: DESULTORY OBSERVATIONS ON THE SITUATION, EXTENT, CLIMATE, POPULATION, MANNERS, CUSTOMS, COMMERCE, CONSTITUTION, GOVERNMENT, ETC., OF THE STATE FROM THE REVOLUTION TO THE CIVIL WAR RECORDED BY THIRTEEN TRAVELLERS. Edited by Mills Lane. Savannah, Ga., The Beehive Press, 1973.

10 × 7 inches; xxxiv + 233 pages; illustrated; map; bibliography.
White cloth over boards; wrapper; slipcase. (17217)

610

RECONSIDERATIONS OF SCULPTURE BY LEONARDO DA VINCI: A BRONZE STATUETTE IN THE J. B. SPEED ART MUSEUM. By Michael Hall. Louisville, Ky., J. B. Speed Art Museum, 1973 (The Bulletin, Vol. XXIX, November 1973).

11 × 8½ inches; 59 + [2] pages including 18 pages of plates.
Smythsewn and glued into printed white paper cover. (57303)

611

ROYAL ART OF CAMEROON: THE ART OF THE BAMENDA-
TIKAR. By Tamara Northern. Hanover, N.H., Hopkins
Center Art Galleries, 1973.

9 × 7½ inches; 75 pages; illustrated; map.
Smythsewn and glued into printed white paper cover. (17352)

612

SAVANNAH REVISITED: A PICTORIAL HISTORY. By Mills
Lane. Savannah, Ga., The Beehive Press, 1973.

Second edition.
10¾ × 12¼ inches; 160 pages; illustrated.
Yellow cloth over boards; slipcase covered in printed blue paper. (See
items 419 and 868.) (17330)

613

SKOPAS IN SAMOTHRACE. By Phyllis Williams Lehmann.
Northampton, Mass., Smith College, 1973.

Designed by Phyllis Williams Lehmann and Elliot Offner.
9 × 7½ inches; [18] + 81 pages including 44 pages of plates.
1,000 copies Smythsewn and glued into printed white paper cover.
(47364)

614

SLAVERY TIME WHEN I WAS CHILLUN DOWN ON
MARSTER'S PLANTATION: INTERVIEWS WITH GEORGIA
SLAVES. Edited by Ronald Killion and Charles Waller.
Savannah, Ga., The Beehive Press, 1973.

8½ × 7 inches; xviii + 167 pages; illustrated.
Brown cloth over boards; gold-stamped spine; wrapper. (27262)

615

SPLENDIDE-HÔTEL. By Gilbert Sorrentino. New York,
N.Y., New Directions, 1973.

8¼ × 5½ inches; 61 pages.
350 copies signed by the author; bound in printed white paper and blue

cloth over boards; gold-stamped spine; acetate wrapper. Also issued Smythsewn (dimensions slightly reduced) and glued into printed white paper cover. (47323)

616

THE SPLENDOR OF TURKISH WEAVING: AN EXHIBITION OF SILKS AND CARPETS OF THE 13TH–18TH CENTURIES. By Louise W. Mackie. Foreword by Richard Ettinghausen. Washington, D.C., The Textile Museum, [1973].

Cover design by Crimilda Pontes.
10×7 inches; 86 pages including [44] pages of plates and 5 leaves of colored plates; map.
Perfect-bound in decorated purple and gold paper cover. (77338)

617

THE STORY OF WRIGHT'S SILVER CREAM, 1873–1973. By David R. Proper. Keene, N.H., Privately printed, 1973.

9×6 inches; 41 pages; illustrated.
Smythsewn and glued into dark blue paper cover. (87365)

618

THE STRAVINSKY FESTIVAL OF THE NEW YORK CITY BALLET. Written and edited by Nancy Goldner. With photographs by Martha Swope and others. New York, N.Y., The Eakins Press, 1973.

5¾×7¼ inches; 302 pages.
Red cloth over boards; gold-stamped cover and spine; acetate wrapper. (37328)

619

THOMAS THE OBSCURE. By Maurice Blanchot. New version translated by Robert Lamberton. New York, N.Y., David Lewis, 1973.

Designed by Ronald Gordon at the Oliphant Press.
9½×6¼ inches; 117+[5] pages.
1,500 copies bound in black cloth over boards; gold-stamped spine; wrapper. (57335)

620

TRAVELS THROUGH NORTH AND SOUTH CAROLINA, GEORGIA, EAST AND WEST FLORIDA. By William Bartram. Introduction by Gordon De Wolf. Savannah, Ga., The Beehive Press, 1973.

Facsimile of the 1792 London edition embellished with its nine original plates + 17 additional illustrations.
9¼ × 6 inches; xx + xxiv + 534 pages; illustrated; facsimile; bibliography. Yellow-brown paper and blue quarter cloth over boards; gold-stamped spine; wrapper; slipcase. (17305)

621

TWENTY-FIVE YEARS OF BOOK CELLARING AS RECALLED BY STEPHEN GREENE. [Brattleboro, Vt., Privately printed], 1973.

8¼ × 5½ inches; 36 pages + [8] pages of plates.
Saddlewire stitched into yellow-green paper cover. (47312)

622

WEEDS AND WILDFLOWERS OF EASTERN NORTH AMERICA. From watercolors by T. Merrill Prentice and text by Elizabeth D. Sargent. Salem, Mass., Peabody Museum and Barre Publishers, 1973.

11¾ × 8¾ inches; [126] leaves including 114 leaves of colored plates numbered 1 to 114.
Green cloth over boards; gold-stamped cover and spine. (87261)

623

WHALERS, WHARVES, AND WATERWAYS: AN EXHIBITION OF PAINTINGS BY CLIFFORD W. ASHLEY. New Bedford, Mass., The Whaling Museum; Chadds Ford, Pa., The Brandywine River Museum, 1973.

10 × 8½ inches; 93 pages including [69] pages of plates (some colored). Smythsewn and glued into printed blue-green paper cover. (37323)

624

WHITE FANG. By Jack London. With an introduction by Ray Gardner and illustrations by Lydia Dabcovich. Avon, Conn., The Limited Editions Club, 1973.

Typography by Charles E. Skaggs.
10¾×7 inches; xiv+245 pages + [5] illustrations printed in color from linoleum blocks.
2,000 copies bound in blue cloth over boards; slipcase. (77235)

[1974]

625

AMERICAN PAINTINGS IN THE RHODE ISLAND HISTOR-ICAL SOCIETY. By Frank H. Goodyear, Jr. Providence, R.I., The Rhode Island Historical Society, 1974.

11¼×8¾ inches; 116 pages including [38] pages of plates (some colored).
Light green cloth over boards; gold-stamped spine; wrapper. (77206)

626

AMERICAN POSTERS OF THE NINETIES. [Introduction by Roberta Wong; foreword by David Brooke and Sinclair Hitchings. Lunenburg, Vt., The Stinehour Press], 1974.

10¼×7¼ inches; 59 pages; illustrated; endleaf; bibliography.
Black cloth over boards; blind-stamped cover and gold-stamped spine.
Also issued Smythsewn and glued into printed white paper cover.
(F97349)

627

AMONG THE CLOUDS. Hanover, N.H., Dartmouth College Library, [1974].

Microfilm edition of Mt. Washington's newspaper published 1877–1917.
Announcement and reel guide to the collection.
Cover title.
9¼×6¼ inches; [4] pages; single folded sheet.
Unbound. (F17414)

628

BENJAMIN FRANKLIN'S PHILADELPHIA PRINTING, 1728–1766: A DESCRIPTIVE BIBLIOGRAPHY. By C. William Miller. Philadelphia, Pa., American Philosophical Society, 1974 (Memoirs of the American Philosophical Society, Vol. 102).

11½×8¾ inches; lxxxv+583 pages; illustrated; bibliography. Brown cloth over boards; wrapper. (17201)

629

BOSTON FURNITURE OF THE EIGHTEENTH CENTURY. [Walter Muir Whitehill, Editor.] Boston, Mass., The Colonial Society of Massachusetts; Distributed by the University Press of Virginia, 1974 (Publications of the Colonial Society of Massachusetts, Vol. 48).

Expanded versions of papers presented at a conference held by the Colonial Society of Massachusetts in May 1972.
9½×6½ inches; xvi+316 pages; illustrated; map; bibliography. Blue buckram over boards; gold-stamped spine. (G37460)

630

COPPÉLIA. Text by Nancy Goldner and Lincoln Kirstein; photographs by Richard Benson. New York, N.Y., Eakins Press Foundation, 1974.

Commemorating the New York City Ballet production choreographed by George Balanchine and Alexandra Danilova that premiered in Saratoga Springs and New York City in 1974.
6¼×61 inch single leaf accordion-folded into 29 pages (6¼×5¼ inches) and glued into printed paper folder. (F77449)

631

DANIEL B. UPDIKE ON TYPOGRAPHY. Lunenburg, Vt., The Stinehour Press, 1974.

Extract from D. B. Updike's *Printing Types* (1951) printed as a keepsake for members of the New Hampshire Library Council.
Cover title.

9¼×6¼ inches; [4] pages; French folded paper in white envelope.
(F47454)

632

DAVID ALONZO JONAH: TRIBUTE TO A LIBRARIAN.
[Providence, R.I.], Commissioned in May 1974 by the
Friends and Colleagues of David A. Jonah.

19×14 inches; broadside. (37438)

633

FOUR CENTURIES OF SCENIC INVENTION: DRAWINGS
FROM THE COLLECTION OF DONALD OENSLAGER. Intro-
duction and catalogue by Donald Oenslager. [Washington,
D.C.], International Exhibitions Foundation, 1974.

8½×10 inches; 187 pages including [113] pages of plates.
Smythsewn and glued into printed off-white paper cover. (G67419)

634

THE FRENCH FORMAL GARDEN. Edited by Elisabeth B.
MacDougall and F. Hamilton Hazlehurst. Washington,
D.C., Dumbarton Oaks, 1974 (Dumbarton Oaks Collo-
quium on the History of Landscape Architecture Vol. III).

10¼×7¼ inches; vi+87 pages and 4 sets of plates numbered I to XII;
I to X; I to XII; I to XII.
Green cloth over boards; gold-stamped cover and spine. (P27457)

635

GIFTS IN HONOR OF THE FIFTIETH ANNIVERSARY. New
York, N.Y., The Pierpont Morgan Library, 1974.

10×7 inches; 63 pages.
Smythsewn and glued into red and gray marbled paper cover; printed
label. (S47461)

636

GILGAMESH. Translated by William Ellery Leonard. Intro-

The Poetry of
ROBERT FROST
Edited by Edward Connery Lathem

I

IMPRINT SOCIETY
BARRE, MASSACHUSETTS, 1971

ENTRY 503

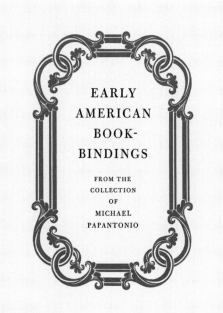

EARLY
AMERICAN
BOOK-
BINDINGS

FROM THE
COLLECTION
OF
MICHAEL
PAPANTONIO

ENTRY 531

ENGLISH
DRAWINGS AND
WATERCOLORS
1550–1850
IN THE COLLECTION OF
MR. AND MRS. PAUL MELLON

THE PIERPONT MORGAN LIBRARY

ROYAL ACADEMY OF ARTS · LONDON

ENTRY 533

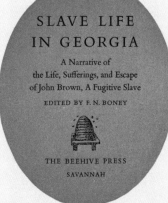

SLAVE LIFE
IN GEORGIA

A Narrative of
the Life, Sufferings, and Escape
of John Brown, A Fugitive Slave

EDITED BY F. N. BONEY

THE BEEHIVE PRESS
SAVANNAH

ENTRY 566

The Visions of Mary

by EDWARD TYLER
with wood engravings by GILLIAN TYLER

ENTRY 570

WEEDS
& WILDFLOWERS
OF EASTERN NORTH AMERICA

FROM WATERCOLORS BY
T. MERRILL PRENTICE

AND TEXT BY
ELIZABETH O. SARGENT

Peabody Museum of Salem & Barre Publishers

ENTRY 622

716 [PENNSYLVANIA. Governor William Denny. Proclamation, July 21, 1759, for preventing sickly Vessels coming up to the City till visited].
[1759]
NOTES: Not seen. Hall charged the Province £1.15.0 for printing this proclamation on July 26, 1759 (Pa. Accounts, 1756-1765, p. 4). The text of this proclamation, concerned with stopping the spread of Yellow Fever from the West Indies to Philadelphia, was reprinted in Pa. Gaz., July 26 and Aug. 2, 1759.
REFERENCES: Evans-Bristol 11246.

717 [PENNSYLVANIA. Governor William Denny. Proclamation, October 17, 1759, appointing October 31 as a Day of Public Thanksgiving].
[1759]
NOTES: Not seen. Hall charged the Province £2.10.0 for printing 200 copies on Oct. 19, 1759 (Pa. Accounts, 1756-1765, p. 5). The text was reprinted in Pa. Gaz., Oct. 18, 1759.
REFERENCES: Evans-Bristol 11245.

718 PENNSYLVANIA. Indian Treaty. Minutes of Conferences held at Easton with the Mohawks in October, 1758. [Second Edition]. 1759
COLLATION: Demy 2° A-H². P: title, 3-31 text of minutes, 32 blank.
CATCHWORDS: no aberrations.
ORNAMENT: 7 No.6.
PAPER: American, marked GHS.
LEAF: 13.3 x 8.5 in.
REF: Evans 8377, Hildeburn 1634, Campbell 636.
NOTES: Advertised for publication on "Saturday next" in Pa. Gaz., Feb. 1, 1759. This second printing is a line-for-line, page-for-page resetting of the 1758 first edition (see No. 696).
COPIES: PPAmP. CSmH, CtY, P, PHi, PPL.

719 RUTTY, John (1698-1775). The Liberty of the Spirit. 1759
COLLATION: Demy 8° A-D⁸. P: title, 3-19 introduction, 20 blank, 21-53 text of tract, 54 blank, 55-64 appendix, etc., Dublin, Aug. 19, 1756.
RUNNING-TITLES: 4-19 The INTRODUCTION. 22-64 [titles vary].

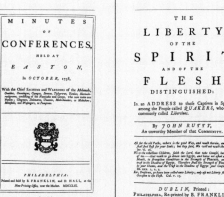

MINUTES OF CONFERENCES, HELD AT EASTON, In OCTOBER, 1758.

With the Chief SACHEMS and WARRIORS of the Mohawks, Oneidas, Onondagos, Cayugas, Senecas, Tuscaroras, Nanticokes, and Conoys, consisting of the Nanticokes and Conoys, who now make one Nation; Chugnuts, Delawares, Unamies, Mohickanders, or Mohicons, Minisinks, and Wapingers, or Pumptons.

PHILADELPHIA:
Printed and sold by B FRANKLIN, and D. HALL, at the New-Printing-Office, near the Market. MDCCLIX.

[718]

CATCHWORDS: 39 Ye
TYPE: Caslon: text in English, notes in long primer.
LEAF: 7.4 x 4.8 in.
REF: Evans 8486, Hildeburn 1642, Campbell 640.
NOTES: First published in Dublin in 1756. Late in 1759 the Society of Friends in Philadelphia ordered the publication of this piece in an edition of 4000 copies, and when informed by the Overseers that DH had about completed the printing in mid-June, 1760, directed that the treatise be distributed in the same proportion as the 1759 Yearly Epistle, i.e., 1000 to stay in Philadelphia, 3000 to be divided among the quarterly meetings in the Provinces of Pennsylvania and New Jersey, and most of the re-

THE LIBERTY OF THE SPIRIT AND OF THE FLESH DISTINGUISHED:

In an ADDRESS to those Captives in Spirit among the People called QUAKERS, who are commonly called Libertines.

By JOHN RUTTY, An unworthy Member of that Community.

As for the old Paths, where is the good Way, and walk therein, and ye shall find Rest for your Souls; but they said, We will not walk therein. Jer. vi. 16.
We is the rebellious Children, saith the Lord, that take Counsel, but not of me—that walk to go down into Egypt, and have not asked at my Mouth, to strengthen themselves in the Strength of Pharaoh, and to trust in the Shadow of Egypt. Therefore shall the Strength of Pharaoh be your Shame, and the Trust in the Shadow of Egypt your Confusion. Ib. xxx. 1, 2, 3.
For, Brethren, ye have been called unto Liberty; only use not Liberty for an Occasion to the Flesh. Gal. v. 13.

DUBLIN, Printed:
PHILADELPHIA, Re-printed by B. FRANKLIN, and D. HALL. 1759.
[719]

mainder to go to Meetings in New England, New York, Maryland, Virginia, and the Carolinas (Minutes of YM II, 134; Minutes of Meeting for Sufferings I, 163, 176).
COPIES: PPAmP. CSmH, CtY(3), DLC, ICN, MdBJ-G, MB, MH, MWA, MiU-C, NjP-T, NN, P(2), PHi, PHC, PPF(2), PPFr, PPL(3), PSC-Hi, PU, RPJCB; FRLL, MNS, NjGbS, Gimbel.

720 SAUNDERS, Richard. A Pocket Almanack for the Year 1760.
[1759]

A POCKET ALMANACK For the Year 1760. Fitted to the Use of PENNSYLVANIA, and the neighbouring Provinces. With several useful ADDITIONS. By R. SAUNDERS, Phil. PHILADELPHIA: Printed and sold by B. FRANKLIN, and D. HALL.

[720]

[Collation, placement of contents, and type like that in A Pocket Almanack for 1749 except for typographical arrangement and text of p. 24. The lines of the table run the length of the page, and the table includes the value and weight of coins as they now pass in England, Pennsylvania, and New York].
PAPER: American, marked GHS.
LEAF: 3.9 x 2.1 in.
BINDING: embossed Dutch paper wrappers.
REFERENCES: Evans 8487, Hildeburn 1643, Campbell 641, Drake 9820.
NOTES: Advertised as "Just Published" in Pa. Gaz., Oct. 25, 1759.
COPIES: PU. CtY, MWA, PHi.

721 SAUNDERS, Richard. Poor Richard Improved for the Year 1760.
[1759]
1-3 preface, 2-3 Finlander's method of reviving drowned persons, 3-4 receipts for hiccoughs, etc., 4 notes, 5 anatomy of man's body, symbols, 6-29 January to December, 29-30 family receipts, 30-31 eclipses, 31 Quaker meetings, 32 table of British rulers, 33 interest table at six per cent, 34-35 court days in Middle

ENTRY 628

ORNAMENTAL INITIALS

THE WOODCUT INITIALS OF CHRISTOPHER PLANTIN A COMPLETE CATALOGUE BY STEPHEN HARVARD

THE AMERICAN FRIENDS OF THE PLANTIN-MORETUS MUSEUM NEW YORK · MCMLXXIV

ENTRY 648

THE FIRST ALPHABETS

series 18, which ranges with series 17, is dated 1563, the year in which Pieter Huys designed thirty-three medium-format greek and roman letters.* Series 17 was easily Plantin's most versatile alphabet, and he used it in more than 230 books of every description over a span of twenty-five years. Another Huys design, the smallest of the suite, replaced the suddenly unfashionable series 25. Like the previous two alphabets, series 26 and the greek 27 were mentioned as being designed by Huys in 1563* and are inscribed, on the N, with that date.

* See the catalogue, series 17.
* See the catalogue, series 26 and 27.

DV DRAGON. CHAP. XX.

Apollon, Draco, Dragon.

IL y a diuerses especes de Dragons entre ceux que nous nommons terrestres, outre celuy lequel du nom de la Mer est nommé Marin, car il y en a de montagniers & de marescagiers, lesquels, selon Philostrate, ont quelque dissemblace. Ils sont aussi dissemblables pour la diuersité des pais, ausquels ils sont engendrez & nourris: si toutefois nous pouuons croire ce que l'on a escript des Dragons Lybiens & Indiens, lesquels me semblent plustost fabuleux, qu'auoir apparence.

I of series 18, designed by Geoffroy Ballain and cut by Arnold Nicolai in 1567. Few blocks of this series exist today, although it appeared in 261 of Plantin's books. From Gesvinus, Deux livres des vertise (1567).

Plantin's new suite of initials in the Paris style was lighter in texture than the popular Antwerp trade initials that appear in his earliest work. While in Paris, the printer had acquired punches and matrices from the widow of Claude Garamond, and with other typographical material by Granjon, Le Bé, and Haultin, Plantin was prepared to produce books of a refinement never before seen in the North. He was to publish grander volumes in the succeeding years, but none more perfect than the modest 8° classical texts of

15

ENTRY 648

ENTRY 651

Haggadah and History

A Panorama in Facsimile of Five Centuries
of the Printed Haggadah from the
Collections of Harvard University and the
Jewish Theological Seminary of America

BY

YOSEF HAYIM YERUSHALMI

The Jewish Publication Society of America
PHILADELPHIA

ENTRY 697

Myopia

A CENTENNIAL CHRONICLE

COMPILED AND EDITED BY

Edward Weeks

1875-1975

Published in 1975 at

HAMILTON · MASSACHUSETTS

ENTRY 710

duced by Leonard Cottrell. Illustrated by Irving Amen. Avon, Conn., For the Members of The Limited Editions Club, 1974.

13 ×9 inches; xvii+[3]+105+[3] pages + [9] pages of color plates. 2,000 copies numbered and signed by the artist; bound in yellow cloth over boards; embossed cover and gold-stamped spine; slipcase. (117327)

637

AN INSIDE VIEW OF SLAVERY: A TOUR AMONG THE PLANTERS. By C. G. Parsons. Introduction by Mrs. H. B. Stowe. Savannah, Ga., The Beehive Press, 1974.

9 ×5½ inches; xi+242 pages.
Gray cloth over boards; together in a slipcase with *A South-Side View of Slavery*. (See item 662.) (37235)

638

IN THE CRUCIBLE OF THE SUN. [Written and illustrated by Tom Lea.] Kingsville, Tex., [Privately printed for King Ranch], 1974.

Designed by Tom Lea.
14¼ × 11¾ inches; 92 pages.
White cloth over boards; acetate wrapper. (F97307)

639

LEAVES FROM MY BOOK OF LIFE. By Guido R. Perera. Boston, Mass., Privately printed, 1974.

Vol. I: *Early Life and Education*; *Business and Professional Life*; *Sporting Life*.
10¼ × 7¼ inches; v+243 pages + [23] pages of plates (some colored); frontispiece portrait.
200 copies bound in red-brown cloth and brown quarter cloth over boards; gold-stamped spine; wrapper. (See items 703 and 847.) (P67407)

640

THE LIMBOURGS AND THEIR CONTEMPORARIES. Text Volume. By Millard Meiss. New York, N.Y., George Braziller and The Pierpont Morgan Library; London, Thames and Hudson, 1974.

At head of title: "French Painting in the Time of Jean De Berry."
Designed by Vincent Torre.
12¼×9¼ inches; x+533 pages; bibliography.
Green cloth over boards; gold-stamped cover and spine; wrapper.
(77347)

641

MAJOR ACQUISITIONS OF THE PIERPONT MORGAN
LIBRARY, 1924–1974. New York, N.Y., The Pierpont
Morgan Library, 1974.

Vol. I: *Autograph Letters and Manuscripts*. Introduction by Herbert Ca-
hoon. xv+103 pages including [50] pages of plates. (117302)
Vol. II: *Drawings*. Introduction by Felice Stampfle. xxx+103 pages including [50] pages of plates. (107336)
Vol. III: *Early Printed Books*. Introduction by Paul Needham. xvi+
[103] pages including 51 pages of plates. (117303)
Vol. IV: *Medieval and Renaissance Manuscripts*. Introduction by William
Voelkle. xvi+106 pages including [51] pages of plates. (117304)
Each volume Smythsewn and glued into gray paper cover stamped in
gold; together in a slipcase covered in red and gray marbled paper and
gray cloth; label printed in gold.

642

A MICROFICHE CATALOGUE OF THE LIBRARY OF JERE-
MIAH SMITH AS PRESERVED IN THE LIBRARY OF DART-
MOUTH COLLEGE. With a biographical introduction by
Richard W. Morin. Hanover, N.H., Dartmouth College
Library, [1974].

Cver title.
4³⁄₄₀×6¼ inches; 24 pages + 10 microfiche; frontispiece portrait.
Together in a brown paper folder; printed front and spine. (F47434)

643

THE MORALS OF CHESS. By Benjamin Franklin. Preface
by Dr. Whitfield Bell. [Lunenburg, Vt., Privately printed],
1974.

Originally appeared in *Chess* by Richard Twiss in London (1787).

$8\frac{3}{4} \times 5\frac{3}{4}$ inches; [4]+[8] pages numbered 141 to 148+[4] pages; facsimile; illustrated.
Handsewn into printed light green paper cover. (107379)

644

MULTIPLE PEPPERS: PHOTOGRAPHS FROM VERMONT'S ARTISTS-IN-SCHOOLS PROGRAM. [Montpelier, Vt.], Vermont Council on the Arts, 1974.

10×8 inches; 33+[3] pages including 31 pages of plates.
Saddlewire stitched into printed white glossy paper cover. (F77443)

645

MUSKETS, CANNON BALLS AND BOMBS: NINE NARRATIVES OF THE SIEGE OF SAVANNAH IN 1779. Edited and translated by Benjamin Kennedy. Savannah, Ga., The Beehive Press, 1974.

$11\frac{1}{4} \times 7$ inches; xv+141 pages; folded map frontispiece.
Red cloth over boards; gold-stamped spine; wrapper. (S77324)

646

THE NATURAL HISTORY OF CAROLINA, FLORIDA AND THE BAHAMA ISLANDS. Containing two hundred and twenty figures of Birds, Beasts, Fishes, Serpents, Insects and Plants by the late Mark Catesby F. R. S. with an introduction by George Frick and notes by Joseph Ewan. Savannah, Ga., The Beehive Press, 1974.

Facsimile reprint of the copy at the Boston Athenaeum (third edition). [Catalogue]: $20\frac{1}{4} \times 14\frac{1}{2}$ inches; xvi+[2]+107+[3] pages including [54] pages of plates; facsimiles; maps on endleaves. Bound in red cloth over boards; gold-stamped spine. [Plates]: 20×14 inches; 50 colored plates numbered I to L. Each in a folder with a descriptive text. 500 sets (numbered 1 to 500) together in a box ($21\frac{3}{4} \times 15\frac{5}{8} \times 3\frac{1}{2}$ inches) covered in green linen cloth; gold-stamped cover and spine. *N.B.* 1,700 copies of the catalogue issued separately (including 30 numbered copies for members of the Walpole Society) bound in olive linen and green quarter linen over boards; gold-stamped cover and spine. (F67143+F97411)

647

OBITER PROSCRIPTA. By F. Lyman Windolph. Lancaster, Pa., Privately published, 1974.

7½×5½ inches; xi+50 pages.
200 numbered copies bound in light brown cloth over boards; gold-stamped spine. (F107411)

648

ORNAMENTAL INITIALS: THE WOODCUT INITIALS OF CHRISTOPHER PLANTIN. A complete catalogue by Stephen Harvard. New York, N.Y., The American Friends of the Plantin-Moretus Museum, 1974.

12¼×9¼ inches; xiii+26+[16] pages + [126] pages of plates; chronological table.
Printed brown paper and red quarter cloth over boards; gold-stamped spine; wrapper. (37358)

649

OUR FIRST VISIT IN AMERICA: EARLY REPORTS FROM THE COLONY OF GEORGIA, 1732–1740. Introduction by Trevor R. Reese. Savannah, Ga., The Beehive Press, 1974.

10¼×7¼ inches; xiv+316 pages; bibliography.
Blue cloth over boards; gold-stamped spine; wrapper. (G77325)

650

PAINTINGS AND DRAWINGS BY FITZ HUGH LANE. Foreword by Edward Hyde Cox. Gloucester, Mass., The Cape Ann Historical Association, 1974.

8¾×10½ inches; [141] pages including 132 pages of plates (some colored).
Orange cloth over boards; illustration laid onto cover; acetate wrapper. (57339)

651

PAYNE HOLLOW: LIFE ON THE FRINGE OF SOCIETY. By Harlan Hubbard. New York, N.Y., The Eakins Press, 1974.

7¼×5¾ inches; 167 pages.
Light gray-green paper over boards; wrapper. (F67316)

652

PERSON AND PLACE: A CANADIAN GARLAND. With a foreword by John Alden. Boston, Mass., G. K. Hall and Co., Christmas 1974.

Facsimiles reprinted from *Les Voyages du Sieur de Champlain Xaintongeois* (Paris, 1613) and *Annapolis Royal* by the Reverend Roger Viets (Halifax, 1788).
8½×5½ inches; [4]+6+[12]+7 pages.
Smythsewn and glued into printed light blue paper cover. (S97449)

653

PETRARCH IN AMERICA. A survey of Petrarchan Manuscripts by Michael Jasenas. Washington, D.C., The Folger Shakespeare Library; New York, N.Y., The Pierpont Morgan Library, 1974.

11×8 inches; xi+63 pages + 24 pages of plates.
Smythsewn and glued into printed blue paper cover. (127309)

654

PUDD'NHEAD WILSON. By Mark Twain. With an introduction by Edward Wagenknecht. Illustrated by John Groth. Avon, Conn., The Limited Editions Club, 1974.

10¾×7½ inches; xiii+164 pages + [8] pages of colored plates.
2,000 numbered copies signed by the artist; bound in printed white cloth over boards; gold-stamped label on spine. Together in a slipcase with "Pudd'nhead Wilson's Calendar" by Mark Twain; illustrated by John Groth (5¼×3½ inches; 32 pages); Smythsewn into brown paper cover and glued into brown marbled paper wrapper. (R117329+R47455)

655

PYGMALION AND CANDIDA. By George Bernard Shaw. With an introduction by Alan Strachan and illustrations by Clarke Hutton. Avon, Conn., The Limited Editions Club, 1974.

Designed by John Dreyfus.
11¾×8½ inches; ix+[7]+169+[3] pages + [8] pages of colored plates.

2,000 copies numbered and signed by the artist; bound in printed cloth and gray quarter cloth over boards; gold-stamped label on spine; slipcase. (F27469)

656

R. Swain Gifford, 1840–1905. [Introduction by Elton W. Hall.] New Bedford, Mass., Old Dartmouth Historical Society, 1974.

10×8½ inches; xvi+113 pages including [105] pages of plates (some colored); frontispiece portrait.
Smythsewn and glued into printed black and white paper cover. (27454)

657

Rare Americana: A Selection of One Hundred and One Books, Maps, and Prints Not in the John Carter Brown Library. Providence, R.I., The Associates of The John Carter Brown Library, 1974.

8¾×5¾ inches; 77 pages.
Smythsewn and glued into printed light yellow paper cover. (127338)

658

Robert Frost, 1874–1963: A Remembrance. Amherst, Mass., The Friends of the Amherst College Library, 1974.

Includes holograph facsimile of "Fragment Written in England in 1914 or 13."
8¾×5¾ inches; [6] pages.
Handsewn into printed gray paper cover. (17420)

659

Robert Frost 100. Compiled by Edward Connery Lathem. Boston, Mass., David R. Godine Publisher, 1974.

One hundred items representative of Frost's books and other printed works.
Typography by Joseph Blumenthal.
9½×6½ inches; viii+104 pages; facsimiles.

Brown cloth over boards; gold-stamped spine; wrapper. Also issued
Smythsewn and glued into printed brown paper cover. (F27430)

660

ROBERT LOWELL: POET OF TERRIBILITÀ. By Stanley
Kunitz. New York, N.Y., The Pierpont Morgan Library,
1974.

9×6¼ inches; [6] pages.
Saddlewire stitched into white paper cover and glued into red paper
wrapper. (17419)

661

SELECTED POEMS AND BALLADS. By Helen Adam. New
York, N.Y., Helikon Press, 1974 (Helikon Press Publication
Number 5).

Designed by Marilan Lund.
10×6¾ inches; 57 pages.
26 copies printed for friends of the poet and 100 copies printed for sale,
numbered and signed by the poet; bound in bright blue paper and
purple quarter cloth over boards. (F67424)

662

A SOUTH-SIDE VIEW OF SLAVERY: THREE MONTHS AT
THE SOUTH. By Nehemiah Adams. Introduction by Mills
Lane. Savannah, Ga., The Beehive Press, 1974.

9×5½ inches; liv+181 pages.
Gray cloth over boards; together in a slipcase with *An Inside View of
Slavery.* (See item 637.) (37236)

663

SUSAN AND MATHER. By Mather Cleveland, M.D. New
London, N.H., Privately printed, 1974.

9¼×6¼ inches; 103 pages.
Blue cloth over boards; gold-stamped spine; wrapper. (17433)

664

THREE NOTES ON EXILE. Northampton, Mass., Alumnae
Association of Smith College, 1974.

Contains "Science and Exile" by Waltraut Seitter; "Printing and Exile"
by Elliot Offner; "Existence as Exile" by Thomas S. Derr.
9×6 inches; 11 pages.
Saddlewire stitched into printed light brown paper cover. (F57403)

665

TOBACCO ROAD. By Erskine Caldwell. With photographs
by Margaret Bourke-White. Savannah, Ga., The Beehive
Press, 1974.

9×6 inches; viii+184 pages + [17] pages of plates.
Brown cloth over boards; gold-stamped spine; wrapper. (S117317)

666

TOUMBA TOU SKOUROU: THE MOUND OF DARKNESS: A
BRONZE AGE TOWN ON MORPHOU BAY IN CYPRUS. By
Emily T. Vermeule. Cambridge, Mass., Harvard Univer-
sity; Boston, Mass., The Museum of Fine Arts, 1974.

11×8½ inches; [69] pages including 49 pages of plates.
Smythsewn and glued into printed gray paper cover. (S97429)

667

UNCLE REMUS: TALES BY JOEL CHANDLER HARRIS.
Selected and introduced by John Tumlin. Savannah, Ga.,
The Beehive Press, 1974.

10×7¼ inches; xxvii+206 pages + [18] pages of plates; bibliography.
Green cloth over boards; gold-stamped spine; wrapper. (F67303)

668

UNIVERSITY AND COLLEGE POETRY PRIZES, 1967–72.
Edited by Daniel Hoffman. [New York, N.Y.], The Academy of American Poets, 1974.

At head of title: "The Academy of American Poets."
9¼×6 inches; 95 pages.
Smythsewn and glued into printed blue paper cover. (127364)

669

VAGARIES MALICIEUX: TWO STORIES BY DJUNA BARNES.
New York, N.Y., Frank Hallman, 1974.

9½×6 inches; 41 pages.
500 numbered copies bound in white cloth over boards; gold-stamped
spine. (F37449)

670

VENETIAN DRAWINGS FROM AMERICAN COLLECTIONS.
Introduction and catalogue by Terisio Pignatti. [Washing-
ton, D.C.], International Exhibitions Foundation, 1974.

11×8½ inches; xiii+57 pages + [121] pages of plates.
Smythsewn and glued into printed blue-green paper cover. (G67402)

671

WALLACE LOWRY. By Walker Lowry. [Lunenburg, Vt.,
Privately printed], 1974.

10¼×7¼ inches; 197 pages.
150 copies bound in brown cloth and green quarter cloth over boards;
gold-stamped spine; slipcase. (57323)

672

WALT WHITMAN'S AUTOGRAPH REVISION OF THE ANAL-
YSIS OF LEAVES OF GRASS (FOR DR. R. M. BUCKE'S
WALT WHITMAN). Introductory essay by Quentin Ander-
son; text notes by Stephen Railton. New York, N.Y., New
York University Press, 1974.

11¼×8 inches; 191 pages including 35 pages of manuscript facsimile.
Green cloth over boards; gold-stamped spine. (57344)

673

"WAR IS HELL!": WILLIAM T. SHERMAN'S PERSONAL
NARRATIVE OF HIS MARCH THROUGH GEORGIA. Edited
by Mills Lane. Savannah, Ga., The Beehive Press, 1974.

9½×9 inches; xxvi+196 pages + [41] pages of plates; maps on
endleaves.
Blue cloth over boards; gold-stamped spine; wrapper. (F107307)

674

WE, THE PEOPLE. By Elizabeth Yates. Illustrated by Nora Unwin. Hanover, N.H., Published for the Regional Center for Educational Training by The Countryman Press, 1974.

8¾×5¾ inches; 39 pages.
Smythsewn and glued into printed blue and white paper cover. Also issued saddlewire stitched into printed blue and white paper cover. (F67444)

[1975]

675

ARCHITECTURAL, ORNAMENT, LANDSCAPE AND FIGURE DRAWINGS COLLECTED BY RICHARD WUNDER. Middlebury, Vt., Middlebury College, 1975.

11×8½ inches; 200 pages including 121 pages of plates.
Smythsewn and glued into printed light blue paper cover. (F87437)

676

THE BOOK OF THE JACOB WENDELL SCHOLARS. [Cambridge, Mass.], Privately printed, 1975.

9¼×6¼ inches; xv+91 pages; portraits.
200 copies Smythsewn and glued into printed light blue paper cover. (G87433)

677

BOSTON: DISTINGUISHED BUILDINGS AND SITES WITHIN THE CITY AND ITS ORBIT AS ENGRAVED ON WOOD BY RUDOLPH RUZICKA. With a commentary by Walter Muir Whitehill. Boston, Mass., David R. Godine Publisher, 1975.

9×6 inches; xxiii+117+[3] pages including [29] pages of colored plates. Marbled paper and blue quarter leather over boards; gold-stamped spine. (G107417)

678

A CENTENNIAL REVIEW: THE MASSACHUSETTS GEN-
ERAL HOSPITAL SCHOOL OF NURSING, 1873–1973. By
Sylvia Perkins. [Boston, Mass.], School of Nursing, Nurses
Alumnae Association, 1975.

9×6 inches; xiv+593 pages; illustrated (portraits).
Smythsewn and glued into blue glossy paper cover; gold-stamped cover
and spine. (17360)

679

CHINESE EXPORT SILVER, 1785 TO 1885. By H. A. Crosby
Forbes, John Devereux Kernan, and Ruth S. Wilkins. Milton, Mass., Museum of the American China Trade, 1975.

11½×8¾ inches; xvi+303 pages including 91 pages of plates;
bibliography.
Bound in two cloths in two shades of blue over boards; gold-stamped
spine; wrapper. (S77437)

680

CLASSIC MAYA POTTERY AT DUMBARTON OAKS. By
Michael D. Coe. Washington, D.C., Dumbarton Oaks, 1975.

11×8½ inches; 30 pages; illustrated; bibliography.
Smythsewn and glued into printed white paper cover. (G97525)

681

CLASSIC PHOTOGRAPHS OF NEW YORK CITY: VIEWS OF
LOWER MANHATTAN. New York, N.Y., Eakins Press Foundation, 1975 (Eakins Pocket Album Number 2).

6×34 inches; 13+[1] pages.
Text and illustrations on single leaf accordion-folded into an album
(6×4¼ inches). (L67542)

682

THE CONQUEST AND SETTLEMENT OF THE ISLAND OF
BORIQUEN OR PUERTO RICO. By Captain Gonzalo Fer-
nandez de Oviedo y Valdés. Translated and edited by Day-

mond Turner. Illustrated with drawings by Jack and Irene Delano. Avon, Conn., Printed for the Members of The Limited Editions Club, 1975.

Contains three sections extracted from *The Natural and General History of the Indies* by Oviedo y Valdés.

$12\frac{1}{4} \times 7\frac{3}{4}$ inches; xxviii+143 pages + 8 pages of color serigraphs.
2,000 copies signed by the illustrators; bound in orange cloth and white quarter paper over boards; gold-embossed cover and spine; slipcase. (L67547)

683

COUSIN HECTOR AND MOP. By Walker Lowry. [Lunenburg, Vt., Privately printed], 1975.

$9\frac{1}{2} \times 4\frac{3}{4}$ inches; 141 pages.
125 copies Smythsewn and glued into white paper cover; glued into red paper wrapper. (F117406)

684

DANDELION AND OTHER POEMS. By Bert Penny; selected by Sally Penny. Birmingham, Mich., Privately printed, 1975.

$8\frac{1}{2} \times 5\frac{3}{4}$ inches; [6]+120 pages; frontispiece portrait.
Green cloth over boards; gold-stamped spine; wrapper. (P27505)

685

THE DELIGHTS OF A RARE BOOK LIBRARIAN. By Frederick R. Goff. Boston, Mass., Trustees of the Public Library of the City of Boston, 1975 (Maury A. Bromsen Lecture in Humanistic Bibliography Number 2).

$8\frac{1}{2} \times 5\frac{1}{2}$ inches; vi+30 pages; illustrated.
1,000 copies Smythsewn and glued into printed white paper cover. (F117423)

686

THE DIARY OF AN ARTILLERY SCOUT. By Horatio Rogers. North Andover, Mass., [Privately printed], 1975.

$10\frac{1}{4} \times 7\frac{1}{4}$ inches; [13]+268 pages.
Red cloth over boards; gold-stamped spine. (F67411)

687

DJUNA BARNES: A BIBLIOGRAPHY. By Douglas Messerli. Lunenburg, Vt., David Lewis, 1975.

Designed by Ronald Gordon at the Oliphant Press.
9½×6¼ inches; xvii+131 pages.
500 copies bound in dark blue cloth over boards; gold-stamped spine. (F97548)

688

DRAWINGS BY BENJAMIN WEST AND HIS SON RAPHAEL LAMAR WEST. By Ruth S. Kraemer. New York, N.Y., The Pierpont Morgan Library, 1975.

11¾×9 inches; xiv+104 pages + plates numbered 1 to 106.
Smythsewn and glued into green paper cover. Also issued in a casebound edition by David R. Godine Publisher. (S57437)

689

DRAWINGS FROM THE COLLECTION OF MR. AND MRS. EUGENE V. THAW. Catalogue by Felice Stampfle and Cara D. Denison with an introduction by Eugene V. Thaw. New York, N.Y., The Pierpont Morgan Library, 1975.

11×8 inches; 105 pages + 115 pages of plates (some colored).
Smythsewn and glued into printed light yellow paper cover. (R117422)

690

EARLY CHILDREN'S BOOKS AND THEIR ILLUSTRATION. By Gerald Gottlieb; essay by J. H. Plumb. New York, N.Y., The Pierpont Morgan Library; Boston, Mass., David R. Godine Publisher, 1975.

12×9¼ inches; xxx+263 pages + [21] pages of colored plates; bibliography.
Red cloth over boards; gold-stamped spine; wrapper. Also issued (by The Pierpont Morgan Library) Smythsewn and glued into printed paper cover. (S47551)

691

THE EARLY HISTORY AND MANAGEMENT PHILOSOPHY

of Richardson-Merrell. By Smith Richardson. New York, N.Y., [Privately printed], 1975.

10¼×6¾ inches; 135 pages; illustrated.
Dark blue cloth over boards; gold-stamped cover and spine. (F27404)

692

The Early History of Richardson-Merrell. By Smith Richardson. New York, N.Y., [Privately printed], 1975.

10×6½ inches; 92 pages; illustrated.
Smythsewn and glued into printed brown paper cover. (F27404)

693

Eucharistic Vessels of the Middle Ages. Cambridge, Mass., The Busch-Reisinger Museum of Harvard University, 1975.

8½×5½ inches; xii+130 pages including 12 pages of plates.
Smythsewn and glued into printed white paper cover. (S17511)

694

Free Joe. Stories by Joel Chandler Harris. Selected and introduced by John Tumlin. Savannah, Ga., The Beehive Press, 1975.

10×7¼ inches; xxiii+232 pages.
Black cloth over boards; gold-stamped spine; wrapper. (F67302)

695

General Oglethorpe's Georgia. Edited by Mills Lane. Savannah, Ga., The Beehive Press, 1975.

10¼×7½ inches; Vol. I: *Colonial Letters, 1733–1743* (i.e. 1733–1737), xxxvi+321 pages; illustrated; map. Vol. II: *Colonial Letters, 1733–1743* (i.e. 1738–1743), 350 pages numbered 325 to 674; illustrated; map. Each volume bound in dark blue buckram over boards; gold-stamped spine; together in a slipcase. (S47437+S57440)

696

GEORGIA SCENES: CHARACTERS, INCIDENTS, ETC., IN
THE FIRST HALF CENTURY OF THE REPUBLIC. By a
native Georgian, Augustus B. Longstreet. Introduction by
Richard Harwell. Savannah, Ga., The Beehive Press, 1975.

9¼×6¼ inches; xix+249 pages.
Light green cloth over boards; gold-stamped label on spine; wrapper.
(S47416)

697

HAGGADAH AND HISTORY: A PANORAMA IN FACSIMILE
OF FIVE CENTURIES OF THE PRINTED HAGGADAH FROM
THE COLLECTIONS OF HARVARD UNIVERSITY AND THE
JEWISH THEOLOGICAL SEMINARY OF AMERICA. By Yosef
Hayim Yerushalmi. Philadelphia, Pa., The Jewish Publi-
cation Society of America, 1975.

11¾×8¾ inches; 494+[4] pages including 200 pages of plates; illustrated endleaves; bibliography.
5,000 copies, of which 252 copies were set aside for a special bibliophilic
issue [not seen] boxed in half leather, of which 200 are numbered, and
52, *hors commerce*, are marked I to LII. This issue contains a portfolio of
16 plates reproducing the 8 extant leaves of the oldest illustrated printed
Haggadah, with an introductory study by Yosef Hayim Yerushalmi.
The remaining copies bound in white cloth over boards; gold-stamped
cover and spine; wrapper. (See item 765.) (S107362)

698

HENRY MOORE: PRINTS, 1969–1974. Introduction by
David Mitchinson. Washington, D.C., The International
Exhibitions Foundation, 1975.

11×8½ inches; 32 pages including 18 pages of plates; bibliography.
Smythsewn and glued into printed white paper cover. (S77528)

699

HOW TO READ A POEM. By Robert Frost. Lancaster, N.H.,
New England Books (Small-Tall Editions), 1975.

Originally appeared in *The Pendulum* (October–November 1960).
$4\frac{3}{4} \times 2$ inches; 15 pages; illustrated.
Smythsewn and glued into white paper cover and glued into gray paper wrapper. (F127411)

700

JANE AUSTEN: LETTERS AND MANUSCRIPTS IN THE PIER-PONT MORGAN LIBRARY. Preface by Charles Ryskamp. New York, N.Y., The Pierpont Morgan Library, 1975.

$10\frac{1}{4} \times 7$ inches; 30 pages + [4] pages of plates.
Sewn into decorated light green paper cover. (R87510)

701

THE JANUS PRESS, 1955–75. Catalogue raisonné by Ruth Fine Lehrer. Burlington, Vt., The Robert Hull Fleming Museum, The University of Vermont, 1975.

$8\frac{1}{2} \times 5\frac{1}{2}$ inches; 43 pages; illustrated.
Smythsewn and glued into yellow-green paper cover. (S57505)

702

THE JOURNAL OF KATE CUMMING, A CONFEDERATE NURSE, 1862–1865. Edited by Richard Harwell. Savannah, Ga., The Beehive Press, 1975.

$10\frac{1}{4} \times 7\frac{1}{4}$ inches; xx+288 pages.
Blue cloth and beige quarter cloth over boards; wrapper. (S87423)

703

LEAVES FROM MY BOOK OF LIFE. By Guido R. Perera. Boston, Mass., Privately printed, 1975.

Vol. II: *Washington and War Years.*
$10\frac{1}{4} \times 7\frac{1}{4}$ inches; xi+252 pages + 10 pages of plates; colored frontispiece portrait.
250 copies bound in red-brown cloth and brown quarter cloth over boards; gold-stamped spine; wrapper. (See items 639 and 847.) (P117420)

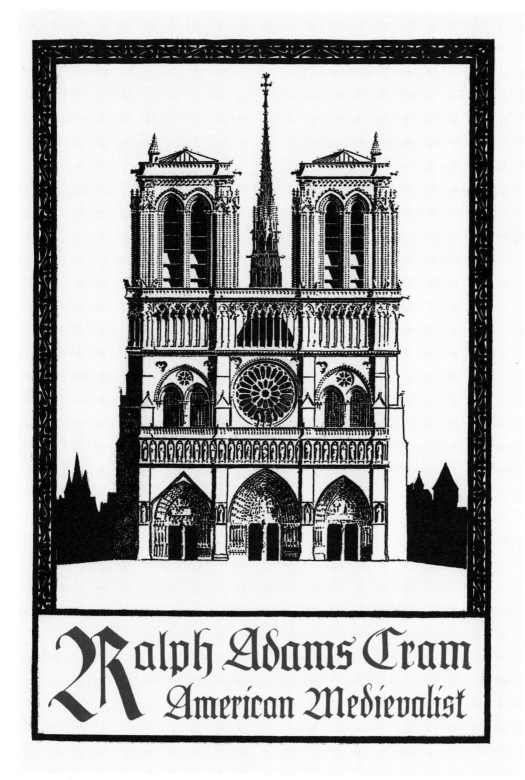

Ralph Adams Cram
American Medievalist

ROYALTON VERMONT

BY HOPE NASH

The Town of Royalton

South Royalton Woman's Club

Royalton Historical Society

1975

Twenty-five Books
of The Stinehour Press

Twenty-five Years
of The Stinehour Press

 is published by
Dartmouth College Library
Hanover, New Hampshire
to celebrate the first quarter-
century of The Stinehour Press
Lunenburg, Vermont

1950–1975

George
Christian Gebelein
Boston Silversmith
1878–1945

A BIOGRAPHICAL SKETCH BY
Margaretha Gebelein Leighton

IN COLLABORATION WITH
ESTHER GEBELEIN SWAIN AND
J. HERBERT GEBELEIN

Boston Massachusetts
1976

THE
PRINTED BOOK
IN AMERICA

BY JOSEPH BLUMENTHAL

DAVID R. GODINE · PUBLISHER
BOSTON · MASSACHUSETTS
IN ASSOCIATION WITH
THE DARTMOUTH COLLEGE LIBRARY

ENTRY 860

704

THE LONDON SCENE: FIVE ESSAYS BY VIRGINIA WOOLF. New York, N.Y., Frank Hallman, 1975.

Designed by Ronald Gordon.
9½×6¼ inches; 44 pages.
750 copies bound in gray cloth over boards; gold-stamped spine. (F77445)

705

A MATTER OF TIME. [Photographs] by Rosamond Wolff Purcell. Afterword by Dennis W. Purcell. Boston, Mass., David R. Godine, 1975 (Contemporary Photographers Series Number 1).

7¼×7¾ inches; vii+72 pages including 69 pages of plates.
Gray cloth over boards; silver-stamped cover and spine; illustration laid onto cover; acetate wrapper. Also issued Smythsewn and glued into printed gray paper cover. (R17563)

706

METAMORPHOSES IN NINETEENTH-CENTURY SCULPTURE. Edited by Jeanne L. Wasserman. Cambridge, Mass., Fogg Art Museum; Distributed by Harvard University Press, 1975.

10¾×9¼ inches; xvi+267 pages; illustrated; bibliography.
Red cloth over boards; gold-stamped spine; wrapper. (S57556)

707

THE MINT JULEP. By Richard Barksdale Harwell. Savannah, Ga., The Beehive Press, 1975.

8¼×5¼ inches; 59 pages.
300 copies bound in decorated green paper and light gray quarter cloth over boards; silver-stamped covers and spine. (S37541)

708

MONADNOCK JOURNAL. By Richard F. Merrifield. Drawing by Nora S. Unwin. Taftsville, Vt., The Countryman Press, 1975.

9¼×6¼ inches; [4]+108 pages.
Green paper over boards; wrapper. (F17515)

709

MY DAY: THREE PIECES BY JEAN RHYS. New York, N.Y., Frank Hallman, 1975.

Designed by R. Schaubeck.
5×7¼ inches; [30] pages.
750 copies (26 bound and signed by the author) bound in light brown cloth over boards. Also issued Smythsewn and glued into printed paper cover. (F87519)

710

MYOPIA . . . 1875–1975: A CENTENNIAL CHRONICLE. Compiled and edited by Edward Weeks. Hamilton, Mass., Privately printed, 1975.

A history of the Myopia Hunt Club.
10¼×7¼ inches; xx+151 pages; illustrated.
Yellow paper and red quarter cloth over boards; gold-stamped spine. (L67526)

711

NEW BEDFORD AND OLD DARTMOUTH: A PORTRAIT OF A REGION'S PAST. [Compiled by the Staff of the Whaling Museum, New Bedford, Massachusetts]; introduction by Richard C. Kugler. New Bedford, Mass., Trustees of the Old Dartmouth Historical Society, 1975.

11×8½ inches; xiii+253 pages; illustrated.
Red cloth over boards; illustration laid onto cover; gold-stamped spine; acetate wrapper. Also issued Smythsewn and glued into printed white paper cover. (F87531)

712

ON CONCILIATION WITH THE COLONIES AND OTHER

PAPERS ON THE AMERICAN REVOLUTION. By Edmund Burke. Edited by Peter J. Stanlis. Illustrated with wood engravings by Lynd Ward. Lunenburg, Vt., Printed for the Members of The Limited Editions Club at The Stinehour Press, 1975.

10¼×7½ inches; xxix+267+[1] pages + [12] pages of wood engravings.
2,000 copies numbered and signed by the artist; bound in printed cloth over boards; gold-stamped brown cloth label on spine; slipcase. (R107423)

713

ON THE PRACTICE OF LAW. By Abraham Lincoln. Lancaster, N.H., New England Books (Small-Tall Editions), 1975.

From Lincoln's *Complete Works* edited by John G. Nicolay and John Hay.
4¾×2 inches; 16 pages; frontispiece caricature.
Smythsewn and glued into white paper cover and glued into paper wrapper. (F87421)

714

AN OUTCAST OF THE ISLANDS. By Joseph Conrad. With an introduction by Clifton Fadiman and illustrations by Robert Shore. Avon, Conn., Printed for the Members of The Limited Editions Club, 1975.

Designed by John O. C. McCrillis.
11½×8¾ inches; ix+[2]+212+[2] pages + [2] pages of colored illustrations.
2,000 copies numbered and signed by the artist; bound in decorated brown cloth over boards; gold-stamped spine; slipcase. (F27509)

715

THE PEOPLE OF GEORGIA: AN ILLUSTRATED SOCIAL HISTORY. By Mills Lane. Savannah, Ga., The Beehive Press, 1975.

11¼×10¼ inches; 350 pages; illustrated; bibliography.
Brown cloth over boards; slipcase. (S127342)

716

RALPH ADAMS CRAM, AMERICAN MEDIEVALIST.
By Douglass Shand Tucci. Boston, Mass., Boston Public
Library, 1975.

10¼×7¼ inches; [6]+49 pages; illustrated; portrait; checklists;
bibliography.
1,000 copies bound in printed gray paper over boards. (S97566)

717

REMBRANDT: THE HUNDRED GUILDER PRINT. [Note by
A. Hyatt Mayor.] New York, N.Y., Eakins Press Foundation, 1975 (Eakins Pocket Album Number 1).

6×34 inches; 14 pages; illustrated.
Text and illustrations on single leaf accordion-folded into an album
(6×4¼ inches). (F17547)

718

ROYALTON, VERMONT. By Hope Nash. Royalton, Vt.,
The Town of Royalton, South Royalton Woman's Club,
and Royalton Historical Society, 1975.

11¼×7½ inches; xiv+299 pages; illustrated; maps.
1,000 copies bound in green cloth; gold-stamped cover and spine;
wrapper. (F67425)

719

RULES OF CIVILITY AND DECENT BEHAVIOUR IN
COMPANY AND CONVERSATION. By George Washington.
Lancaster, N.H., New England Books (Small-Tall
Editions), 1975.

Reprinted from Moncure D. Conway's *George Washington's Rules of Civility* (1890).
4¾×2 inches; 42 pages; frontispiece silhouette.
Smythsewn and glued into white paper cover and glued into gray paper
wrapper. (F127410)

720

SELECTED WORKS OF ALICE ROYCE: BATIK, POETRY,

and Other Writings. Montréal, Quebec, The Alithea Press, 1975.

7×5 inches; [62] pages including 23 pages of reproductions (some colored) laid in.
100 numbered copies bound in batik cloth over boards; slipcase. (F17524)

721

Sir Arthur Sullivan: Composer and Personage. By Reginald Allen in collaboration with Gale R. D'Luhy. New York, N.Y., The Pierpont Morgan Library; London, England, Chappell and Co., Ltd., 1975.

11½×8¼ inches; xxviii+215 pages; illustrated; bibliography.
Light brown cloth over boards; wrapper. Also issued Smythsewn and glued into printed yellow paper cover. (R77451)

722

Strange Days Ahead. By Michael Brownstein. Calais, Vt., Z Press, 1975.

9×6 inches; [10]+91 pages.
1,500 copies (26 lettered and signed) Smythsewn and bound in printed paper cover. (G67556)

723

Three Tales. By Paul Bowles. New York, N.Y., Frank Hallman, 1975.

7¼×5 inches; 27 pages.
1,000 copies Smythsewn and glued into printed brown paper cover. 100 copies casebound and signed by the author. (F47501)

724

To the King's Taste: Richard II's Book of Feasts and Recipes Adapted for Modern Living. By Lorna J. Sass. New York, N.Y., The Metropolitan Museum of Art, 1975.

Designed by Peter Oldenburg.
8¾×5 inches; 144 pages; illustrated.
Printed yellow paper over boards; printed cover and spine. (F37546)

725

THE TRIAL. By Franz Kafka. Translated from the German by Willa and Edwin Muir. With an introduction by Erich Heller and illustrations by Alan E. Cober. Avon, Conn., The Limited Editions Club, 1975.

Designed by Peter Oldenburg.
9¾×7¾ inches; xiii+220 pages + [10] pages of colored plates.
2,000 copies signed by the illustrator; bound in red oasis leather; blind-stamped cover and gold-stamped cover and spine; slipcase. (F107544)

726

TROPICALISM. By Kenward Elmslie. Calais, Vt., Z Press, 1975.

9×6 inches; 77 pages.
2,000 copies (26 lettered and signed) Smythsewn and glued into printed white paper cover. Some copies issued in printed pink paper cover. (P67511)

727

TWENTY-FIVE BOOKS OF THE STINEHOUR PRESS, TWENTY-FIVE YEARS OF THE STINEHOUR PRESS. Hanover, N.H., Dartmouth College Library, 1975.

Published by Dartmouth College to celebrate the first quarter-century of The Stinehour Press, 1950–1975.
9¾×6¼ inches; [16] pages; illustrated.
Handsewn into printed brown paper cover; 125 copies created especially for The Typophiles, New York, Christmas 1975. (F107548)

728

VERMONT FARM AND THE SUN. By Constance and Raymond Montgomery. Photographs by Dennis Curran. Waitsfield, Vt., Vermont Crossroads Press, 1975.

11¼×8¾ inches; 31+[1] pages.
Oversewn and glued into printed paper over boards. (L67545)

729

VERMONT ROADBUILDER. By Constance and Raymond

Montgomery. Photography by Larry Burns. Waitsfield, Vt., Vermont Crossroads Press, 1975.

11¼×8¾ inches; 31 pages; illustrated.
Printed black and white cloth over boards; library binding. (L67544)

730

VITA NUOVA: A MEMOIR OF PRISCILLA BARTON MOR-
ISON. By Samuel Eliot Morison. Northeast Harbor, Me.,
[Privately printed], 1975.

9¼×6¼ inches; xviii+414 pages + [31] leaves of plates (some colored).
Blue-green cloth over boards; gold-stamped spine. (P17526)

731

A WEEK ON THE CONCORD AND MERRIMACK RIVERS.
By Henry David Thoreau. With an introduction by Charles
R. Anderson and illustrations by R. J. Holden. Avon, Conn.,
The Limited Editions Club, 1975.

Designed by Robert L. Dothard.
10¼×6¾ inches; xv+327 pages.
2,000 copies signed by the illustrator; bound in green marbled paper and green quarter cloth over boards; gold-stamped spine; slipcase. (P87436)

[1976]

732

AN ALBUM OF LINCOLN PHOTOGRAPHS AND WORDS.
New York, N.Y., Eakins Press Foundation, 1976 (Eakins
Pocket Album Number 3).

6×34 inches; [14] pages.
Text and illustrations on single leaf accordion-folded into an album (6×4¼ inches). (F27613)

733

AMERICA FROM AMERIGO VESPUCCI TO THE LOUISIANA

PURCHASE. [Preface by Charles Ryskamp.] New York, N.Y.,
The Pierpont Morgan Library, 1976.

10 × 7 inches; x+66 pages including [16] pages of plates; portraits.
Smythsewn and glued into red, white, and blue marbled paper cover;
printed on front. Reissued in 1976 in a similar format (title page and
pagination vary) by the Amon Carter Museum, Fort Worth, and The
Lyndon Baines Johnson Library, Austin, Tex. (S37617)

734

ANCIENT MESOPOTAMIAN ART AND SELECTED TEXTS.
New York, N.Y., The Pierpont Morgan Library, 1976.

10 × 7 inches; 42 pages including 11 pages of plates.
Smythsewn and glued into printed blue and brown paper cover. (S87634)

735

ANGLING FOR ATLANTIC SALMON. By Shirley E. Woods.
Illustrated by Tom Hennessey. Goshen, Conn., The Angler's
and Shooter's Press, 1976.

10 × 6¾ inches; xiv+219 pages + [4] pages of plates (some colored).
990 copies signed by the author and artist; bound in red cloth over
boards; gold-stamped cover and spine; slipcase. (R57630)

736

ANGLO-SAXON VERNACULAR MANUSCRIPTS IN AMERICA.
By Rowland L. Collins. New York, N.Y., The Scheide Library and The Pierpont Morgan Library, 1976.

10 × 7 inches; 86 pages including 12 pages of plates; bibliography.
Smythsewn and glued into patterned brown and white paper cover; red
spine. Patterned paper cover, title page border, and chapter head orna-
ments especially created for the edition by Stephen Harvard. (R97547)

737

THE ARCHITECTURE OF GEORGIA. Text by Frederick
Doveton Nichols; photographs by Van Jones Martin and
Frances Benjamin Johnston; drawings by Frederick Spitz-

miller; edited by Mills Lane. Savannah, Ga., The Beehive Press, 1976.

11½×10 inches; [6]+436 pages.
Brown cloth over boards; gold-stamped spine; wrapper. (97523)

738

THE ASSEMBLY HOUSE. By Gerald W. R. Ward; foreword by Bryant F. Tolles, Jr. Salem, Mass., Essex Institute, 1976 (Historic House Booklet Number 3).

9×6 inches; 31 pages + [4] pages of plates.
Saddlewire stitched into printed red paper cover. (G107530)

739

THE BIBLIOPHILE OF THE FUTURE: HIS COMPLAINTS ABOUT THE TWENTIETH CENTURY. By Jacques Barzun. Boston, Mass., Trustees of the Public Library of the City of Boston, 1976 (Maury A. Bromsen Lecture in Humanistic Bibliography Number 4).

8½×5½ inches; vi+19 pages.
1,000 copies Smythsewn and glued into printed white paper cover. (G77606)

740

BICENTENNIAL ADDRESS. By Wilmarth S. Lewis. Farmington, Conn., Farmington Historical Society, 1976.

8¾×5¾ inches; 17+[1] pages.
1,000 copies saddlewire stitched into printed light blue paper cover.

741

THE BOOK OF TRADES IN THE ICONOGRAPHY OF SOCIAL TYPOLOGY. By Hellmut Lehmann-Haupt. Boston, Mass., Boston Public Library, 1976 (Maury A. Bromsen Lecture in Humanistic Bibliography Number 1).

8½×5½ inches; vi+12 pages + [14] pages of plates.
1,000 copies Smythsewn and glued into printed white paper cover. (F127515)

742

THE BOOKS OF ISAAC NORRIS (1701–1766) AT DICK-
INSON COLLEGE. By Marie Elena Korey with an introduction by Edwin Wolf 2nd. Carlisle, Pa., Dickinson College,
1976.

9½×6½ inches; [6]+315 pages + [16] pages of plates.
Gray cloth over boards; wrapper. (F37508)

743

BUILDING A GREAT LIBRARY: THE COOLIDGE YEARS
AT HARVARD. By William Bentinck Smith. Cambridge,
Mass., Harvard University Libraries, 1976.

10½×7½ inches; xiii+218 pages; illustrated.
Blue cloth over boards; gold-stamped cover and spine; acetate wrapper.
(P27526)

744

CAPTAIN SAMUEL TUCKER (1747–1833), CONTINENTAL
NAVY. By Philip Chadwick Foster Smith. Foreword by
Robert G. Albion. Salem, Mass., Essex Institute, 1976.

First appeared in the Institute's *Historical Collections*, Vol. 112, Number 3.
9¼×6¼ inches; xv+115 pages + [5] leaves of plates.
500 copies bound in blue cloth over boards; gold-stamped cover and
spine. (G47624)

745

CATALOGUE OF THE ITALIAN PAINTINGS BEFORE 1800.
By Peter Tomory. [Sarasota, Fla.], The John and Mable
Ringling Museum of Art, 1976.

10¼×8¼ inches; xiii+198 pages; illustrated (some colored).
Blue cloth over boards; gold-stamped cover and spine. (P117527)

746

CAXTON: AN AMERICAN CONTRIBUTION TO THE QUIN-
CENTENARY CELEBRATION. Edited by Susan Otis Thomp-

son. New York, N.Y., The Typophiles, 1976 (Typophile Chap Book Number 52).

7¼×4¾ inches; xvi+54 pages + [3] pages of plates; map.
1,250 copies printed on acid-free Curtis Rag Antique (here used for the first time). Of the total, 250 for the Caxton International Congress; 500 for the Curtis Paper Co.; 500 for The Typophiles and their friends. Bound in green cloth over boards; blind-stamped cover and gold-stamped spine; wrapper. (R67607)

747

CELEBRATION: 1925–1975. A poem read by David Mc-Cord . . . at the Fall Assembly of The Harvard College Fund . . . 26 September 1975. [Cambridge, Mass., Printed for the Fund, 1976].

9×6¼ inches; 32 pages; illustrated.
Saddlewire stitched into printed light brown paper cover. (S87628)

748

CHRISTIAN GULLAGER: PORTRAIT PAINTER TO FEDERAL AMERICA. By Marvin Sadik. Washington, D.C., National Portrait Gallery, Smithsonian Institution, 1976.

Designed by Leonard Baskin.
11×8½ inches; 108 pages including 30 pages of plates.
Smythsewn and glued into printed paper cover. (F97546)

749

CLASSIC PLAYS. By Dick Higgins. New York, N.Y., and Barton, Vt., Unpublished Editions, 1976.

9¼×6 inches; 4+xlvii pages.
750 copies Smythsewn and glued into printed paper cover. 50 copies bound in blue cloth over boards; gold-stamped spine; glassine wrapper. (R77628)

750

THE DECLARATION OF INDEPENDENCE. Two essays by

Howard Mumford Jones and Howard H. Peckham. Worcester, Mass., American Antiquarian Society, 1976.

First appeared in the Society's *Proceedings*, Vol. 85, Parts 1 and 2.
9¼×6¼ inches; 37 pages.
Saddlewire stitched into printed light blue paper cover. (R107545)

751

DISCOVERING YOSEMITE: HISTORIC PHOTOGRAPHS BY PIONEER PHOTOGRAPHERS: DESCRIPTIONS BY JOHN MUIR. New York, N.Y., Eakins Press Foundation, 1976 (Eakins Pocket Album Number 4).

6×34 inches; [14] pages.
Text and illustrations on single leaf accordion-folded into an album (6×4¼ inches). (F27606)

752

DR. CHURCH'S "HOAX": AN ASSESSMENT OF DR. WILLIAM CHURCH'S TYPOGRAPHICAL INVENTIONS IN WHICH IS ENUNCIATED CHURCH'S LAW. By Richard E. Huss. Lancaster, Pa., Graphic Crafts, Inc., 1976.

9¼×6¼ inches; xiv+78 pages; illustrated; bibliography.
500 copies bound in blue cloth over boards; gold-stamped cover and spine; wrapper. (R97550).

753

DREAM OF A DREAM. By Robert Penn Warren. [Boston, Mass.], G. K. Hall and Co., Christmas 1976.

4½×6¼ inches; 5 panels accordion-folded.
Unbound. (F97605)

754

EUROPEAN DRAWINGS FROM THE FITZWILLIAM. Introduction by Michael Jaffé. [Washington, D.C.], International Exhibitions Foundation, 1976.

10×7½ inches; xiv+84 pages + [121] pages of plates.
Smythsewn and glued into printed red paper cover. (G77632)

755

FACT AND FANTASY: ILLUSTRATED BOOKS FROM A PRI-
VATE COLLECTION. Catalogue by David P. Becker. Cam-
bridge, Mass., Harvard College Library Department of
Printing and Graphic Arts, 1976.

8½×5½ inches; 32 pages + 70 pages of plates.
Smythsewn and glued into printed cream paper cover. (S37651)

756

THE FIRST HUNDRED YEARS OF WESLEYAN COLLEGE,
1836–1936. By Samuel Luttrell Akers. Macon, Ga., Wesleyan College; Savannah, Ga., The Beehive Press, 1976.

9½×6½ inches; 160 pages; illustrated; portraits; schematic plans.
Orange-brown paper over boards; gold-stamped spine; wrapper.
(F127530)

757

FORTY YEARS MORE: A HISTORY OF GROTON SCHOOL,
1934–1974. By Acosta Nichols. Groton, Mass., The Trustees of Groton School, 1976.

9½×6½ inches; xviii+257 pages; illustrated.
Red cloth over boards; gold-stamped spine; wrapper. (F27608)

758

FROM FLESH IS HEIR: TWO UNPUBLISHED PARAGRAPHS.
[By Lincoln Kirstein. Lunenburg, Vt., Privately printed],
1976.

Cover title: "For Lincoln Kirstein."
8×5 inches; [8] pages; frontispiece photograph tipped in.
17 copies printed on handmade Amatruda paper; handsewn into printed
handmade light brown paper wrapper. (F37647)

759

FROM SEED TO FLOWER: PHILADELPHIA 1681–1876:
A HORTICULTURAL POINT OF VIEW. Philadelphia, Pa.,
The Pennsylvania Horticultural Society, 1976.

9½×7¼ inches; 119 pages including 41 pages of plates.

Light brown cloth over boards; gold-stamped cover and spine. Also issued Smythsewn and glued into printed green paper cover. (L17611?)

760

THE GARDNER-PINGREE HOUSE. By Gerald W. R. Ward. Foreword by Bryant F. Tolles, Jr. Salem, Mass., Essex Institute, 1976 (Historic House Booklet Number 5).

9×6 inches; 27 pages + [8] pages of plates.
Saddlewire stitched into printed green paper cover. (G107528)

761

GENERAL JOHN GLOVER'S LETTERBOOK, 1776–1777. Edited and with an introduction by Russell W. Knight. Foreword by Walter Muir Whitehill. Salem, Mass., Essex Institute, 1976.

First appeared in the Institute's *Historical Collections*, Vol. 112, Number 1.
9¼×6¼ inches; xvi+64 pages; illustrated; frontispiece portrait; bibliography.
500 copies bound in red-brown cloth over boards; gold-stamped spine; wrapper. (107554)

762

GEORGE CHRISTIAN GEBELEIN, BOSTON SILVERSMITH, 1878–1945. A biographical sketch by Margaretha Gebelein Leighton in collaboration with Esther Gebelein Swain and J. Herbert Gebelein. Boston, Mass., Privately printed, 1976.

9½×6¼ inches; xix+118 pages; illustrated.
Dark red cloth over boards; silver-stamped spine; wrapper. (S107610)

763

GEORGE WASHINGTON'S COPY OF POEMS ON SEVERAL OCCASIONS BY NATHANIEL EVANS. A facsimile edition with an introduction by Andrew Breen Myers. New York, N.Y., Fordham University Press, 1976.

Includes facsimile of the Philadelphia (1772) edition.
8×4¾ inches; 59+xxviii+160+24 pages.
500 copies bound in brown-gray cloth over boards; gold-stamped spine. (F97638)

764

GRAN PARTITA, K. 361. By Wolfgang Amadeus Mozart.
With an introduction by Alfred Einstein. Washington, D.C.,
Library of Congress, 1976.

A facsimile of the holograph of Serenade, K. 370ª (361) B♭ major in the
Whittall Foundation Collection.
10½×13¾ inches; 11 pages + [98] pages of holograph facsimile.
Blue paper and black quarter cloth over boards; gold-stamped cover
and spine. (L67557)

765

HAGGADAH AND HISTORY: A PANORAMA IN FACSIMILE
OF FIVE CENTURIES OF THE PRINTED HAGGADAH FROM
THE COLLECTIONS OF HARVARD UNIVERSITY AND THE
JEWISH THEOLOGICAL SEMINARY OF AMERICA. By Yosef
Hayim Yerushalmi. Philadelphia, Pa., The Jewish Publi-
cation Society of America, 1976.

Second, corrected edition.
11¾×8¾ inches; 494+[4] pages including 200 pages of plates; illustrated endleaves; bibliography.
White cloth over boards; gold-stamped cover and spine; wrapper. (See
item 697.) (L17618)

766

THE HARVARD LAMPOON HUNDREDTH ANNIVERSARY,
1876–1976. Cambridge, Mass., The Harvard Lampoon,
Inc., 1976.

9¼×6¼ inches; x+182 pages; illustrated.
Red cloth over boards; gold-stamped cover and spine. (S117542)

767

HISTORIC PHOTOGRAPHS OF WASHINGTON, D.C. New
York, N.Y., Eakins Press Foundation, 1976 (Eakins Pocket
Album Number 5).

6×34 inches; [14] pages; illustrated.
Text and illustrations on single leaf accordion-folded into an album
(6×4¼ inches). (F27612)

768

I THINK THEY'LL LAY MY EGG TOMORROW. By Geof
Hewitt. Lunenburg, Vt., The Vermont Council on the Arts
and The Stinehour Press, 1976 (Vermont Poetry Chapbooks
edited by Hayden Carruth).

9 ×6 inches; 27 pages.
Smythsewn and glued into patterned yellow and white paper cover.
(F17609)

769

THE ILLUSTRATOR AND THE BOOK IN ENGLAND FROM
1790 TO 1914. By Gordon N. Ray. New York, N.Y., The
Pierpont Morgan Library and Oxford University Press,
1976.

12 ×9¼ inches; xxxiii+336 pages including 100 pages of plates;
bibliography.
Blue cloth embossed in gold over boards; acetate wrapper. Also issued
(published by The Pierpont Morgan Library) Smythsewn and glued
into blue paper cover embossed in gold. (R37547)

770

AN INVENTORY OF THE PAPERS OF JOHN WINGATE
WEEKS (1860–1926) IN THE LIBRARY OF DARTMOUTH
COLLEGE. Hanover, N.H., Dartmouth College Library,
1976.

9¼ ×6 inches; 11 pages + [6] pages of plates.
Brown cloth over boards; gold-stamped spine; wrapper. Also issued
Smythsewn and glued into printed light brown paper cover. (F47345)

771

AN INVENTORY OF THE PAPERS OF SINCLAIR WEEKS
(1893–1972) IN THE LIBRARY OF DARTMOUTH COL-
LEGE. Hanover, N.H., Dartmouth College Library, 1976.

9½ ×6¼ inches; 54 pages + [12] leaves of plates.
Brown cloth over boards; gold-stamped spine; wrapper. Also issued
Smythsewn and glued into printed paper cover. (F47346)

772

THE ISLAMIC GARDEN. Edited by Elisabeth B. MacDougall and Richard Ettinghausen. Washington, D.C., Dumbarton Oaks, 1976 (Dumbarton Oaks Colloquium on the
History of Landscape Architecture).

10¼×7¼ inches; [8]+135 pages + 36 plates numbered I to XXXVI.
Green cloth over boards; gold-stamped cover and spine. (P57574)

773

IZAAK WALTON: THE COMPLEAT ANGLER AND HIS
TURBULENT TIMES. By J. Lawrence Pool and Angeline
Pool. Lunenburg, Vt., The Stinehour Press, 1976.

9¼×6½ inches; xiii+134 pages including [9] pages of plates + [2]
pages of illustrations tipped in; frontispiece portrait; maps on endleaves;
bibliography.
Green cloth over boards; gold-stamped spine; wrapper. (S67642)

774

JOHN HILLS, ASSISTANT ENGINEER. By Peter J. Guthorn.
Brielle, N.J., Portolan Press, [1976].

10×6 inches; [6]+58 pages.
Smythsewn and glued into printed gray paper cover. Accompanied by
a folder (16¼×11 inches) containing 15 manuscript maps (some folded)
in facsimile. (F57640)

775

THE JOURNAL OF CHARLES CARROLL OF CARROLLTON
AS ONE OF THE CONGRESSIONAL COMMISSIONERS TO
CANADA IN 1776. Edited by Allan S. Everest. Fort Ticon-
deroga, N.Y., Champlain–Upper Hudson Bicentennial
Committee, 1976.

8¾×5¾ inches; 64 pages.
Light blue-gray paper over boards. (F67602)

776

JURGEN, A COMEDY OF JUSTICE. By James Branch Cabell.

With an introduction by Edward Wagenknecht. Illustrations by Virgil Burnett. Westport, Conn., Printed for the Members of The Limited Editions Club, 1976.

Designed by Ted Gensamer.
11 × 7¼ inches; xvi+290 pages + [8] pages of colored plates.
2,000 copies signed by the illustrator and numbered; bound in purple cloth over boards; gold-stamped cover and spine; slipcase. (F37646)

777

LANDMARKS OF OLD CHESHIRE. [Edited by Howard Tredennick Dedel.] Cheshire, Conn., The Cheshire Bicentennial Committee, 1976.

10¼ × 7¼ inches; xx+176 pages; illustrated; bibliography.
Red cloth over boards; gold-stamped spine; wrapper. 200 copies numbered and signed. (P107624)

778

LETTERS AND DOCUMENTS OF EZEKIEL WILLIAMS OF WETHERSFIELD, CONNECTICUT. Introduction and notes by John C. Parsons. [Middletown], Conn., The Acorn Club, 1976.

8¾ × 5¾ inches; xvii+95+[2] pages.
White paper over boards. Also issued Smythsewn and glued into white paper cover. (F37645)

779

LOVE POEMS: POETRY [with] ILLUSTRATIONS FROM LITHOGRAPHS BY HENRI MATISSE. . . . New York, N.Y., Eakins Press Foundation, 1976 (Eakins Pocket Album Number 6)

6 × 34 inches; [14] pages; illustrated.
Text and illustrations on single leaf accordion-folded into an album (6 × 4¼ inches). (F27605)

780

MARIA BOSOMWORTH AND WILLIAM ROGERS. By

Eleanor West. [Ossabaw Island, Ga., Privately printed];
Savannah, Ga., The Beehive Press, 1976.

7½×9¼ inches; [66] pages including 31 pages of plates; map.
Light green paper over boards. Also issued Smythsewn and glued into
green paper cover. (G87509)

781

MEMOIRS OF A VICTORIAN COUNTRY LAD. By J. Harrison
Heckman. [Edited by Marianne H. Hancock. Exeter, N.H.,
Privately printed], 1976.

9½×6½ inches; x+262 pages; illustrated; frontispiece portrait.
Red cloth over boards; gold-stamped spine; wrapper. (F97609)

782

NAMU DAI BOSA: A TRANSMISSION OF ZEN BUDDHISM
TO AMERICA. By Nyogen Senzaki, Soen Nakagawa, Eido
Shimano. Edited with an introduction by Louis Nordstrom.
New York, N.Y., Theatre Arts Books, 1976 (The Bhaisaja-
guru Series).

9¼×6¼ inches; xxix+262 pages; illustrated; portraits; bibliography.
1,000 copies signed and numbered; printed on Curtis Rag Natural laid
paper and bound in light brown paper and brown quarter cloth over
boards; gold-stamped spine; slipcase. Another edition bound in light
brown cloth over boards; gold-stamped spine; wrapper. Another edition
Smythsewn and glued into decorated orange and black paper cover.
(F127537)

783

NEW ENGLANDERS IN NOVA ALBION: SOME 19TH CEN-
TURY VIEWS OF CALIFORNIA. By James D. Hart. Boston,
Mass., Trustees of the Public Library, 1976 (Maury A.
Bromsen Lecture in Humanistic Bibliography Number 3).

8½×5½ inches; vi+34 pages; illustrated; portraits.
Smythsewn and glued into white paper cover; printed on cover and
spine. (F97506)

784

OCTET FOR STRINGS, OPUS 20. By Felix Mendelssohn. With an introduction by Jon Newsom. Washington, D.C., Library of Congress, 1976.

Facsimile of the holograph in the Whittall Foundation Collection. 14½×11¼ inches; 8 pages + [41] pages of manuscript facsimile. Purple paper and black quarter cloth over boards; gold-stamped cover and spine. (67313)

785

ONE SEASON HERE: POEMS 1943–1946. By Francis Coleman Rosenberger. Charlottesville, Va., University Press of Virginia, [1976].

9½×6½ inches; 85+[2] pages. Green cloth over boards; gold-stamped spine; wrapper. (G127531)

786

OUR CULTURAL HERITAGE: WHENCE SALVATION. By Louis B. Wright. THE USES OF THE PAST. By Gordon N. Ray. [Washington, D.C., Association of Research Libraries], 1976.

9×6 inches; [2]+42 pages. Saddlewire stitched into printed white paper cover. (G117636)

787

POWERS. By Martha Zweig. Lunenburg, Vt., The Vermont Council on the Arts and The Stinehour Press, 1976 (Vermont Poetry Chapbooks edited by Hayden Carruth).

9×6 inches; 27 pages. Smythsewn and glued into patterned red and white paper cover. (F17610)

788

A PRINTER'S EMBLEMS. . . . Text and calligraphic panels by Stephen Harvard. [Lunenburg, Vt., The Stinehour Press], 1976.

Keepsake in honor of Roderick Stinehour compiled and printed by his friends and associates.
5 ×6 inches; [20] pages including 4 pages printed in color.
Saddlewire stitched into dark blue gold-embossed paper cover. (F27652?)

789
READINGS. By Peter Heitkamp. Lunenburg, Vt., The Vermont Council on the Arts and The Stinehour Press, 1976 (Vermont Poetry Chapbooks edited by Hayden Carruth).

9 ×6 inches; 27 pages.
Smythsewn and glued into patterned brown and white paper cover. (F17606)

790
RECOLLECTIONS OF A COLLECTOR. By Lessing J. Rosenwald. Jenkintown, Pa., The Alverthorpe Gallery, 1976.

10¼×6¾ inches; [8]+148 pages; illustrated; frontispiece portrait.
250 copies bound in brown cloth and black quarter leather over boards; gold-stamped cover and spine; slipcase covered in brown cloth. (R67501)

791
RHYMES REVERENT AND IRREVERENT. Written over the years by Dorothy Hall Leavitt. [Norwich, Vt., Privately printed], 1976.

9 ×6 inches; 67 pages.
Smythsewn and glued into white paper cover. (F37636)

792
ROXANA, THE FORTUNATE MISTRESS. . . . By Daniel Defoe. With an introduction by James Sutherland and woodcuts by Bernd Kroeber. Avon, Conn., Printed for the Meml bers of The Limited Editions Club, 1976.

Designed by Adrian Wilson.
11½×8½ inches; xiv+236 pages + [12] pages of colored plates.
2,000 copies signed by the artist and numbered; bound in red and white quarter cloth over boards; stamped in white on the covers and in red and gold on the spine; slipcase. (F37626)

793

SAINT PAUL'S CHURCH, LANCASTER, NEW HAMPSHIRE, 1876–1976. [Lunenburg, Vt.], Printed at The Stinehour Press, [1976].

9 × 6 inches; 36 pages.
Saddlewire stitched into printed blue paper cover. (F77635)

794

SAMUEL JONES AND THE NEW YORK SOCIETY LIBRARY. Reflections in the National Bicentennial Year by Harvey Simmonds. New York, N.Y., Trustees of the New York Society Library, 1976.

9¼ × 6¼ inches; 28 pages including [2] pages of facsimile manuscript; medallion portrait on title page and cover.
550 copies handsewn into printed red-brown paper cover. (F67637)

795

DER SCHAUSPIELDIREKTOR: THE IMPRESARIO, A COM-EDY WITH MUSIC IN ONE ACT, K. 486. By Wolfgang Amadeus Mozart. New York, N.Y., The Pierpont Morgan Library, 1976.

Facsimile of the autograph manuscript in the Mary Flagler Cary Music Collection.
9¾ × 13¼ inches; xvi+85 pages including [89] pages of holograph facsimile.
Smythsewn and glued into printed blue paper cover. (F57612)

796

SELECTED SERMONS. By Theodore Parker Ferris. Boston, Mass., Trinity Church, 1976.

9½ × 6½ inches; xv+368 pages; frontispiece portrait.
Red cloth over boards; gold-stamped spine; wrapper. (F77619)

797

SESTINA FOR THE QUEEN. By David McCord. [Boston, Mass.], The Bostonian Society, 1976.

Issued in honor of Her Majesty the Queen and His Royal Highness the Prince Philip on the occasion of their visit to The Old State House in Boston, 11 July 1976.
26 × 16 inches; broadside.
300 [sic] copies: 15 copies on handmade light gray paper (watermark HMP); 175 copies on Rives; 25 copies on SP book. Another 400 copies on Mohawk SF white. (R67614)

798

Seventeenth-Century Dutch Landscape Drawings and Selected Prints from American Collections. An exhibition organized by Curtis O. Baer. Poughkeepsie, N.Y., Vassar College Art Gallery, 1976.

8½ × 5½ inches; 69+[2] pages + [50] pages of plates + [3] pages. Smythsewn and glued into printed yellow paper cover. (P127526)

799

76 United Statesiana: Seventy-six Works of American Scholarship Relating to America as Published During Two Centuries from the Revolutionary Era of the United States Through the Nation's Bicentennial Year. Edited by Edward Connery Lathem. Washington, D.C., Association of Research Libraries, 1976.

9½ × 7¼ inches; [164] pages including 76 pages of plates.
Red cloth over boards; blind-stamped cover and silver-stamped spine; wrapper. Also issued Smythsewn and glued into printed red, white, and blue paper cover. (R67609)

800

"Should the liberty of the press be once destroyed...." By Isaiah Thomas. Lunenburg, Vt., Printed at The Stinehour Press, 1976.

Designed by Joseph Blumenthal.
21 × 15 inches; broadside printed on handmade Tovil paper.
Together with 15 additional broadsides and an introductory note (each 21 × 15 inches) laid into a portfolio bearing the title *A Little Rebellion Now and Then* (Santa Cruz, Calif., William James Association) covered in blue buckram; gold-stamped cover; 200 copies. (117501)

801

SIN ONE WAY ECONOMY CLASS. By Lucy Caldwell. Princeton, N.J., Privately printed, 1976.

8½ × 5½ inches; xi + 135 pages.
Smythsewn and glued into black and white printed paper cover.
(F77617)

802

A SMALL PORTRAIT OF LEILA MOORE WILLIAMS, CO-FOUNDER WITH LEWIS KEMPER WILLIAMS OF THE HISTORIC NEW ORLEANS COLLECTION. New Orleans, La., The Historic New Orleans Collection; Savannah, Ga., The Beehive Press, 1976.

9¼ × 6¼ inches; 16 pages; frontispiece portrait.
Handsewn into printed blue paper wrapper. (F117540)

803

SWAGGER HILL. By Walker Lowry. [Lunenburg, Vt., Privately printed], 1976.

9½ × 4¾ inches; 148 pages.
125 copies Smythsewn and glued into light blue paper cover; glued into light blue paper wrapper. (F107534)

804

TWO CONTINENTS. By Lyle Glazier. Lunenburg, Vt., The Vermont Council on the Arts and The Stinehour Press, 1976 (Vermont Poetry Chapbooks edited by Hayden Carruth).

9 × 6 inches; 27 pages.
Smythsewn and glued into patterned green and white paper cover.
(F17605)

805

VISIONS OF COURTLY INDIA: THE ARCHER COLLECTION OF PAHARI MINIATURES. Introduction and catalogue by W. G. Archer. Washington, D.C., International Exhibitions Foundation; Distributed by Sotheby Parke Bernet Publications (New York and London) and Oxford University Press (Delhi and Karachi), 1976.

10¼×9¾ inches; xiii+156 pages including 80 pages of plates (some colored); bibliography.
Blue cloth over boards; gold-stamped cover and spine; wrapper. (F57581)

806

THE WELL. By Carol Henrikson. Lunenburg, Vt., The Vermont Council on the Arts and The Stinehour Press, 1976 (Vermont Poetry Chapbooks edited by Hayden Carruth).

9×6 inches; 27 pages.
Smythsewn and glued into patterned blue and white paper cover. (F17607)

807

WHAT SO PROUDLY WE HAILED. By Raymond Holden. Taftsville, Vt., The Countryman Press, 1976.

7¼×9¼ inches; 53+[3] pages.
Red and white paper over boards. (F127517)

808

WHERE LIBERTY DWELLS: 19TH CENTURY ART BY THE AMERICAN PEOPLE: WORKS OF ART FROM THE COLLECTION OF MR. AND MRS. PETER TILLOU. Catalogue by Peter H. Tillou. [Buffalo, N.Y., Albright-Knox Art Gallery], 1976.

10×8½ inches; 114 pages including 85 pages of plates (some colored); bibliography.
Smythsewn and glued into printed red-brown paper cover. (G107536)

809

WILLARD LEROY METCALF: A RETROSPECTIVE. Selection and catalogue by Francis Murphy. With a biographical essay by Elizabeth De Veer. Springfield, Mass., Museum of Fine Arts, 1976.

8½×10¼ inches; xix+58 pages including 48 pages of plates (some colored).
Smythsewn and glued into printed white paper cover. (G27632)

810

WILLIAM MORRIS AND THE ART OF THE BOOK. With essays on William Morris as Book Collector by Paul Needham, as Calligrapher by Joseph Dunlap, and as Typographer by John Dreyfus. New York, N.Y., The Pierpont Morgan Library; London, England, Oxford University Press, 1976.

12×9¼ inches; 140 pages + cxiv pages of plates; portraits; facsimiles; illustrated endleaves.
Light green cloth and dark green quarter cloth over boards; gold-stamped spine; wrapper. Also issued (by The Pierpont Morgan Library) Smythsewn and glued into patterned green and white paper cover. (S47636)

811

WORLD WAR I THROUGH MY SIGHTS. By Horatio Rogers. San Rafael, Calif., Presidio Press, 1976.

9½×6¼ inches; [14]+268 pages + [13] leaves of plates.
Blue cloth over boards; gold-stamped cover and spine; wrapper. (F37603)

⌈1977⌉

812

ALCHEMY AND THE OCCULT: A CATALOGUE OF BOOKS AND MANUSCRIPTS FROM THE COLLECTION OF PAUL AND MARY MELLON GIVEN TO YALE UNIVERSITY LIBRARY. Compiled by Laurence C. Witten II and Richard Pachella. With an introduction by Pearl Kibre and additional notes by William McGuire. New Haven, Conn., Yale University Library, 1977.

Designed by Joseph Blumenthal.

12½×9½ inches; Vol. III: *Manuscripts 1225–1671*, lxiv+402 pages including [139] pages of plates (some colored). Vol. IV: *Manuscripts 1675–1922*, xciv+[451] pages numbered 403 to 853 including [179] pages of plates (some colored). *N.B.* Vols. I and II printed at Spiral Press.
500 sets bound in blue cloth and white quarter cloth over boards; gold-stamped black labels on spines; together in a slipcase covered in dark blue cloth; label on spine. (117042)

813

AMERICAN ART AT THE CENTURY. By A. Hyatt Mayor and Mark Davis. [New York, N.Y.], The Century Association, 1977.

11¼×8¾ inches; xxviii+161 pages including 60 pages of plates (some colored).
Red paper over boards; gold-stamped cover and spine. (F37625)

814

LE BESTIAIRE OU CORTÈGE D'ORPHÉE. By Guillaume Apollinaire. Illustrated with woodcuts by Raoul Dufy. Translations by Lauren Shakely. New York, N.Y., The Metropolitan Museum of Art, 1977.

Facsimile reprint of the Paris (1911) edition with new English translation.
13¼×10¼ inches; [46] pages including 30 pages of plates.
Light brown cloth over boards; gold-stamped spine; slipcase. (R37704)

815

CARVING MYSELF: POEMS FROM A WOODCUTTER. By William F. Herrick [with illustrations by the author]. Lunenburg, Vt., Published by Phyllis and William F. Herrick, 1977.

9¼×6¼ inches; xiii+133 pages.
300 numbered copies bound in brown cloth over boards; gold-stamped spine; slipcase. Also issued Smythsewn and glued into printed paper cover. (F47715)

816

A CHECK LIST OF WESTERN MEDIEVAL MANUSCRIPTS

AND INCUNABULA [in] THE FRANCIS FITZ RANDOLPH RARE BOOK ROOM. Poughkeepsie, N.Y., Vassar College Library, 1977.

10 ×7 inches; 19 pages + [11] pages of plates including colored frontispiece.
2,000 copies Smythsewn and glued into printed blue paper cover. (F117626)

817

CHEKHOV ON THE WEST HEATH. By Denise Levertov. Andes, N.Y., Woolmer/Brotherson, Ltd.; Printed for Cornell University Library Associates, 1977.

10 ×8¼ inches; [14] pages.
26 copies lettered A to Z (not for sale); 200 copies numbered and signed by the author; 400 copies for Cornell University Library Associates; saddlewire stitched into white paper cover and glued into green and white marbled paper wrapper. (F67707)

818

THE COMPLETE WORKS OF WILLIAM BILLINGS. Hans Nathan, Editor. Boston, Mass., The American Musicological Society and The Colonial Society of Massachusetts; Distributed by the University Press of Virginia, 1977.

Vol. II: *The Singing Master's Assistant* (1778); *Music in Miniature* (1779). 12 ×9¼ inches; xv +362 pages; scores; facsimiles.
Dark blue cloth over boards; gold-stamped spine. (G57609)

819

CONVERSATIONS, OR, THE BAS BLEU: ADDRESSED TO MRS. VESEY. [Compiled by Sidney Ives.] Cambridge, Mass, The Houghton Library, 1977.

11 ×8 inches; vii +75 pages; illustrated; bibliography.
900 copies Smythsewn and glued into white paper cover; glued into blue paper wrapper. 150 copies for The Johnsonians have as a cover ornament a reproduction of a portrait of Mr. and Mrs. Donald F. Hyde; 750 copies (including 500 copies for The Friends of The Harvard Col-

lege Library) have as an ornament a reproduction of Mrs. Vesey's bookplate. (S77706)

820

CORPUS VASORUM ANTIQUORUM: THE LOS ANGELES COUNTY MUSEUM OF ART. By Pamela M. Packard and Paul A. Clement. Berkeley, Calif., University of California Press, 1977 (The Los Angeles County Museum of Art Fasicule 1 [U.S.A. Fasicule 18]).

At head of title: "Union Académique Internationale."
13 × 9¾ inches; [x] + 67 pages; bibliography.
Smythsewn and glued into printed light brown paper cover. (P47630)

821

CYRIACUS OF ANCONA'S EGYPTIAN VISIT AND ITS REFLECTIONS IN GENTILE BELLINI AND HIERONYMUS BOSCH. By Phyllis Williams Lehmann. Locust Valley, N.Y., J. J. Augustin Publisher, [1977].

10¼ × 7 inches; [10] + 34 pages + 47 pages of plates numbered 1 to 47.
White cloth over boards; gold-stamped cover and spine. (G87712)

822

THE DAILY NEWS. By Brad Gooch. Calais, Vt., Z Press, 1977.

9 × 6 inches; 40 pages; portrait.
500 copies (26 lettered and signed) Smythsewn and glued into printed black paper cover. (P97631)

823

"DEAR MOTHER: DON'T GRIEVE ABOUT ME. IF I GET KILLED, I'LL ONLY BE DEAD": LETTERS FROM GEORGIA SOLDIERS IN THE CIVIL WAR. Edited by Mills Lane. Savannah, Ga., The Beehive Press, 1977.

8¾ × 10¾ inches; xxxi + 353 pages including 73 pages of plates; bibliography.
Black cloth over boards; wrapper. (F107627)

824

THE DEDICATION OF THE ROBERT FROST INTERPRE-
TATIVE TRAIL IN RIPTON, VERMONT, AUGUST 28, 1976.
By Victor E. Reichert and Hyde Cox. Lunenburg, Vt.,
[Privately printed], 1977.

8¾×5¾ inches; 13 pages.
Handsewn into white paper cover and glued into green paper wrapper.
(S17717)

825

DR. BENTLEY'S SALEM: DIARY OF A TOWN. Salem,
Mass., Essex Institute, 1977.

First appeared in the Institute's *Historical Collections*, Vol. 113, Number 3.
9×6 inches; 86 pages + [8] pages of plates.
500 copies perfect-bound and glued into printed yellow paper cover.
(G37721)

826

DONALD OENSLAGER: WITH A CATALOGUE OF DRAW-
INGS FROM HIS COLLECTION "FOUR CENTURIES OF SCE-
NIC INVENTION." Austin, Tex., College of Fine Arts, The
University of Texas, 1977 (E. William Doty Lectures in
Fine Arts, First Series, 1975).

Includes catalogue published separately in 1974.
8½ × 10 inches; xlviii+187 pages including [113] pages of plates.
Smythsewn and glued into light brown paper cover. (L107740)

827

THE ENGLISH ANCESTRY OF ROGER GOODSPEED.
Boston, [Mass.], Charles E. Goodspeed and Co., 1977.

Reprinted from *The New England Historical and Genealogical Register*, October 1928.
9¾×6½ inches; 15 pages.
Printed blue paper cover. (F97725)

828

ENGLISH LANDSCAPE, 1630–1850: DRAWINGS, PRINTS

AND BOOKS FROM THE PAUL MELLON COLLECTION. By Christopher White. New Haven, Conn., Yale Center for British Art, 1977.

11×8½ inches; xxv+126 pages + [91] leaves of plates (some colored) numbered I to CLXXXI.
Smythsewn and glued into printed light blue paper cover. (P67522)

829

EVERYONE HAS SHER FAVORITE (HIS OR HERS). By Dick Higgins. New York, N.Y., and Barton, Vt., Unpublished Editions, 1977.

9×6 inches; 86 pages.
50 copies numbered and signed; bound in red-purple cloth over boards; gold-stamped spine. 700 copies Smythsewn and glued into printed black and white paper cover. (F57702)

830

A FACULTY LOOKS EAST: FAR EASTERN OBJECTS IN THE POSSESSION OF COLUMBIA FACULTY MEMBERS. New York, N.Y., Low Memorial Library, 1977.

10½×7¾ inches; 37 pages.
Saddlewire stitched into light violet paper cover. (F37735)

831

A FAMILY CHRONICLE: A RECORD OF CERTAIN MEMBERS OF THE HOOSE, LOWDEN, SCHOFF, AND WHITNEY FAMILIES, PIONEERS IN UPSTATE NEW YORK. By James Stanley Schoff. Lunenburg, Vt., Privately printed, 1977.

Designed by Ronald Gordon at The Oliphant Press.
9½×6½ inches; xi+100 pages + [4] pages of plates.
125 copies, of which 100 are numbered, bound in dark red cloth over boards; gold-stamped spine. (F37701)

832

FAST ASLEEP. By Pat Nolan. Calais, Vt., Z Press, 1977.

9×6 inches; 41 pages.
500 copies (26 lettered and signed) Smythsewn and glued into printed paper cover. (P97630)

833

FIVE SEASONS: SELECTED POEMS AND ESSAYS OF GOD-FREY JOHN. Cambridge, Mass., Foursquare Press, 1977.

9¼×6¼ inches; xvii+219 pages.
Green cloth over boards; gold-stamped spine; wrapper. Also issued Smythsewn and glued into printed light green paper cover. (F127622)

834

GEORGE HERBERT'S PATTERN POEMS: IN THEIR TRA-DITION. By Dick Higgins. West Glover, Vt., and New York, N.Y., Unpublished Editions, 1977.

9¾×6¾ inches; 79 pages; bibliography.
Purple cloth over boards; gold-stamped spine. Also issued Smythsewn and glued into gray paper cover. (F37741)

835

GOD'S LITTLE ACRE. By Erskine Caldwell. Savannah, Ga., The Beehive Press, 1977.

Includes photographic illustrations from the archives of the Farm Security Administration at the Library of Congress.
9¼×6¼ inches; ix+[3]+221+[1] pages + [22] pages of plates.
Green cloth over boards; gold-stamped spine; wrapper. (S57540)

836

HELEN DRUSILLA LOCKWOOD: A MEMOIR AND APPRE-CIATION. By Barbara Swain. Poughkeepsie, N.Y., Vassar College, 1977.

10×7 inches; [4]+38 pages; illustrated; frontispiece portrait.
Smythsewn and glued into printed light brown paper cover. (F27720)

837

HELEN LOCKWOOD'S COLLEGE YEARS, 1908–1912. A convocation address by Alan Simpson. Poughkeepsie, N.Y., Vassar College, 1977.

10×7 inches; [4]+54+[1] pages; illustrated; frontispiece portrait.
Smythsewn and glued into printed yellow paper cover. (F37722)

838

HEROIC EMBLEMS. By Ian Hamilton Finlay and Ron Costley. Introduction and commentaries by Stephen Bann.
Calais, Vt., Z Press, 1977.

9 ×6 inches; ix+53 pages.
750 copies (26 numbered and signed) Smythsewn and glued into printed
light green paper cover. (F77712)

839

THE HOME BOOK: PROSE AND POEMS, 1951–1970.
By James Schuyler. Edited by Trevor Winkfield. Calais,
Vt., Z Press, 1977.

9 ×6 inches; 97 pages.
1,000 copies (26 lettered and signed) bound in printed white paper
cover. (P107603)

840

HOPKINS OF DARTMOUTH: THE STORY OF ERNEST MAR-
TIN HOPKINS AND HIS PRESIDENCY OF DARTMOUTH
COLLEGE. By Charles E. Widmayer. Hanover, N.H., Published by Dartmouth College through The University Press
of New England, 1977.

9¼ ×6¼ inches; viii+312 pages; illustrated; frontispiece portrait.
Green cloth over boards; gold-stamped spine; wrapper. (F117638)

841

IMAGES OF CHILDHOOD: AN EXHIBITION OF PICTURES
AND OBJECTS FROM NINETEENTH-CENTURY NEW BED-
FORD HELD AT THE OLD DARTMOUTH HISTORICAL SO-
CIETY. New Bedford, Mass., Old Dartmouth Historical
Society, 1977.

11 ×8½ inches; x+67 pages; illustrated.
Smythsewn and glued into printed blue paper cover. (F117634)

842

THE J D R 3RD FUND AND ASIA, 1963–1975. Text by

Elaine Moss. New York, N.Y., The J D R 3rd Fund, 1977.
8½×8¾ inches; 244 pages; illustrated.
Smythsewn and glued into printed white paper cover. (P17845)

843

JOHN SLOAN DICKEY: THE DARTMOUTH EXPERIENCE.
Edited by Edward Connery Lathem. Hanover, N.H., Published by Dartmouth College through The University Press
of New England, 1977.
9½×6½ inches; xiii+308 pages; illustrated.
Green cloth over boards; gold-stamped spine; wrapper. (F27714)

844

JOYCE'S NOTES AND EARLY DRAFTS FOR ULYSSES: SE-
LECTIONS FROM THE BUFFALO COLLECTION. Edited by
Phillip F. Herring. Charlottesville, Va., Published for the
Bibliographical Society of the University of Virginia by the
University Press of Virginia, 1977.
9¼×6¼ inches; xii+275+[1] pages.
Brown cloth over boards. (67115)

845

KEEPSAKE OF AN EXHIBITION CONSISTING OF TYPOG-
RAPHY, PRINTS, DRAWINGS, SKETCHES, AND WATER-
COLORS BY RUDOLPH RUZICKA SHOWN IN THE GAL-
LERY OF THE CENTURY ASSOCIATION TO CELEBRATE
MR. RUZICKA'S COMPLETION OF FIFTY YEARS OF MEM-
BERSHIP, 1926–1976. New York, N.Y., The Century Asso-
ciation, 1977.
9¼×8½ inches; [4] pages; single leaf, French folded.
Unbound. (R47717)

846

LAURENCE SICKMAN. [By Marc F. Wilson. New York,
N.Y., Privately printed], 1977.
Designed by Joseph Blumenthal.
10×7¼ inches; [12] pages.
Handsewn into white paper cover and glued into golden brown paper
wrapper, printed on front. (F37729)

847

LEAVES FROM MY BOOK OF LIFE. By Guido R. Perera.
Boston, Mass., Privately printed, 1977.

Vol. III: *Family and Friends.*
10¼×7¼ inches; 156 pages; illustrated (includes colored frontispiece
portrait).
200 copies bound in red-brown cloth and brown quarter cloth over
boards; gold-stamped spine. (See items 639 and 703.) (R127610)

848

MARK TWAIN GOES BACK TO VASSAR: AN INTRODUC-
TION TO THE JEAN WEBSTER MCKINNEY FAMILY PA-
PERS. By Alan Simpson. Poughkeepsie, N.Y., Vassar Col-
lege, 1977.

10×7 inches; [4]+20 pages; illustrated; frontispiece portrait.
Smythsewn and glued into printed yellow-brown paper cover. (F37714)

849

OCCASIONS FOR LOVE AND OTHER ESSAYS AT RECOL-
LECTION. By Oscar Handlin. [Lunenburg, Vt., Privately
printed], 1977.

9¼×6¼ inches; 77 pages.
250 copies bound in light blue cloth and dark blue quarter cloth over
boards; gold-stamped covers and spine. (S17721)

850

OLD MASTER DRAWINGS FROM THE GORDON COLLEC-
TION. Framingham, Mass., The Danforth Museum, 1977.

11×8½ inches; [6] pages + [3] pages of plates.
Saddlewire stitched into printed white paper cover. (97713)

851

OLD ORANGE COUNTY: A COLLECTION OF DRAWINGS
AND ENGRAVINGS. Edited by Julien Cornell and Carolyn
C. Arno. Central Valley, N.Y., Smith Clove Press, 1977.

9×11¼ inches; 72+[1] pages including [32] pages of plates.
Red cloth over boards; gold-stamped spine; wrapper. (F27745)

852

ON FIRST GLANCING AT A BOSTON BILLBOARD. By David McCord. [Boston, Mass., Club of Odd Volumes], 1977.

19×11 inches; broadside.
80 copies. (S17716)

853

ONE HUNDRED GIFTS TO THE WATKINSON LIBRARY, 1952–1977: A REPRESENTATIVE SELECTION CELEBRATING ITS FIRST TWENTY-FIVE YEARS AT TRINITY COLLEGE. Hartford, Conn., The Watkinson Library, Trinity College Library Associates, 1977.

11×7½ inches; 38 pages + [75] pages of plates.
Smythsewn and glued into patterned green and white paper cover; blue spine. (S37750)

854

THE ORIGINAL CONSTITUTION OF THE STATE OF VERMONT, 1777: A FACSIMILE. Montpelier, Vt., The Vermont Historical Society, 1977.

9¾×5¾ inches; 24 pages.
500 copies saddlewire stitched into green paper cover and glued into green paper wrapper; gold-stamped cover. (F127628)

855

PAUL SAMPLE: SOME GLIMPSES OF THE MAN AND HIS WORK. [Hanover, N.H.], Dartmouth College Library, [1977].

Cover title.
11½×8¾ inches; [16] pages including 10 pages of plates.
Folded, uncut printer's proof sheets; unbound. (S57742)

856

A PERSONAL NOTE ON THE D. T. McCORD LIBRARY. [Boston, Mass.], Boston Center for Adult Education, 1977.

15½×10 inches; broadside.
450 copies. (F87746)

857

PERSUASION. By Jane Austen. With an introduction by Louis Auchincloss and illustrations by Tony Buonpastore. Westport, Conn., Printed for the Members of The Limited Editions Club, 1977.

Designed by Robert L. Dothard.
10½ ×7 inches; x+241 pages + [8] pages of plates.
1,600 copies signed by the artist; bound in brown cloth over boards; gold-stamped spine; slipcase. (F97632)

858

PETER MILTON: COMPLETE ETCHINGS 1960–1976. Commentary and editing by Kneeland McNulty with essays by the artist. Boston, Mass., Published by Impressions Workshop, 1977.

Designed by Samuel Maitin.
11½ ×8¾ inches; 137 pages including 88 pages of plates.
Brown cloth over boards; gold-stamped cover and spine; wrapper. (G127627)

859

PREACHERS AND POLITICIANS: TWO ESSAYS ON THE ORIGINS OF THE AMERICAN REVOLUTION. By Jack P. Greene and William G. McLoughlin. Worcester, Mass., American Antiquarian Society, 1977.

9¼ ×6¼ inches; 73 pages.
Smythsewn and glued into printed light yellow paper cover. (G97701)

860

THE PRINTED BOOK IN AMERICA. By Joseph Blumenthal. Boston, Mass., David R. Godine Publisher in Association with The Dartmouth College Library, 1977.

11 ×7½ inches; xvi+250 pages including 70 pages of plates; bibliography.
Maroon cloth over boards; gold-stamped spine; wrapper. (R67608)

861

PRINTS BY PETER MILTON: AN EXHIBITION OF PRINTS
FROM THE COLLECTION OF THE ARTIST. Introduction by
Kneeland McNulty. [Washington, D.C.], International
Exhibitions Foundation, 1977.

11 ×8¾ inches; 32 pages including [18] pages of plates; bibliography.
Smythsewn and glued into printed blue and white paper cover. (F67709)

862

A PRIVATE EYE: FIFTY NINETEENTH-CENTURY AMER-
ICAN PAINTINGS, DRAWINGS, AND WATERCOLORS FROM
THE STEBBINS COLLECTION. Catalogue by Carol L.
Troyen. Huntington, N.Y., The Heckscher Museum, 1977.

9½ ×7½ inches; 108+[4] pages including [50] pages of plates.
Smythsewn and glued into printed gray paper cover. (F57733)

863

PROMISED GIFTS '77: AN EXHIBITION ORGANIZED AND
SPONSORED BY FRIENDS OF THE VASSAR ART GALLERY.
Foreword by A. Hyatt Mayor; introduction by Eugene A.
Carroll. Poughkeepsie, N.Y., Vassar College, 1977.

8½ ×9¾ inches; xix+[1]+122 pages including [59] pages of plates
(some colored).
Smythsewn and glued into brown and white paper cover; printed on
front. (R97635)

864

RACHAEL PLUMMER'S NARRATIVE OF TWENTY-ONE
MONTHS SERVITUDE AMONG THE COMMANCHEE IN-
DIANS. Reproduced from the only known copy with a pref-
ace by Archibald Hanna and an introduction by William
S. Reese. Austin, Tex., Jenkins Publishing Co., 1977.

8¾ ×5¾ inches; [32] pages including [10] pages of facsimile reprint.
400 copies bound in light brown paper and dark brown quarter cloth
over boards; gold-stamped cover and spine. (S17722)

865

RENAISSANCE AND BAROQUE DRAWINGS FROM THE COL-
LECTIONS OF JOHN AND ALICE STEINER. Edited by Kon-
rad Oberhuber. Cambridge, Mass., Fogg Art Museum,
1977.

8½×5½ inches; 172 pages including [62] pages of plates; bibliography.
Smythsewn and glued into printed brown paper cover. (S127616)

866

REVISIONS. By Sarah Swenson. Introduction by Rudolf
Baranik. Johnson, Vt., French Hill Press, 1977.

14¼×11¼ inches; [4] pages of text + [14] leaves of plates.
Together, unbound, in a portfolio of heavy black paper; cover illustration laid on. (F37732)

867

THE SATIRES [of] LODOVICO ARIOSTO. Translated by
Rudolf B. Gottfried. Lunenburg, Vt., Privately printed,
1977.

9×6 inches; 63 pages.
150 copies Smythsewn and glued into printed brown paper cover.
(F47712)

868

SAVANNAH REVISITED: A PICTORIAL HISTORY. Text by
Mills Lane, research by Mary Morrison, new photographs
by Van Jones Martin. Savannah, Ga., The Beehive Press,
1977.

Third edition.
10¾×11¼ inches; 214+[2] pages; illustrations (some colored).
Blue cloth over boards; gold-stamped spine; wrapper. (See items 421
and 612.) (F27744)

869

SEVENTEENTH-CENTURY DUTCH DRAWINGS FROM AMERican Collections. By Franklin W. Robinson. [Washington, D.C.], International Exhibitions Foundation, 1977.

10 × 7½ inches; xvii + 189 pages including 87 pages of plates.
Smythsewn and glued into printed gray paper cover.

870

Snowfall: A New Poem. By Joyce Carol Oates. [Boston, Mass.], G. K. Hall and Co., Christmas 1977.

Cover title.
5¼ × 7¾ inches; [4] pages; leaflet.
Unbound.

871

The Stamp of Whistler. Catalogue by Robert H. Getscher. Introduction by Allen Staley. Oberlin, Ohio, Allen Memorial Art Museum, Oberlin College, 1977.

11¼ × 8¾ inches; x + 285 pages including [152] pages of plates.
Smythsewn and glued into printed blue paper cover. (G117630)

872

The Story of Dick Hall's House: Fiftieth Anniversary, 1977. [Hanover, N.H.], Dartmouth College, 1977.

Cover title.
8 × 5½ inches; 35 + [1] pages; illustrated.
Saddlewire stitched into printed green paper cover. (F117631)

873

Strider Theater: Dedication in Prose and Verse, 30 April 1977. By David McCord. Waterville, Me., Colby College, 1977.

9 × 6¼ inches; 18 pages; illustrated.
Saddlewire stitched into white paper cover and glued into light brown wrapper. (S67728)

874

A Tale of Treasure Trove. By Julien Cornell. Central Valley, N.Y., Smith Clove Press, 1977.

9½×6½ inches; viii+82 pages.
Light green cloth over boards; gold-stamped spine. (F27810)

875

Teresa de Jesús: A Secular Appreciation. By Walker Lowry. [Lunenburg, Vt., Privately printed], 1977.

10¼×7¼ inches; [4]+91 pages.
125 copies bound in off-white cloth over boards; wrapper. (F97651)

876

Thirteen Colonial Americana: A Selection of Publications Issued in the British Provinces of North America During the Final Half-Century of the Colonial Era. Edited by Edward Connery Latham. Washington, D.C., Association of Research Libraries, 1977.

11¼×8¾ inches; [54] pages including 13 pages of illustrations in facsimile.
1,000 copies bound in blue cloth over boards; blind-stamped cover and gold-stamped spine; wrapper. (R67715)

877

The Town of Lunenburg, Vermont, 1763–1976. Text by Nellie M. Streeter. Lunenburg, Vt., The Town of Lunenburg Historical Society, 1977.

11¼×8¾ inches; 80 pages; illustrated.
250 numbered copies bound in light green cloth over boards; gold-stamped spine. 750 copies issued Smythsewn and glued into printed paper cover. (G57626)

878

Trouble in July. By Erskine Caldwell. Savannah, Ga., The Beehive Press, 1977.

9¼×6¼ inches; ix+159 pages including [22] pages of plates.
Brown cloth over boards; gold-stamped spine; wrapper. (F127626)

879

UNION JACK: THE NEW YORK CITY BALLET. Edited by
Lincoln Kirstein. Photographs by Martha Swope and Richard Benson. New York, N.Y., The Eakins Press Foundation,
1977.

6×9 inches; 107 pages including 33 pages of plates.
Smythsewn and glued into decorated white paper cover. (F47722)

880

LA VIE DE NOSTRE BENOIT SAUVEUR IHESUCRIST & LA
SAINCTE VIE DE NOSTRE DAME: TRANSLATEE A LA RE-
QUESTE DE TRES HAULT ET PUISSANT PRINCE IEHAN,
DUC DE BERRY. [Introduction and notes by Millard Meiss
and Elizabeth H. Beatson.] New York, N.Y., Published by
New York University Press for the College Art Association
of America, 1977 (Monographs on Archaeology and the
Fine Arts No. 32).

11¼×8¾ inches; xxxvi+186 pages including 16 pages of plates.
Red cloth over boards; gold-stamped cover and spine. (F57632)

881

WASH AND GOUACHE: A STUDY OF THE DEVELOPMENT
OF THE MATERIALS OF WATERCOLOR. By Marjorie B.
Cohn. Catalogue of the exhibition by Rachel Rosenfield.
Cambridge, Mass., Published by The Center for Conserva-
tion and Technical Studies, Fogg Art Museum, and The
Foundation of the American Institute for Conservation,
1977.

8×10 inches; 116 pages including 6 pages of colored plates; bibliography.
Smythsewn and glued into printed green paper cover. (S127615)

882

WASHINGTON AND THE POET. Edited by Francis Coleman
Rosenberger. Charlottesville, Va., University Press of Virginia, 1977.

Issued as a special volume of the *Records* of the Columbia Historical Society.

9½×6½ inches; vii+79 pages.

1,250 copies (50 for the poets, 600 for members of the Columbia Historical Society, and 600 for sale) bound in maroon cloth over boards; gold-stamped spine. (F57744)

883

WELLSPRINGS OF A NATION: AMERICA BEFORE 1801. Text by Rodger D. Parker. Worcester, Mass., American Antiquarian Society, 1977.

11×8½ inches; v+141 pages including 57 pages of plates. Smythsewn and glued into light brown paper cover. (F127620)

[1978]

884

AN ALPHABET. By Francis Coleman Rosenberger. Charlottesville, Va., University Press of Virginia, 1978.

9½×6½ inches; [34] pages.
Dark blue cloth over boards; gold-stamped spine; wrapper. (F117711)

885

AMERICAN LIBRARIES AS CENTERS OF SCHOLARSHIP: PROCEEDINGS OF A CONVOCATION HELD AT DARTMOUTH COLLEGE ON JUNE 30TH, 1978. . . . Edited by Edward Connery Lathem. Hanover, N.H., Dartmouth College, 1978.

9¼×6¼ inches; 107 pages; illustrated.
Green cloth over boards; gold-stamped spine; wrapper. (R87837)

886

L'APRÈS-MIDI D'UN FAUNE: NIJINSKI: 1912. Thirty-three photographs by Baron Adolphe de Meyer (palladium prints by Richard Benson). New York, N.Y., Produced by the

Eakins Press Foundation; London, England, Dance Books, Ltd., [1978].

18¼ × 15¾ inches; [8] leaves + [33] folders (each holding one palladium print) + [8] leaves.
250 copies signed by Richard Benson in an exhibition binding; covered with gray-green buckram; label laid onto front cover. (R27819)

887

THE ARTFUL ROUX: MARINE PAINTERS OF MARSEILLE. Including a catalogue of the Roux Family paintings at the Peabody Museum of Salem. By Philip Chadwick Foster Smith. Salem, Mass., Peabody Museum of Salem, 1978.

11 × 8½ inches; 73 pages + [12] pages of colored plates; bibliography. Smythsewn and glued into printed light blue and white paper cover. (F87835)

888

A BAKER'S DOZEN OF BAKER'S TREASURES: A KEEP-SAKE MARKING THE FIFTIETH ANNIVERSARY, IN 1978, OF THE FISHER AMES BAKER MEMORIAL LIBRARY OF DARTMOUTH COLLEGE. [Hanover, N.H., Printed for the Friends of the Dartmouth College Library], 1978.

Cover title.
9 × 6 inches; [28] pages including 13 pages of plates.
1,500 copies saddlewire stitched into printed green paper cover. (R87842)

889

BIRDS IN FLIGHT. By Eliot Porter. Santa Fe, N.Mex., and New York, N.Y., Bell Editions, [1978].

Designed by Eleanor Morris Caponigro.
Cover title.
24 × 20 inches; portfolio; [4] pages; single untrimmed leaf of Guarro paper.
20 copies (plus 6 artist's copies) each with 8 photographs (original dye transfer prints); calligraphy by Stephen Harvard; together in a case with *The Way Birds Fly*. (See item 946.) (F107801)

890

BITS AND PIECES. By Margaret B. Owen. Weston, Mass., [Privately printed], 1978.

8¾×5¾ inches; 53 pages; illustrated.
Light green cloth over boards; gold-stamped cover and spine; wrapper. (F57840)

891

BRODIE CARLYLE. By Walker Lowry. [Lunenburg, Vt., Privately printed], 1978.

9½×4¾ inches; 131 pages.
100 copies Smythsewn and glued into white paper cover and glued into green paper wrapper. (P17813)

892

THE BROKEN BLOCKHOUSE WALL. By John Peck. Boston, Mass., David R. Godine, 1978 (Godine Poetry Chapbook, Third Series).

8¾×5¾ inches; 44 pages.
Smythsewn and glued into patterned gray and white paper over boards. (G127747)

893

CHARLES F. MONTGOMERY AND FLORENCE M. MONT- GOMERY: A TRIBUTE. Edited by Barbara M. Ward and Gerald W. R. Ward. New Haven, Conn., Yale University Art Gallery, June 1978.

Design and typography by Howard I. Gralla.
9½×6¼ inches; 71 pages including 8 pages of plates; chronologies; bibliographies.
Blue buckram over boards; printed label on cover; gold-stamped spine. (F17851)

894

CHINA JOURNAL. By Virginia S. Cornell. With foreword and appendices by Julien Cornell. Central Valley, N.Y., Smith Clove Press, 1978.

$9\frac{1}{4} \times 6\frac{1}{4}$ inches; viii+104 pages + [21] pages of photographic plates. Smythsewn and glued into red paper cover; gold-stamped spine. Also issued without plates. (P127736)

895

A CHRONOLOGICAL BIBLIOGRAPHY OF THE PUBLISHED WORKS OF VILHJALMUR STEFANSSON (1879–1962) COMPRISING BOOKS, ARTICLES, REVIEWS, AND INTRODUCTIONS TO OTHER WORKS. By Robert W. Mattila. With an introductory essay byEvelyn Stefansson Nef. Hanover, N.H., Dartmouth College Libraries (The Stefansson Collection), 1978.

9×6 inches; xii+66 pages; frontispiece portrait.
Smythsewn and glued into printed blue paper cover. (F37813)

896

THE CLASSICAL TRADITION IN RAJPUT PAINTING FROM THE PAUL F. WALTER COLLECTION. By Pratapaditya Pal. New York, N.Y., The Pierpont Morgan Library and The Gallery Association of New York State, 1978.

$10\frac{1}{4} \times 9\frac{1}{2}$ inches; xii+210 pages including 83 pages of plates (some colored); bibliography. (Page 182 with corrected text laid in.)
Red-purple silken cloth over boards; gold-stamped spine; slipcase covered in orange paper. Also issued Smythsewn and glued into white paper cover; glued into printed white wrapper. (R67809)

897

THE COMMON PRESS; BEING A RECORD, DESCRIPTION AND DELINEATION OF THE EARLY EIGHTEENTH-CENTURY HANDPRESS IN THE SMITHSONIAN INSTITUTION. With a history and documentation of the press by Elizabeth Harris and drawings and advice on construction by Clinton Sisson. Boston, Mass., David R. Godine, 1978.

[Vol. I]: Text, $11 \times 8\frac{1}{2}$ inches; 62 pages. [Vol. II]: Illustrations, $22 \times 16\frac{3}{4}$ inches (folded to $11 \times 8\frac{1}{8}$ inches); 8 pages.
2,000 sets; text Smythsewn and glued into printed golden brown paper cover; illustrations in printed golden brown paper folder; together in a slipcase covered in printed golden brown paper. (S37703)

898

THE COSMOS CLUB OF WASHINGTON: A CENTENNIAL HISTORY, 1878–1978. Written by Wilcomb E. Washburn. Washington, D.C., The Cosmos Club, 1978.

9¼×6¼ inches; xv+406 pages; illustrated; portraits.
Red-brown cloth over boards; gold-stamped spine. (R27801)

899

THE DANNIE AND HETTIE HEINEMAN COLLECTION. New York, N.Y., The Pierpont Morgan Library, 1978.

9½×6¼ inches; x+109 pages + [12] pages of plates.
250 copies bound in dark red cloth over boards; gold-stamped cover and spine.

900

DAVID HOCKNEY: PRINTS AND DRAWINGS. Introduction by Gene Baro. Washington, D.C., International Exhibitions Foundation, 1978.

11×8½ inches; 32 pages including [18] pages of plates; colored frontispiece.
Smythsewn and glued into printed green paper cover. (F47836)

901

DES SAUVAGES. By Samuel de Champlain. With an introduction by Prof. Marcel Trudel. Montreal, Que., [Privately printed], 1978.

7½×5¼ inches; 13+[8] pages + 36 leaves; facsimile.
100 copies printed for Mr. Gregory Javitch; bound in maroon cloth over boards; gold-stamped spine. (R57843)

902

DESPERATE MEASURES. By George Starbuck. Boston, Mass., David R. Godine, 1978 (Godine Poetry Chapbook, Third Series).

8¾×5¾ inches; 59 pages.
Patterned green and white paper over boards. (G127710)

903

Dr. William W. Herrick: A Measure of the Man. Letters, addresses, and tributes collected by his daughter Eunice Herrick Trowbridge for family and friends. [Lunenburg, Vt., Privately printed], 1978.

10¼×7¼ inches; 68 pages; illustrated; frontispiece portrait.
500 copies bound in decorated light brown cloth and brown quarter cloth over boards; gold-stamped spine. (F87742)

904

80 Flowers. By Louis Zukofsky. Lunenburg, Vt., [Privately printed], 1978.

5¾×6¾ inches; 80 pages.
80 copies signed and dated by the author; bound in light brown cloth over boards; gold-stamped blue label on spine. (F27807)

905

The Epickall Quest of the Brothers Dichtung and Other Outrages. By Dick Higgins. Illustrated by Ken Friedman. New York, N.Y., Printed Editions, 1978.

8½×5¾ inches; 108 pages.
750 copies (50 numbered and signed by the author) bound in blue cloth over boards; gold-stamped spine; glassine wrapper. Also issued Smythsewn and glued into light green paper cover. (F37828)

906

Erlkönig (The Erlking, D. 328). By Franz Peter Schubert. New York, N.Y., The Pierpont Morgan Library, 1978.

Facsimile of the autograph manuscript in the Dannie and Hettie Heineman Collection.
12½×9½ inches; 39 pages including [5] pages of manuscript score; illustrated; bibliography.
Smythsewn and glued into printed gray paper cover. (R107814)

907

An Exhibition in Memory of Agnes Rindge Claflin,

1900–1977. Poughkeepsie, N.Y., The Vassar Art Gallery, 1978.

10×7 inches; 43 pages including 9 pages of plates (some colored). Smythsewn and glued into printed red-brown paper cover. (F17809)

908

FAMILY FAVORITES FROM THE RECIPE COLLECTION OF VIRGINIA S. CORNELL. Central Valley, N.Y., Smith Clove Press, 1978.

7×5¼ inches; 110 pages. Spiral bound with black plastic spine and red-orange paper cover. (F27810)

909

FONS SAPIENTIAE: RENAISSANCE GARDEN FOUNTAINS. Edited by Elisabeth B. MacDougall. Washington, D.C., Dumbarton Oaks, 1978 (Dumbarton Oaks Colloquium on the History of Landscape Architecture Number V).

10¼×7¼ inches; x+206 pages + 68 pages of plates numbered I to IV, I to VIII, I to XVI, I to XXIV, I to XVI+[4] folded leaves of plates laid in. Green cloth over boards; gold-stamped cover and spine. (G67821)

910

GEORGE COPE, 1855–1929. Exhibition and catalogue prepared by Joan H. Gorman. Essay and notes by Gertrude Grace Sill. Chadds Ford, Pa., Brandywine River Museum, 1978.

8½×10 inches; 75 pages; bibliography. Smythsewn and glued into printed brown paper cover. (F37839)

911

GEORGIA O'KEEFFE: A PORTRAIT BY ALFRED STIEG-LITZ. With an introduction by Georgia O'Keeffe. New York, N.Y., Metropolitan Museum of Art, 1978.

14¼×10¾ inches; [8] pages + 51 leaves of plates + [6] pages.

Gray paper over boards and white quarter cloth; gold-stamped cover and spine; slipcase covered in gray paper. (F107822)

912

A GUIDE TO THE MICROFILM EDITION OF THE EURO-PEAN JOURNALS OF GEORGE AND ANNA TICKNOR. Edited by Steven Allaback and Alexander Medlicott, Jr. Hanover, N.H., Dartmouth College Library, 1978.

9½×6½ inches; vi+101 pages.
Blue cloth over boards; gold-stamped spine; wrapper. Also issued Smyth-sewn and glued into printed off-white paper cover.

913

THE ILLUSTRATOR'S MOMENT: WORKS BY ABBEY, FO-GARTY, LEYENDECKER, PYLE, RACKHAM, N. C. WYETH. By Diana Strades. Stockbridge, Mass., The Old Corner House, 1978.

8½×9 inches; 99 pages including [64] pages of plates; bibliography.
Smythsewn and glued into printed paper cover. (F37830)

914

IN/DIRECTION. By Alvin Greenberg. Boston, Mass., David R. Godine, 1978 (Godine Poetry Chapbook, Third Series).

8¾×5¾ inches; 31 pages.
Brown and white patterned paper over boards. (G127708)

915

AN INVITATION TO THE WEDDING MASQUE CELEBRAT-ING THE MARRIAGE OF ANNE ELIZABETH WILLIFORD AND TODD STEPHEN THOMPSON. New York, N.Y., [Privately printed, 1978].

Cover title: "The Masque." Reprinted from *The Tempest*, IV, i; V, i.
11×8½ inches; [8] pages.
50 copies with calligraphy by Stephen Harvard; handsewn into printed light blue paper cover. (S17858)

916

JAMES AUGUSTINE HEALY COLLECTION OF NINETEENTH
AND TWENTIETH CENTURY IRISH LITERATURE. Com-
piled and edited by Cheryl Abbott and J. Fraser Cocks III.
Waterville, Me., Colby College, 1978.

9×6 inches; 38 pages + [3] pages of plates.
Perfect-bound in printed gold paper cover. (F37829)

917

THE JOHN TUCKER DALAND HOUSE. By Bryant F. Tolles,
Jr. Foreword by Anne Farnam. Salem, Mass., Essex Institute, 1978 (Historic House Booklet Number 7).

9½×6¼ inches; 27 pages; illustrated.
Saddlewire stitched into printed paper cover. (P107746)

918

A JOURNEY THROUGH THE GENESEE COUNTRY, FINGER
LAKES REGION AND MOHAWK VALLEY FROM PATRICK
CAMPBELL'S TRAVELS IN THE INHABITED PARTS OF
NORTH AMERICA IN THE YEARS 1791 AND 1792. With
an introduction by Henry W. Clune and a preface by Robert L. Volz. Rochester, N.Y., The Friends of the University
of Rochester Libraries, 1978.

Facsimile reprint of the Edinburgh (1793) edition.
8½×5¼ inches; 17+[72] pages including 4 pages of plates; frontispiece portrait; maps on endleaves.
Light brown paper and brown quarter cloth over boards; gold-stamped
spine; slipcase. (F107728)

919

LIFE AND LABOR ON ARGYLE ISLAND: LETTERS AND
DOCUMENTS OF A SAVANNAH RIVER RICE PLANTATION,
1833–1867. Edited with an introduction by James M. Clifton. Savannah, Ga., The Beehive Press, 1978.

10×6½ inches; xlvi+365 pages; illustrated.
Yellow cloth over boards; gold-stamped spine. (F67704)

920

THE LOVER'S FAMILIAR. By James McMichael. Boston, Mass., David R. Godine, 1978 (Godine Poetry Chapbook, Third Series).

8¾×5¾ inches; 47 pages.
Patterned orange and white paper over boards. (G127702)

921

M ALVAREZ BRAVO. By Jane Livingston with an essay by Alex Castro and documentation by Frances Fralin. Boston, Mass., David R. Godine; Washington, D.C., The Corcoran Gallery of Art, 1978.

Designed at The Hollow Press by Caroline Orser and Alex Castro.
11×8½ inches; xlv+82 pages of plates numbered 1 to 82; frontispiece.
Smythsewn and glued into printed light brown paper cover. (G77819)

922

MAJABIGWADUCE: CASTINE, PENOBSCOT, BROOKSVILLE. By Ellenore W. Doudiet. Castine, Me., Castine Scientific Society, 1978.

9×11½ inches; viii+116 pages; illustrated.
1,000 copies bound in green cloth over boards; gold-stamped spine; wrapper. (F47706)

923

THE MAN WITH THE VELLUM VALISE. By David T. McCord. [Boston, Mass.], Club of Odd Volumes, May 1978.

18×12½ inches; broadside.
151 copies. (R57828)

924

MASACCIO: THE DOCUMENTS. By James Beck with the collaboration of Gino Conti. Locust Valley, N.Y., J.J. Augustin Publishers, 1978 (Villa I Tatti, The Harvard University Center for Italian Renaissance Studies Number 4).

10×7 inches; [8]+60 pages.
Maroon cloth over boards; gold-stamped cover and spine. (R47809)

925

NETHERLANDISH SCROLLED GABLES OF THE SIXTEENTH
AND EARLY SEVENTEENTH CENTURIES. By Henry-Russell
Hitchcock. New York, N.Y., Published by New York University Press for the College Art Association of America,
1978 (Monographs on Archaeology and Fine Arts No. 34).

11¼×8¾ inches; xvi+157 pages including 33 pages of plates.
Orange buckram over boards; gold-stamped cover and spine; glassine
wrapper. (117727)

926

NEW ENGLAND SAMPLERS TO 1840. By Glee Krueger.
Sturbridge, Mass., Old Sturbridge Village, 1978.

8½×7 inches; xv+227 pages including [93] pages of plates.
Smythsewn and glued into printed blue paper cover. (F77710)

927

NEWPORT IN 1780. Newport, R.I., Society for French
Historical Studies, 1978.

Includes map reprinted from *The American Campaigns of Rochambeau's
Army*, translated and edited by Howard C. Rice, Jr., and Anne S. K.
Brown.
12×9¾ inches; [4] pages including map (colored facsimile).
500 numbered copies handsewn into printed blue paper cover. (F127727)

928

NICCOLÒ DI GIOVANNI FIORENTINO AND VENETIAN
SCULPTURE OF THE EARLY RENAISSANCE. By Anne Markham Schulz. New York, N.Y., Published by New York
University Press for the College Art Association of America,
1978 (Monographs on Archaeology and Fine Arts No. 33).

11¼×8¾ inches; xxiv+136 pages including [33] pages of plates.
Brown cloth over boards; gold-stamped cover and spine. (F77720)

929

NIGHTFIRE. By Gail Mazur. Boston, Mass., David R.
Godine, 1978 (Godine Poetry Chapbook, Third Series).

8¾×5¾ inches; 47 pages.
Patterned black and white paper over boards. (G127729)

930

PLEASURE AND PAIN: REMINISCENCES OF GEORGIA IN
THE 1840's. By Emily Burke. Introduction by Felicity Calhoun. Savannah, Ga., The Beehive Press, 1978.

First published in a slightly different form in Oberlin, Ohio (1850).
10 ×6¼ inches; xii+97 pages; frontispiece portrait.
Decorated light green paper over boards. (F107733)

931

POE AT WORK: SEVEN TEXTUAL STUDIES. Edited by
Benjamin Franklin Fisher IV. Baltimore, Md., The Edgar
Allan Poe Society, 1978.

9¼×6¼ inches; [2]+110 pages + [2] pages of plates; bibliography.
Purple buckram over boards; gold-stamped spine. (G107753)

932

POEMS. By Edwin George Astle, Sr. [Lunenburg, Vt.,
Privately printed, 1978.]

9 ×6 inches; 55 pages.
Saddlewire stitched into white paper cover and glued into red paper
wrapper. (F117829)

933

A PORTFOLIO HONORING HAROLD HUGO FOR HIS CON-
TRIBUTION TO SCHOLARLY PRINTING. [Foreword by
Walter Muir Whitehill; epilogue by Julian P. Boyd. Lunen-
burg, Vt.], Produced by The Committee to Honor Harold
Hugo, 1978.

Designed by P. J. Conkwright.
12¼×9½×1¾ inches; [36] unsewn signatures including [42] leaves of
plates (facsimiles, portraits, map; some colored).
Together in a hinged box by Coman and Southworth; lined with decorated papers designed by Stephen Harvard. Box covered with red-
brown cloth; gold-stamped leather label laid onto spine. (37759)

934

THE PROVIDENCE PUBLIC LIBRARY: A CENTURY OF

SERVICE, 1878–1978. By Stuart C. Sherman. Providence, R.I., Providence Public Library, 1978.

8½×5½ inches; 39 pages including 8 pages of plates; portraits.
Smythsewn and glued into printed blue paper cover. (G127748)

935

ELS QUATRE GATS: ART IN BARCELONA AROUND 1900. By Marilyn McCully. Princeton, N.J., Princeton University Art Museum; Distributed by Princeton University Press, 1978.

11¼×8½ inches; 160 pages including [63] pages of plates; colored frontispiece; bibliography.
Green cloth over boards; blind-stamped cover and spine stamped in gold and silver; wrapper. Also issued Smythsewn and glued into printed green paper cover. (107749)

936

ROMAN SARCOPHAGI IN THE METROPOLITAN MUSEUM OF ART. By Anna Marguerite McCann. New York, N.Y., Metropolitan Museum of Art, 1978.

Designed by Peter Oldenburg.
11¼×9 inches; 151 pages; illustrated.
Rust-red cloth over boards; gold-stamped cover and spine. (F107741)

937

THE ROWFANT MANUSCRIPTS. By H. Jack Lang with an introduction by Herman W. Liebert. Cleveland, Ohio, The Rowfant Club, 1978.

10¼×7 inches; ix+65 pages including 24 pages of plates; frontispiece.
400 numbered copies bound in brown paper and brown quarter cloth over boards; gold-stamped cover and spine. (F117728)

938

THE SPANISH FORGER. By William Voelkle. New York, N.Y., The Pierpont Morgan Library, 1978.

$11\frac{1}{4} \times 8\frac{3}{4}$ inches; 77 pages + [132] pages of plates (some colored); colored frontispiece laid in.
Blue cloth over boards; gold-stamped spine; color plate laid onto cover. Also issued Smythsewn and glued into printed blue paper cover; gold-stamped cover and spine. (R17835)

939

STEICHEN: THE MASTER PRINTS, 1895–1914: THE SYMBOLIST PERIOD. By Dennis Longwell. New York, N.Y., The Museum of Modern Art; Distributed by the New York Graphic Society, Boston, Mass., 1978.

Designed by James M. Eng and Stevan A. Baron.
$11\frac{1}{4} \times 9\frac{1}{4}$ inches; 180 pages including 72 pages of plates + colored frontispiece.
Light brown cloth over boards; gold-stamped cover and spine. (P117704)

940

TENNIEL'S ALICE: DRAWINGS BY SIR JOHN TENNIEL FOR ALICE'S ADVENTURES IN WONDERLAND AND THROUGH THE LOOKING-GLASS. [Introduction by Eleanor M. Garvey and W. H. Bond.] Cambridge, Mass., Department of Printing and Graphic Arts, Harvard College Library, in association with The Metropolitan Museum of Art, 1978.

$8\frac{3}{4} \times 6$ inches; 75 pages including 32 pages of plates.
Maroon cloth over boards; gold-stamped spine; wrapper. Also issued Smythsewn and glued into printed white paper cover. (S87829)

941

THEMES IN THE HISTORY OF THE FAMILY. Edited by Tamara K. Hareven. Worcester, Mass., American Antiquarian Society, 1978.

$9\frac{1}{4} \times 6\frac{1}{4}$ inches; 72 pages; illustrated; graphs; tables.
Smythsewn and glued into green paper cover. (G37834)

942

THERE IS NO BALM IN BIRMINGHAM. By Ann Deagon.

THIRTEEN
COLONIAL
AMERICANA

Association of Research Libraries

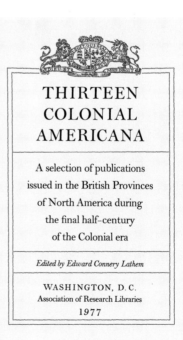

THIRTEEN
COLONIAL
AMERICANA

A selection of publications
issued in the British Provinces
of North America during
the final half-century
of the Colonial era

Edited by Edward Connery Lathem

WASHINGTON, D.C.
Association of Research Libraries
1977

The Common Press

Being a Record, Description & Delineation
of the Early Eighteenth-Century Handpress
in the Smithsonian Institution

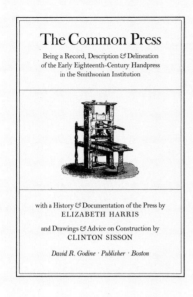

with a History & Documentation of the Press by
ELIZABETH HARRIS

and Drawings & Advice on Construction by
CLINTON SISSON

David R. Godine · Publisher · Boston

ENTRY 897

A PORTFOLIO HONORING

HAROLD HUGO

FOR HIS CONTRIBUTION TO

SCHOLARLY PRINTING

———

1978

ENTRY 933

The Rowfant Manuscripts

THE manuscripts of the Rowfant Club are not as well known as its renowned collection of books. The manuscripts have been treated somewhat as stepchildren by Club librarians of the past. And perhaps understandably so. The Rowfant books have given abiding reading pleasure to its members, and some first and special editions have greater inherent value than the autograph letters and documents. This is true of such scarce items as the first edition of Walt Whitman's *Leaves of Grass*, Johnson's *Plan of a Dictionary*, dedicated to Lord Chesterfield, and the many early editions of the dictionary itself. But, this is not always the case. Consider the choice, first edition of Cardinal Newman's *Apologia Pro Vita Sua*. It was given to Frederick Locker-Lampson by Alfred Lord Tennyson whose son Lionel was married to Locker's daughter Eleanor. It bears the bookplates and autograph inscriptions of both Locker and Tennyson—a fine collector's item. Yet, one early cataloguer observed that of even more value are the two original letters of John Henry Newman laid in its pages. This appraisal may

1

ENTRY 937

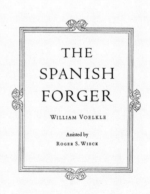

THE
SPANISH
FORGER

WILLIAM VOELKLE

Assisted by
ROGER S. WIECK

The Pierpont Morgan Library
NEW YORK

ENTRY 938

THE LYRICAL POEMS OF

In the original French, & in the English versions by
Algernon Charles Swinburne, Dante Gabriel
Rossetti, William Ernest Henley, John
Payne, and Léonie Adams; selected
by Léonie Adams. With an
introductory essay by
Robert Louis
Stevenson

THE LIMITED EDITIONS CLUB

NEW YORK · MCMLXXIX

ENTRY 976

BALLADE DES SEIGNEURS DU TEMPS JADIS

Qui plus, ou est le tiers Calixte,
Dernier decedé de ce nom,
Qui quatre ans tint le papaliste?
Alphonce le roy d'Arragon,
Le gracieux duc de Bourbon,
Et Artus le duc de Bretaigne,
Et Charles septiesme le bon?
Mais ou est le preux Charlemaigne?

Semblablement, le roy Scotiste
Qui demy face ot, ce dit on,
Vermeille comme une amatiste
Depuis le front jusqu'au menton?
Le roy de Chippre de renon,
Helas! et le bon roy d'Espaigne
Duquel je ne sçay pas le nom?
Mais ou est le preux Charlemaigne?

D'en plus parler je me desiste;
Le monde n'est qu'abusion.
Il n'est qui contre mort resiste
Ne qui treuve provision.
Encor fais une question:
Lancelot le roy de Behaigne,
Ou est il? Ou est son tayon?
Mais ou est le preux Charlemaigne?

Ou est Claquin le bon Breton?
Ou le conte Daulphin d'Auvergne
Et le bon feu duc d'Alençon?
Mais ou est le preux Charlemaigne?

(42)

BALLAD OF THE LORDS OF OLD TIME

What more? Where is the third Calixt,
Last of that name now dead and gone,
Who held four years the Papalist?
Alfonso, king of Aragon,
The gracious lord, duke of Bourbon,
And Arthur, duke of old Britaine?
And Charles the Seventh, that worthy one?
Even with the good knight Charlemain.

The Scot too, king of mount and mist,
With half his face vermilion,
Men tell us, like an amethyst
From brow to chin that blazed and shone;
The Cypriote king of old renown,
Alas! and that good king of Spain,
Whose name I cannot think upon?
Even with the good knight Charlemain.

No more to say of them I list;
'Tis all but vain, all dead and done:
For death may no man born resist,
Nor make appeal when death comes on.
I make yet one more question;
Where's Lancelot, king of far Bohain?
Where's he whose grandson called him son?
Even with the good knight Charlemain.

Where is Guesclin, the good Breton?
The lord of the eastern mountain-chain,
And the good late duke of Alençon?
Even with the good knight Charlemain.

(43)

ENTRY 976

THE PROMISE
OF LIGHT

RICHARD OUTRAM

Anson-Cartwright Editions

TORONTO · 1979

ENTRY 986

CHAPTER FOUR

NORDURÁ

THE famous Nordurá, about which much has been written, remains to this day one of Iceland's more productive rivers.

It is a west coast river of the Borgarnes District, a tributary to the milky glacial river Hvitá (not to be confused with the south coast glacial river of the same name). It is one of Iceland's larger salmon waters. Being on the west coast, it is considered an early July river. Iceland allows limited netting of its rivers with glacial origins, thus influencing the salmon population of all clear-water tributaries. In this instance not only the Nordurá but the Pvera (Kjarrá), Grímsá, Flokadalsa, and the Reykjadalsa are all fine salmon waters with little apparent harm being caused by the current level of commercial fishing.

The Nordurá lodge is very comfortable with the original building containing a lodge room with a fireplace, dining room, sauna, and individual rooms sharing a hall bath. New motel-style rooms have been completed and located in a nearby separate building. The food and service at the Nordurá was as good as any I have had anywhere, and

[145]

ENTRY 991

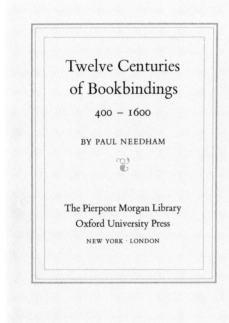

Twelve Centuries
of Bookbindings

400 – 1600

BY PAUL NEEDHAM

The Pierpont Morgan Library

Oxford University Press

NEW YORK · LONDON

ENTRY 1001

---

and Morgan *Schatzbehalters* are different, though both were bound in the same shop.
8. This Bible with commentaries, Hain 3170, was a very substantial work, of 1432 folio leaves in double columns; it seems likely that waste material from it might belong either to 1492 or 1493.
9. Three other Nuremberg bindings in the Morgan Library deserve special notice, as they come from the library of the famous physician-geographer-book collector Hieronymus Münzer. The finest of these is his copy (1) of Boccaccio *Genealogia deorum* (Reggio Emilia, 6 Oct. 1481, Hain 3319), PML 25593. It comes from the anonymous

bindery referred to by Kyriss as 'Blumenstock I' (*Verzierte gotische Einbände* 94–95 no. 116; *Tafelband* II pls. 233–34). The binding is illustrated by E. P. Goldschmidt *Hieronymus Münzer* pl. 2. Also from this bindery is (2) Münzer's copy of Aulus Gellius (Brescia, 3 Mar. 1485, Hain 7521) bound with P. Orosius *Historiae* (Venice, 30 July 1483, Hain 12102), PML 46898. Its central boss and clasp plates seem to be stamped from the same dies as those of (1). Münzer's copy of (3) L. Valla *De vero bono* (Louvain, 1483, Hain 15816), PML 33824, is in a binding from Kyriss's 'Madonna' shop (*Verzierte gotische Einbände* 99–100 no. 120; *Tafelband* II pls. 241–42). Its clasp plates are stamped 'ave'.

---

31 ❧ *Gold-tooled binding from Buda for King Wladislaus II, ca. 1490–1500*

Johannes Angelus. Astrolabium. Augsburg: Erhard Ratdolt, 1488. 4to. PML 55078.

Dark brown calf over wooden boards, gold-tooled; two pairs of clasps on fore-edge, catching on upper cover; edges gilt and gauffered. 24 × 17.5 × 3.5 cm.

PROVENANCE: Wladislaus II, king of Hungary – C. W. Dyson Perrins (*Sotheby's,* 10 Mar. 1947, lot 348, illus.) – Maj. J. R. Abbey (*Sotheby's,* I, 21 June 1965, lot 31, illus.) – PML (1965). Purchased on the Lathrop C. Harper Trust Fund.

REFERENCES: FR 1965–66: 40; Schunke 'Ungarische Nachlese'; Csapodi *The Corvinian library* no. 36.

THE kingdom of Hungary was brought into the orbit of the Italian Renaissance during the reign of Matthias Corvinus (1458–90), son of the great crusader John Hunyadi. Corvinus was a figure of legendary proportions: a tireless warrior battling Christians and Turks alike; a shrewdly calculating diplomat; and withal a patron of learning and avid bibliophile. He collected and commissioned hundreds of manuscripts from Italy and eventually established (it would seem) a palace scriptorium in Buda. As one aspect of his refined bibliophily, he introduced the art of gold-tooled bookbinding into Central Europe. Corvinus was probably influenced in this by the example of the Aragonese library in Naples; he was married to Beatrice, sister of King Ferrante, and her brother Cardinal Giovanni d'Aragona was papal legate to Hungary. But the Corvinus bindings are in a class by themselves. They contain Italian elements—punch dotting and cablework tools besides gilding—but are quite distinctive in their exuberant use of naturalistic flower tools and of coloring. The anonymous binder for Corvinus was an original craftsman.[1]

When Corvinus died, aged only forty-seven, his son was passed over and the crown given to Wladislaus Jagellon, king of Bohemia, who thereby regained peaceably the extensive Bohemian lands lost to Corvinus in battle. Wladislaus possessed none of his predecessor's distinctions, either as monarch or as patron, but recent research has discovered a number of royal Hungarian bindings from his reign, indicating (if tenuously) a continuity in the famed royal library. Several bindings from the beginning of the reign were made by the Corvinus binder, substituting Wladislaus' arms for those of Matthias but otherwise identical in style. These cover manuscripts commissioned by Matthias, but not yet bound at his death.

112

ENTRY 1001

Boston, Mass., David R. Godine, 1978 (Godine Poetry Chapbook, Third Series).

8¾×5¾ inches; 47 pages.
Patterned yellow and white paper over boards. (G117732)

943

"This Is the Mark or Device of The Stinehour Press. . . ." [Lunenburg, Vt., The Stinehour Press, 1978.]

Keepsake produced for The Stinehour Press; title from first line on first leaf.
11¼×8¾ inches; [5] leaves each with an inscription and illustrated with a pressmark or calligraphic cut.
Together unbound in a golden brown paper folder; gold-stamped cover. Calligraphy by Stephen Harvard. (F17822)

944

THREE PLAYS. By John Ashbery. Calais, Vt., Z Press, 1978.

Includes "The Heroes," "The Compromise," "The Philosopher."
9×6 inches; [6]+160 pages.
1,000 copies Smythsewn and glued into printed pink paper cover. Also issued in hardcover (500 numbered copies and 26 lettered and signed copies). (F87716)

945

29 MINI-ESSAYS. By Joe Brainard. Calais, Vt., Z Press, 1978.

3×5 inches; [32] pages.
500 numbered copies (first 50 signed by the author) perfect-bound and glued into printed blue paper cover. (F107707)

946

THE WAY BIRDS FLY. [By Eliot Porter. Lunenburg, Vt., Printed for Eliot Porter and Bell Editions], 1978.

Designed by Eleanor Morris Caponigro.
Cover title.
13½×10¼ inches; [8] pages; single untrimmed signature.
34 copies; unbound, together in a case with *Birds in Flight*. (See item 889.) (F107801)

947

WILLIAM ALLEN WALL: AN ARTIST OF NEW BEDFORD. By Richard C. Kugler. New Bedford, Mass., Old Dartmouth Historical Society, 1978.

11¼×8½ inches; v+72 pages including 55 pages of plates (some colored); frontispiece portrait.
Smythsewn and glued into printed paper cover. (F67818)

948

WINDOWS INTO CHINA: THE JESUITS AND THEIR BOOKS, 1580–1730. By John Parker. Boston, Mass., Trustees of the Public Library of the City of Boston, 1978 (Maury A. Bromsen Lecture in Humanistic Bibliography Number 5).

8½×5½ inches; xi+[1]+36 pages including 12 pages of plates.
1,000 copies Smythsewn and glued into printed white paper cover. 350 additional copies printed for the Associates of the James Ford Bell Library. (G87737)

949

WINESBURG, OHIO. By Sherwood Anderson. With an introduction by Malcolm Cowley and illustrations by Ben F. Stahl. New York, N.Y., Limited Editions Club, 1978.

Designed by Harry A. Rich.
12¼×10 inches; xviii+[2]+152+[2] pages + [13] pages of plates; colored frontispiece.
1,600 copies numbered and signed by the artist; bound in brown cloth and green quarter leather over boards; gold-stamped cover and spine; slipcase covered in brown-green paper over boards; gold-stamped spine. (F67815)

950

WRITING THROUGH FINNEGANS WAKE. By John Cage. New York, N.Y., Printed Editions, 1978 (University of Tulsa Monograph Series Number 16).

Published as a supplement to *James Joyce Quarterly*, Vol. 15.
11¼×9¾ inches; [180] pages.
200 copies signed and numbered and bound in light brown paper and quarter cloth over boards; blind-stamped cover. (F57731)

951

AMERICAN FRIENDS. By Celia Zukofsky. New York, N.Y.,
C. Z. Publications, Inc., 1979.

7×4¾ inches; 83 pages.
Perfect-bound in light brown-gray paper cover. 200 copies signed and
numbered by the author. (F27907)

952

ARCHITECTURE IN COLONIAL MASSACHUSETTS. Boston,
Mass., The Colonial Society of Massachusetts; Distributed
by the University Press of Virginia, 1979 (Publications of
the Colonial Society of Massachusetts, Vol. 51).

9½×6½ inches; xv+234 pages; illustrated.
Blue buckram over boards; gold-stamped spine; wrapper. (97115)

953

BEGGAR ON HORSEBACK: THE AUTOBIOGRAPHY OF
THOMAS D. CABOT. Boston, Mass., David R. Godine,
1979.

9½×6¼ inches; ix+[3]+191+[3] pages + [64] pages of plates; frontispiece portrait.
4,000 copies bound in dark blue cloth over boards; gold-stamped spine;
wrapper. (F77806)

954

THE BIRTH OF A NATION: A FORMAL SHOT-BY-SHOT
ANALYSIS TOGETHER WITH MICROFICHE. By John Cuniberti. [Woodbridge, Conn.,] Research Publications, Inc.,
1979 (Cinema Editions on Microfiche).

11¾×9 inches; 232 pages + [5] microfiche in envelopes in pocket;
bibliography.
Smythsewn and glued into black cloth over boards; silver-stamped cover
and spine. (F17923)

955

BY THEIR CHINS YE SHALL KNOW THEM. Lunenburg, Vt., The Walpole Society, 1979.

9 × 6 inches; [40] pages including 31 pages of silhouettes.
125 copies saddlewire stitched into decorated red, white, and green paper cover. (F117922)

956

CATALOGUE OF THE ITALIAN PAINTINGS. By Fern Rusk Shapley. Washington, D.C., National Gallery of Art, 1979.

Designed by Klaus Gemming.
Vol. I: *Text*, 9¼ × 5¾ inches; xii + 591 + [5] pages; addenda; indexes.
Vol. II: *Plates*, 9¼ × 8 inches; [410] pages of plates + [3] pages.
Each volume Smythsewn and glued into printed orange glossy paper cover. (F87801)

957

THE COLLECTION OF GERMAIN SELIGMAN: PAINTINGS, DRAWINGS, AND WORKS OF ART. Edited by John Richardson. Privately printed for E. V. Thaw and Co., New York, N.Y.; Artemis S. A., Luxembourg; David Carritt, Ltd., London, England, 1979.

11¾ × 9 inches; [224] pages including 125 catalog entries illustrated with plates; frontispiece portrait.
500 copies Smythsewn and glued into green paper cover; gold-stamped cover and spine; slipcase covered with green and white marbled paper. (R127810)

958

THE DEFENSE OF THE SUGAR ISLANDS: A RECRUITING POSTER. By Turner Cassity. Los Angeles, Calif., The Symposium Press, 1979.

10¼ × 7¼ inches; 23 pages.
300 copies (25 lettered A to AA and 275 numbered and signed by the author) handsewn into white paper cover and glued into printed blue-green paper wrapper. (S37922)

959

THE DEVELOPMENT OF PHOTOGRAPHY IN BOSTON, 1840–1875. Exhibition and catalogue prepared by Pamela Hoyle. Boston, Mass., Boston Athenaeum, 1979.

8½×11 inches; 64 pages including 22 pages of plates; bibliography. Saddlewire stitched into printed white paper cover. (S37925)

960

DOCUMENTS, DRAWINGS AND COLLAGES: FIFTY WORKS ON PAPER FROM THE COLLECTION OF MR. AND MRS. STEPHEN D. PAINE. Williamstown, Mass., Williams College Museum of Art, 1979.

9¾×8 inches; 123 pages including 52 pages of plates; bibliography. Smythsewn and glued into printed white paper cover. (F127818)

961

DRAWINGS BY MICHELANGELO FROM THE BRITISH MUSEUM. New York, N.Y., The Pierpont Morgan Library, 1979.

11¾×9 inches; 111 pages including [41] pages of plates (some colored). Smythsewn and glued into printed orange paper cover. (R97823)

962

DUCKS, DOGS AND FRIENDS. By John Eugene Clay, Jr. Savannah, Ga., [Privately printed], 1979.

8¾×5¾ inches; 47 pages; illustrated.
2,000 copies bound in decorated brown paper and brown quarter leather over boards; gold-stamped spine. (F87841)

963

THE EDGE OF THE WOODS: A MEMOIR. By Hildegarde Lasell Watson. [Lunenburg, Vt., Privately printed], 1979.

Designed by Janet Zweig.
10¼×7¼ inches; xiv+[2]+165 pages; illustrated.
1,000 copies bound in green cloth over boards; colored portrait laid onto cover; gold-stamped cover and spine. (F127816)

964

EDITH NEWTON'S NEW MILFORD. Introduction by Philip Kappel. Edited by Charles Beach Barlow. New Milford, Conn., New Milford Historical Society, 1979.

9 × 10¼ inches; xiv+87 pages; illustrated.
Orange buckram over boards; wrapper. (F77933)

965

EIGHTEENTH CENTURY MASTER DRAWINGS FROM THE ASHMOLEAN. Introduction and catalogue by Kenneth J. Garlick. [Washington, D.C.], International Exhibitions Foundation, 1979.

10¼ × 7½ inches; xii+28 pages + 89 pages of plates.
Smythsewn and glued into printed brown paper cover. (P37932)

966

FIFTEEN FOURTEENERS FROM GIOVANNI DELLA CASA. Translated by Rudolf B. Gottfried. Bloomington, Ind., [Privately printed], 1979.

7 × 6 inches; [28] pages.
150 copies Smythsewn and glued into light brown paper cover.(F107907)

967

FLYING THE OCEANS: A PILOT'S STORY OF PAN AM, 1935–1955. By Horace Brock. Lunenburg, Vt., The Stinehour Press, 1979.

9½ × 6½ inches; 323 pages + [50] pages of plates; photographs; maps; tables.
Dark blue cloth over boards; gold-stamped spine; wrapper. (F77807)

968

H. M. VANDEVEER AND COMPANY: ONE HUNDRED YEARS OF THE VANDEVEER FAMILY. By Vida Seaman Baxter. Taylorville, Ill., [Privately printed, 1979].

9½ × 6¾ inches; ix+[1]+434 pages + [16] pages of plates + [1] chart (folded); frontispiece portrait; bibliographical and genealogical references.

Decorated blue paper and black quarter paper over boards; gold-stamped cover and spine. (R37909)

969

THE HARVEST FESTIVAL: A PLAY IN THREE ACTS. By Sean O'Casey. With a foreword by Eileen O'Casey and an introduction by John O'Riordon. New York, N.Y., The New York Public Library, Astor, Lenox and Tilden Foundations and Readex Books, 1979 (The Harcourt Brace Jovanovich Fund Publication Number 1).

Designed by Marilan Lund.
First edition.
9¼×6¼ inches; 91 pages.
1,000 copies bound in red buckram over boards; blind-stamped cover and gold-stamped spine. (G77926)

970

JAPANESE LACQUER. By Ann Yonemura. Washington, D.C., The Freer Gallery of Art, Smithsonian Institution, 1979.

Designed by Crimilda Pontes.
11¾×8¼ inches; vi+106 pages + [12] pages of colored plates; bibliography.
Smythsewn and glued into printed white paper cover. (R47926)

971

THE JUNIUS B. BIRD PRE-COLUMBIAN TEXTILE CONFERENCE, MAY 19TH & 20TH, 1973. Edited by Ann Pollard Rowe, Elizabeth P. Benson, Anne-Louise Schaffer. Washington, D.C., The Textile Museum and Dumbarton Oaks, 1979.

11½×8¾ inches; 278 pages + [2] leaves of tables folded in pocket; bibliography.
Brown cloth over boards; gold-stamped cover and spine. (F17868)

972

THE LETTERS OF FRANZ LISZT TO OLGA VON MEYENDORFF, 1871–1886, IN THE MILDRED BLISS COLLECTION

AT DUMBARTON OAKS. Translated by William R. Tyler. Introduction and notes by Edward N. Waters. Washington, D.C., Dumbarton Oaks; Distributed by Harvard University Press, 1979.

9½×6¼ inches; xxi+532 pages + [3] leaves of plates; illustrated endleaves.
Black cloth over boards; gold-stamped cover and spine; wrapper. (F97625)

973

LIBRARY OF THE BOSTONIAN SOCIETY. [Boston, Mass., Printed for the Society, 1979.]

Cover title.
9½×6¼ inches; [8] pages.
Printer's proof sheet, single fold, uncut, unbound; together with a broadside (20×14½ inches) on handmade paper. (F37919)

974

LIFE AND TIMES IN SHOE CITY: THE SHOE WORKERS OF LYNN. Salem, Mass., Essex Institute, 1979.

First appeared in the Institute's *Historical Collections*, Vol. 115, Number 5.
9×6 inches; vii+83 pages + [16] pages of plates.
500 copies perfect-bound and glued into printed light brown paper cover. (G77906)

975

LUCY PORTER TO DR. JOHNSON: HER ONLY KNOWN LETTER. With an introduction by James L. Clifford. [Cambridge, Mass.], The Johnsonians, 1979.

Cover title; first reproduced here to commemorate the 270th birthday of Dr. Johnson.
11×8½ inches; 7 pages including 2 pages of plates; illustrated.
200 copies handsewn into printed white paper cover. (F77902)

976

THE LYRICAL POEMS OF FRANÇOIS VILLON. In the original French and in the English versions by Algernon Charles

Swinburne, Dante Gabriel Rossetti, William Ernest Henley, John Payne, and Léonie Adams; selected by Léonie Adams with an introductory essay by Robert Louis Stevenson. New York, N.Y., Limited Editions Club, 1979.

11×7½ inches; 145+[3] pages.
2,000 copies bound in green cloth over boards; gold-stamped cover and spine; glassine wrapper; slipcase covered in green cloth and patterned green paper; numbered and signed by Stephen Harvard who provided the typography, calligraphy, and decorated paper on the endleaves. (S47901)

977

MASTER DRAWINGS FROM THE COLLECTION OF INGRID AND JULIUS S. HELD. By Laura Giles, Elizabeth Milray, Gwendolyn Owens. Williamstown, Mass., Trustees of Williams College and Trustees of the Sterling and Francine Clark Art Institute, 1979.

9¾×8 inches; 139 pages including [64] pages of plates.
Smythsewn and glued into printed light yellow paper cover. (F127817)

978

MEMORIAL SERVICE [for] LESSING J. ROSENWALD . . . [at the] PHILADELPHIA MUSEUM OF ART, SEPTEMBER 10, 1979. Jenkintown, Pa., Alverthorpe Gallery, 1979.

9¼×6¼ inches; 29 pages.
Handsewn into printed light brown paper cover. (F117914)

979

MORE MARINE PAINTINGS AND DRAWINGS IN THE PEABODY MUSEUM. By Philip Chadwick Foster Smith. Salem, Mass., Peabody Museum, 1979.

11¾×8¾ inches; ix+[3]+166+[2] pages + [14] pages of colored plates interleaved with the text.
3,000 copies bound in red buckram over boards; gold-stamped spine; wrapper. (R37905)

980

OLD SAINT JO: GATEWAY TO THE WEST, 1799–1932.
By Sheridan A. Logan; color illustrations by John Falter.
[Lunenburg, Vt.], J. S. Logan Foundation, 1979.

9½×6½ inches; x+464 pages; portraits.
Dark blue cloth over boards; gold-stamped spine; wrapper. (G17852)

981

THE ONE-HUNDREDTH ANNIVERSARY OF THE FOUND-
ING OF THE COSMOS CLUB OF WASHINGTON, D.C. Washington, D.C., The Cosmos Club, 1979.

8½×5½ inches; 122 pages; illustrated.
Smythsewn and glued into printed brown paper cover. (R57907)

982

THE PEDIGREE OF FLETCHER GARRISON HALL. By Garrison Kent Hall. Boston, Mass., New England Historic
Genealogical Society, 1979.

8¾×6 inches; xii+479 pages; illustrated; portraits.
Dark blue cloth over boards; gold-stamped spine; wrapper. (P57851)

983

PERSIAN GARDENS AND GARDEN PAVILIONS. By Donald
Newton Wilber. Washington, D.C., Dumbarton Oaks, 1979.

Second edition.
10½×7¼ inches; xiv+104 pages + [44] leaves of plates (some colored);
bibliography.
Green cloth over boards; gold-stamped cover and spine. (P57725)

984

PIRANESI'S CARCERI: SOURCES OF INVENTION. By William L. MacDonald. Northampton, Mass., Smith College,
1979 (Twenty-first Annual Katharine Asher Engel Lecture).

Designed by William L. MacDonald and Lucinda S. Brown.
9×6 inches; 38 pages + 32 pages of plates + [7] pages; illustrated;
bibliography.
1,000 copies Smythsewn and glued into white paper cover. (F17937)

985

PLAIN & ELEGANT, RICH & COMMON: DOCUMENTED NEW HAMPSHIRE FURNITURE, 1750–1850. Concord, N.H., New Hampshire Historical Society, 1979.

11 × 7½ inches; 153 pages including [59] pages of plates.
Smythsewn and glued into printed red paper cover. (S17909)

986

THE PROMISE OF LIGHT. By Richard Outram. Toronto, Ont., Anson-Cartwright Editions, 1979.

9¼ × 5¾ inches; [8] + 117 pages.
250 copies bound in dark blue marbled paper and dark blue quarter cloth over boards; gold-stamped spine. (F77907)

987

RADCLIFFE IN RUNOVER RHYME. By David McCord. [Cambridge, Mass., Radcliffe College], 1979.

11¾ × 6¼ inches; broadside; folded to insert in a brochure. (R97802)

988

RANDOM THOUGHTS AND MEMORIES. By Fritz Scholder. Scottsdale, Ariz., A R C Press, 1979.

3 × 2½ inches; [12] double leaves; frontispiece portrait.
500 copies bound in white cloth and black quarter cloth over boards; gold-stamped spine. (F77832)

989

ROMAN BLACK-AND-WHITE FIGURAL MOSAICS. By John R. Clarke. New York, N.Y., Published by New York University Press for the College Art Association of America, 1979 (Monographs on Archaeology and Fine Arts No. 35).

11¼ × 8¾ inches; xxiv + 147 pages including 32 pages of plates.
White buckram over boards; cover and spine printed in black; glassine wrapper. (F127825)

990

RUBENS AND REMBRANDT IN THEIR CENTURY: FLEMISH AND DUTCH DRAWINGS OF THE 17TH CENTURY FROM THE PIERPONT MORGAN LIBRARY. By Felice Stampfle. New York, N.Y., The Pierpont Morgan Library; Oxford, England, Oxford University Press, 1979.

11¼×8¾ inches; 298 pages including [136] pages of plates + [20] pages of tables, indices, and notes.
Orange cloth over boards; gold-stamped spine; wrapper. Also issued (published by The Pierpont Morgan Library) Smythsewn and glued into printed orange and white paper cover. (R37843)

991

SALMON-SALMON; WITH A CHAPTER ON ICELAND. By Joseph P. Hubert. Illustrations by Harvey D. Sandstrom. Goshen, Conn., Privately printed; Published by The Angler's and Shooter's Press, 1979.

13×10½ inches; xx+[2]+165+[7] pages + [12] leaves of plates (some colored and signed by the illustrator) + [10] colored plates and [5] folded maps laid in.
100 copies printed on Rives mould-made paper bound by hand in blue leather; gold-stamped cover and spine; marbled endleaves; Icelandic coin (2s flóirin) embedded in inside back cover; slipcase covered in gray buckram. (R17905)

992

SERENADE. By Bernard Welt. Calais, Vt., Z Press, 1979.

9×6 inches; 65 pages.
750 copies (26 lettered and signed) Smythsewn and glued into printed white paper cover. (F67922)

993

SOME RECENT SNOWFLAKES (AND OTHER THINGS). By Dick Higgins. New York, N.Y., and West Glover, Vt., Printed Editions, 1979.

8½×5¾ inches; vi+94 pages.
50 copies, signed and numbered, bound in brown and white cloth over

boards; blind-stamped cover with blue label laid on and gold-stamped spine. 700 additional copies issued Smythsewn and glued into printed paper cover. (F37904)

994

SOMETHING OF GREAT CONSTANCY: ESSAYS IN HONOR OF THE MEMORY OF J. GLENN GRAY, 1913–1977. Edited by Timothy Fuller. Colorado Springs, Colo., The Colorado College, 1979.

9¼×6¼ inches; xi+198 pages; frontispiece portrait; bibliography. Brown cloth over boards; gold-stamped spine; wrapper. (S127811)

995

THE SPIRIT OF THE ENTERPRISE. By Peter Mayer. New York, N.Y., R. R. Bowker Co., 1979 (R. R. Bowker Memorial Lectures, New Series, Number 6).

Designed by Philip Grushkin.
8¾×6 inches; 22 pages.
Saddlewire stitched into decorated light brown paper cover. (P37923)

996

STANLEY MORISON AND D. B. UPDIKE: SELECTED CORRESPONDENCE. Edited by David McKitterick. New York, N.Y., The Moretus Press, 1979.

9½×6½ inches; xxxiv+217 pages including 20 pages of plates. Blue cloth over boards; gold-stamped spine; wrapper. (R27939)

997

A TALE OF VEENY, A DOWN-MAINE CHIPMUNK. By T. Robley Louttit. [Lunenburg, Vt., Privately printed], 1979.

5½×8½ inches; 89 pages.
Smythsewn and glued into printed paper cover. (F47929)

998

A TESTAMENT OF FAITH: A LEAF FROM A COPY OF THE

First American Bible, Translated into the Language of the Algonquian Indians by John Eliot and Printed at Cambridge in New England in the Year 1663. With a commentary on its origins by John Alden. Boston, Mass., Charles E. Goodspeed and Co., 1979.

8¼×6½ inches; 10 pages.
87 copies bound in dark blue cloth over boards; gold-stamped spine; glassine wrapper; slipcase covered in dark blue cloth. (F27910)

999

Tools and Technologies: America's Wooden Age. Edited by Paul B. Kebabian and William C. Lipke. Burlington, Vt., Robert Hull Fleming Museum, University of Vermont, 1979.

11×8½ inches; vii+111 pages; illustrated.
Smythsewn and glued into printed brown paper cover. (F57928)

1000

"Towards a National Spirit": Collecting and Publishing in the Early Republic to 1830. By Whitfield J. Bell, Jr. Boston, Mass., Trustees of the Public Library of the City of Boston, 1979 (Maury A. Bromsen Lecture in Humanistic Bibliography Number 6).

8½×5½ inches; ix+37 pages; illustrated.
1,500 copies (including 500 for the Friends of the American Philosophical Society Library) Smythsewn and glued into printed white paper cover. (G87816)

1001

Twelve Centuries of Bookbindings, 400–1600. By Paul Needham. New York, N.Y., The Pierpont Morgan Library and Oxford University Press, 1979.

12¼×9¼ inches; xvii+338 pages including [6] colored plates laid in + 100 pages of additional plates; bibliography.
Red cloth over boards; spine printed in black and stamped in gold; wrapper. Also issued Smythsewn and glued into printed white paper cover. (S77851)

1002

VISION AND REVISION: INTRODUCING MERIDEN-STINE-HOUR INCORPORATED. Meriden, Conn., and Lunenburg, Vt., Meriden-Stinehour Inc., 1979.

"This book was undertaken as a cooperative venture of the photographer, B. A. King of Worcester, Massachusetts, and the printers, Harold Hugo and Roderick Stinehour, who also wrote the text. The captions under the photographs were written by Stephen Harvard."
10¾×9¼ inches; [52] pages; illustrated.
Rust-red cloth over boards; gold-stamped spine. A special edition of 100 copies (to honor Parker B. Allen on his 84th birthday) issued Smyth-sewn and glued into brown paper cover. (R17924)

1003

WAR DIARY AND LETTERS OF STEPHEN MINOT WELD, 1861–1865. Boston, Mass., Massachusetts Historical Society, 1979.

Second edition.
10×6¾ inches; xxiv+[2]+433 pages + [69] pages of plates; portraits.
Blue buckram over boards; gold-stamped spine. (F37918)

1004

THE WEAVERS DRAFT BOOK AND CLOTHIERS ASSISTANT. With a new introduction by Rita J. Adrosko. Worcester, Mass., American Antiquarian Society, 1979 (American Antiquarian Society Facsimiles, Number 2).

Facsimile of the edition of Baltimore (1792).
8¼×6½ inches; [18]+28+[2] pages; facsimile.
Saddlewire stitched into printed blue and gray paper cover. (S127806)

1005

WILLIAM AND MARY AND THEIR HOUSE. New York, N.Y., The Pierpont Morgan Library and Oxford University Press, 1979.

12×9¼ inches; 258 pages including [51] leaves of plates + [3] leaves of plates tipped in.
Dark blue cloth over boards; gold-stamped cover and spine; wrapper. (R77901)

1006

WILLIAMS COLLEGE MUSEUM OF ART: HANDBOOK OF
THE COLLECTION. By S. Lane Faison, Jr. Williamstown,
Mass., Williams College, 1979.

10 ×8 inches; xiii+[94] pages + [72] pages of plates.
Smythsewn and glued into printed blue paper cover. (F117721)

SERIAL PUBLICATIONS
PRINTED AT
THE STINEHOUR PRESS

Listed here are the titles of serials printed during the years 1950–1979 at Lunenburg, entries for which are not included within the main body of the bibliography. Some of these publications continue to be produced regularly by Meriden-Stinehour Press, certain others have ceased publication.

Albert H. Wiggin Collection Reports.
> Boston Public Library, Boston, Mass.

American Friends of the Plantin–Moretus Museum Newsletter.
> American Friends of the Plantin–Moretus Museum,
> New York, N.Y.

Archives of Asian Art.
> Asia Society, New York, N.Y.

The Art Quarterly, new series.
> Art Studies, Inc., New York, N.Y.

Books at Brown.
> Friends of the Library of Brown University, Providence, R.I.

Boston University Graduate Journal.
> Boston University, Boston, Mass.

Bulletin of Research in the Humanities.
> New York Public Library, New York, N.Y.

Bulletin of the Currier Gallery of Art.
> Currier Gallery of Art, Manchester, N.H.

Bulletin of The New York Public Library.
> New York Public Library, New York, N.Y.

Central European History.
> Emory University, Atlanta, Ga.

Colloquium on the History of Landscape Architecture.
Center for Studies in Landscape Architecture,
Dumbarton Oaks, Washington, D.C.
Colorado College Studies.
Colorado College, Colorado Springs, Colo.
Dartmouth College Bulletin.
Dartmouth College, Hanover, N.H.
Dartmouth College Library Bulletin.
Baker Library, Dartmouth College, Hanover, N.H.
Dartmouth Quarterly.
Undergraduate Council, Dartmouth College, Hanover, N.H.
Dumbarton Oaks Conference Proceedings.
Dumbarton Oaks, Washington, D.C.
English Literary Renaissance.
Department of English, University of Massachusetts,
Amherst, Mass.
Essex Institute Historical Collections.
Essex Institute, Salem, Mass.
Fogg Art Museum Acquisitions Reports.
Fogg Art Museum, Harvard University, Cambridge, Mass.
Fogg Art Museum Annual Reports.
Fogg Art Museum, Harvard University, Cambridge, Mass.
4-H Premium List.
Lancaster Fair Association, Lancaster, N.H.
Franconia Review.
Franconia College, Franconia, N.H.
Goddard College Bulletin.
Goddard College, Plainfield, Vt.
Grolier Club Gazette.
Grolier Club, New York, N.Y.
Grolier Club Yearbook.
Grolier Club, New York, N.Y.
Harvard Journal of Asiatic Studies.
Harvard-Yenching Institute, Cambridge, Mass.
Hopkins Center Art Galleries Bulletin.
Hopkins Center, Dartmouth College, Hanover, N.H.

Journal of Architectural Education.
    Association of Collegiate Schools of Architecture,
    Washington, D.C.
Journal of Glass Studies.
    Corning Museum of Glass, Corning, N.Y.
Journal of Public Health Policy.
    Journal of Public Health Policy, Inc., Burlington, Vt.
Journal of the American Musical Instrument Society.
    American Musical Instrument Society, Vermillion, S.Dak.
    Vermillion, S.Dak.
Journal of the History of Medicine and Allied Sciences.
    Journal of the History of Medicine and Allied Sciences, Inc.,
    Minneapolis, Minn.
Journal of the Society of Architectural Historians.
    Society of Architectural Historians, Philadelphia, Pa.
Keats-Shelley Journal.
    Keats-Shelley Association of America, Inc., New York, N.Y.
Lancaster Fair Premium List.
    Lancaster Fair Association, Lancaster, N.H.
Lunenburg, Vt., Town Reports.
    Town of Lunenburg, Vt.
MacDowell Colony News.
    MacDowell Colony, New York, N.Y.
Marsyas: Studies in the History of Art.
    Students of the Institute of Fine Arts, New York University,
    New York, N.Y.
Middle American Research Institute Publications.
    Tulane University, New Orleans, La.
New Glass Review.
    Corning Museum of Glass, Corning, N.Y.
Notes on Printing and Graphic Arts. See *Printing and Graphic Arts.*
Perspectives in American History.
    Charles Warren Center for Studies in American
    History, Harvard University, Cambridge, Mass.
Polar Notes.
    Stefansson Collection, Dartmouth College Library,
    Hanover, N.H.

Printing and Graphic Arts.
    The Stinehour Press, Lunenburg, Vt.
Printing History: Journal of the American Printing History Association.
    American Printing History Association, New York, N.Y.
Proceedings of the American Antiquarian Society, new series.
    American Antiquarian Society, Worcester, Mass.
Proceedings of the Cambridge Historical Society.
    Cambridge Historical Society, Cambridge, Mass.
Renaissance Quarterly.
    Renaissance Society of America, New York, N.Y.
Reports to the Fellows of The Pierpont Morgan Library.
    Pierpont Morgan Library, New York, N.Y.
Restoration Quarterly: Studies in Christian Scholarship.
    Abilene Christian University, Abilene, Tex.
Rowfant Club Yearbook.
    Rowfant Club, Cleveland, Ohio
Smith College Studies in History.
    Smith College, Northampton, Mass.
Studies in Pre-Columbian Art and Archaeology.
    Center for Pre-Columbian Studies, Dumbarton Oaks,
    Washington, D.C.
Studies in Romanticism.
    Graduate School, Boston University, Boston, Mass.
Studies in the Renaissance.
    Renaissance Society of America, New York, N.Y.
The University of Pennsylvania Library Chronicle.
    Friends of the University of Pennsylvania Library,
    Philadelphia, Pa.
Vermont History.
    Vermont Historical Society, Montpelier, Vt.
Yale University Library Gazette.
    Yale University Library, New Haven, Conn.

WRITINGS RELATED TO THE STINEHOUR PRESS

"Note Bene." *Bookfair* [November 1953], p. 2.

Thomajan, P. K. "The Stinehour Press." *American Printer and Lithographer* [August 1956], pp. 46–47, 62.

Hitchings, Sinclair. *The Stinehour Press: Notes on Its First Five Years.* Lunenburg, Vt., 1957.

"Scholarly Works in Foreign Languages. . . ." *Caledonian-Record* [St. Johnsbury, Vt.], 22 July 1960, p. 5.

Fry, Ann. "Fine Printing in a Barn." *Vermont Life* [Winter 1965], pp. 47–51.

"Graphic Artist." *Dartmouth Alumni Magazine* [November 1966], p. 33.

Stinehour, Roderick D. "Random Thoughts About Book Design." *Publisher's Weekly* 5 [May 1969], pp. 90, 93–94.

"Two Printing Companies Join in Awards, Recognizing Achievements." *The Courier* [Littleton, N.H.], 12 June 1969, p. 6A.

English, Nancy. "Lunenburg's Stinehour Press Kept Alive by Scholarly Work." *The Burlington* [Vt.] *Free Press*, 9 July [1971].

"For Stinehour Press, Quality Is Keystone to Success." *The Burlington* [Vt.] *Free Press*, 26 June 1972, p. 18.

"Vermont Small Businessman of the Year, 1972: Roderick D. Stinehour." Montpelier, Vt., U.S. Small Business Administration, 1972. Typescript, 5 pages.

"Lunenburg Book Printer Small Businessman of Year." *Caledonian-Record* [St. Johnsbury, Vt.], vol. 56, no. 18.

Ward, Bradley. "Another Bookmaker." *Yankee* [September 1972], pp. 121–122.

"The New Monotype Award for Photoset Composition Is Won by The Stinehour Press. . . ." *Lithoprinter* [October 1975], p. 53.

Nilsen, Solveig. "Rocky Stinehour and The Stinehour Press." Typescript, 23 pages.

Stinehour, Roderick D. "Books are both our luxuries and our daily bread. . . ." [Address to] The Wynkyn de Worde Society, London, 27 November 1975. Typescript, 7 pages.

———. *Twenty-five Books of The Stinehour Press, Twenty-five Years of The Stinehour Press*. Hanover, N.H., Dartmouth College Library, 1975.

"Talk Saturday by Vermont Printer of Rare Books." *White River Valley Herald*, 17 April 1975.

"Roderick Stinehour." *Publisher's Weekly* 6 [December 1976], pp. 28–29.

"Rocky Stinehour of Lunenburg, Vermont's Stinehour Press." *New England Printer and Publisher* [August 1978], pp. 23, 51.

Stinehour, Roderick D. "Papermaking: The State of the Art." *AB Bookman's Weekly* 62:7–14 [August 1978], pp. 683–702.

———. "Testimonial to a Library." *Dartmouth College Library Bulletin* new series 19:1 [November 1978], pp. 2–7.

Sherman, Stuart C. "Roderick Stinehour: Scholar-Printer." *The Book Collector* 27:4 [Winter 1978], pp. 479–493.

Ross, Robert H. "Making Books." *Dartmouth Alumni Magazine* [April 1980], pp. 36–42.

"A New Life of Baker." *Harvard Business School Bulletin* 57:3 [May/June 1981], pp. 60–63.

INDEX OF TITLES

Numbers refer to entries

29 Mini-Essays, 945

Twice-Told Tales, 313

Two Continents, 804

Two Mementoes from the Poe-Ingram Collection, 515

Two Poems, 383

2,000 Years of Calligraphy: A Three-part Exhibition Organized by the Baltimore Museum of Art, the Peabody Institute Library, and the Walters Art Gallery: A Comprehensive Catalogue, 265

Uncle Remus: Tales by Joel Chandler Harris, 667

"Undergraduate and the Graphic Arts, The," 425

Unified Field Theory, A, 234

Union Jack: The New York City Ballet, 879

University and College Poetry Prizes, 1967–72, 668

University Collects: Georgia Museum of Art, The University of Georgia, A, 426

Unto the Generations: The Roots of True Americanism, 384

Uses of the Past, The, 786

Vagaries Malicieux: Two Stories by Djuna Barnes, 669

Vanity of Human Wishes, The, 152

Varujan Boghosian: Artist in Residence, 385

Venetian Bronzes from the Collections of the Correr Museum, Venice, 386

Venetian Drawings from American Collections, 670

Venice and the Defense of Republican Liberty: Renaissance Values in the Age of the Counter-Reformation, 387

Vermont Clock and Watchmakers, Silversmiths and Jewelers, 1778–1878, 470

Vermont Farm and the Sun, 728

Vermont Imprints, 1778–1820: A Checklist of Books, Pamphlets, and Broadsides, 191

Vermont Roadbuilder, 729

Vessel of Sadness, 427

Views from the Circle: Seventy-five Years of Groton School, 117

INDEX OF NAMES

Numbers refer to entries

Anson-Cartwright Editions, 986
Apollinaire, Guillaume, 814
ARC Press, 988
Archer, W. G., 805
Arents, George, 23, 46
Armstrong, James I., 578
Arno, Carolyn C., 851
Arnold, Benedict, 90
Art Institute of Chicago, 12,
    58, 71, 535
Artemis, S. A., 957
Arthur, John, 520
Ashbery, John, 944
Ask, Gilbert, 68
Association of Research Libraries,
    786, 799, 876
Astle, Edwin George, Sr., 932
At the Sign of Al Kalbu al Kabir
    al Aswad, 363, 552
Auchincloss, Louis, 857
Auden, W. H., 352
Audette, Anna H., 456
Austen, Jane, 857
Austin, Gabriel, 168
Ayrault House, Newport, 47

Babbidge, Homer Daniels, Jr.,
    536
Baer, Curtis O., 57, 77, 798
Baker, Anna, 574
Baker, Carlos, 138
Baldwin, Harrison W., 398
Ball, Robert, 516
Bancroft, Charles Parker, 134, 136
Bandelier, Fanny, 557
Bann, Stephen, 838
Bannon, John Francis, 557
Baranik, Rudolf, 866
Barchilon, Jacques, 43
Barlow, Charles Beach, 964
Barnard, Thomas, 437

Barnes, Djuna, 669
Baro, Gene, 900
Baron, Stevan A., 939
Barrall, L. Wethered, 333
Barre Publishers, 175, 197, 253,
    255, 268, 311, 335, 490,
    517, 525, 622
Bartlett, Donald, 76
Bartlett, Fred S., 235
Bartók Archives, 159
Bartram, William, 390, 620
Barzun, Jacques, 739
Baskin, Leonard, 59, 82, 104, 140,
    145, 166, 193, 219, 223, 264,
    355, 358, 374, 399, 407, 426,
    447, 448, 449, 748
Bator, Victor, 159
Baxter, Vida Seaman, 968
Bean, Jacob, 485
Beatson, Elizabeth H., 880
Beck, James, 924
Beck, Sydney, 256
Becker, David P., 755
Bedsole, V. L., 97
Beehive Press, 499, 546, 555, 556,
    562, 566, 583, 609, 612, 614,
    620, 637, 645, 646, 649, 662,
    665, 667, 673, 694, 695, 696,
    702, 707, 715, 737, 756, 780,
    802, 823, 835, 868, 878,
    919, 930
Beerbohm, Max, 26
Bell Editions, 889, 946
Bell, Whitfield J., Jr., 436, 643,
    1000
Belt, Rigel Osborn, 462
Benson, Elizabeth P., 478, 527,
    601, 971
Benson, John, 512
Benson, John Howard, 53
Benson, Richard, 598, 630, 879,
    886

Burns, Larry, 729
Busch-Reisinger Museum (Harvard University), 326, 542, 693
Butcher, S. H., 193
Butler, Samuel, 397
Butterfield, L. H., 246, 380
Buttrey, Theodore V., Jr., 584
Buxbaum, Edwin C., 477
Bynner, Witter, 22, 114

C. Z. Publications, 951
Cabell, James Branch, 776
Caflisch, Max, 528
Cage, John, 950
Cahoon, Herbert, 641
Caldwell, Erskine, 665, 835, 878
Caldwell, Lucy, 801
Calhoun, Felicity, 930
Califano, Joseph A., 558
Calvin Coolidge Memorial Foundation, 524, 581
Cape Ann Historical Association, 650
Caponigro, Eleanor Morris, 889, 946
Carlisle, Lilian Baker, 470
Carnegie Institution of Washington, 124
Carney, William, 406
Carpenter, Ralph E., Jr., 25
Carroll, Eugene A., 863
Carruth, Hayden, 787, 789, 804, 806
Carter, B. Nowland, 120
Carter, David G., 297
Cary, Richard, 339
Casares, Dr. Jorge, 91
Cassity, Turner, 958
Castine Scientific Society, 922
Castro, Alex, 921

Catesby, Mark, F.R.S., 646
Cauthen, Irby B., Jr., 515
Cavell, James Branch, 776
Center for Conservation and Technical Studies, 881
Century Association, 587, 813, 845
Chamberlin, Roy B., 30
Champlain, Samuel de, 901
Champlain–Upper Hudson Bicentennial Committee, 775
Chappell and Co., Ltd., 721
Charles Butcher Fund, 89, 100
Charles E. Goodspeed and Co., 827, 998
Chatsworth (Devonshire Collection), 147, 325, 412
Cheshire Bicentennial Committee, 777
Chetham, Charles Scott, 55, 84
Childs, Charles D., 504, 520
Childs, Francis Lane, 428
Childs, Marquis W., 264
Church of the Holy Trinity, 72
Ciardi, John, 166
Clay, John Eugene, Jr., 962
Clement, Paul A., 820
Cleveland, Mather, M.D., 409, 663
Clifford, J. Garry, 602
Clifford, James L., 975
Clifton, James M., 919
Club of Odd Volumes, 118, 201, 303, 421, 852, 923
Clune, Henry W., 918
Cober, Alan E., 725
Cocks, J. Fraser, III, 916
Coe, Michael D., 370, 680
Coffin, David D., 373
Cohn, Marjorie B., 881
Colby College, 461, 476, 873, 916; Art Museum, 282; Friends of Art, 172; Press, 339
Coleman, Francis, 882, 884

College Art Association of America, 502, 880, 925, 928
College Art Museum, 282
Collins, Philip, 475
Collins, Rowland L., 736
Colonial Dames of America, 169, 301
Colonial Society of Massachusetts, 580, 629, 818, 952
Colorado College, 344, 994
Colorado Springs Fine Arts Center, 235
Columbia University Department of Physics, 469
Columbia University Press, 123, 324
Committee to Honor Harold Hugo, 933
Comstock, Mary B., 544
Concordia Company, Inc., 130
Congressional Press, 248
Conkwright, P. J., 933
Conrad, Joseph, 714
Conti, Gino, 924
Coolidge, Calvin, 391, 524, 581
Coolidge, John, 391
Cooper, James Fenimore, 257
Corcoran Gallery of Art, 921
Cornell, Julien, 851, 874, 894
Cornell University Library Associates, 817
Cornell, Virginia S., 894, 908
Cosmos Club, 283, 898, 981
Costley, Ron, 838
Cottrell, Leonard, 636
Coulter, E. Merton, 546
Council of the Society of Colonial Wars, 479
Countryman Press, 674, 708, 807
Couzens, Michael, 573
Cowley, Malcolm, 949
Cox, Edward Hyde, 308, 650, 824

Crane, Hart, 341
Creasy, Edward S., 398
Crossette, George, 283, 466
Cruikshank, Robert, 46
Cummings, E. E., 341
Cuniberti, John, 954
Curran, Dennis, 728
Currier Gallery of Art, 218, 231
Curtis, Joseph Henry, 464
Curwen, Henry Darcy, 244
Cutler, Robert, 267, 272, 393

D O R Company, 549
D'Luhy, Gale R., 721
Dabcovich, Lydia, 624
Damon, S. Foster, 101, 160, 240
Dance Books, Ltd., 886
Danforth Museum, 850
Dankert, Clyde E., 188
Dartmouth College, 5, 7, 8, 75, 150, 199, 286, 312, 331, 376, 385, 402, 424, 463, 494, 840, 843, 885; Committee on Freshman Reading, 316; Graphic Arts Workshop, 1; Library, 317, 362, 438, 465, 491, 498, 547, 551, 582, 602, 627, 642, 727, 770, 771, 855, 860, 872, 895, 912; College Library, Division of Special Collections, Archives Department, 3, 24; Library Friends, 17, 196, 608, 888; Public Affairs Center, 353, 545; Hopkins Center, 178, 184, 190, 231, 280; Art Galleries, 611; Beaumont-May Gallery, 349; Thayer School of Engineering, 194; Trustees, 607; William Jewett Tucker Foundation, 319

Dartmouth Outing Club, 354
Dartmouth Publications, 30, 39, 51, 54, 76, 88, 113, 116, 138, 141, 182, 187, 220, 233, 242, 243, 263, 294, 334, 353, 356, 395, 399, 420, 467
David Carritt, Ltd., 957
David Lewis, 480, 619, 687
David R. Godine Publisher, 466, 510, 512, 577, 659, 677, 688, 690, 705, 860, 892, 897, 902, 914, 920, 929, 942, 953
Davidson, Suzette Morton, 445
Davis, Burke, 537
Davis, Mark, 813
De Cordova Museum, 282
De Veer, Elizabeth, 809
De Wolf, Gordon, 620
Deagon, Ann, 942
Dedel, Howard Tredennick, 777
Dee, Elaine Evans, 388
Deerfield Academy, 435
Defoe, Daniel, 792
Delacroix, Eugène, 228
Delano, Irene, 682
Delano, Jack, 682
Delphic Arts, 140
Denby, Edwin, 603
Denison, Cara D., 586, 689
DePol, John, 67
Derr, Thomas S., 664
Derthick, Martha, 558
Dickens, Charles, 475
Dickey, John Sloan, 8, 843
Dickinson College, 742
Dickinson, Emily, 383
Diocesan Library, 95
Dobrée, Bonamy, 365
Domjan, Joseph, 398
Dothard, Robert L., 561, 731, 857
Doudiet, Ellenore W., 922

Doyle, Richard, 579
Drachman, Julian M., 404
Dreyfus, John, 251, 365, 655, 810
Dufy, Raoul, 814
Duke University Press, 351
Dumbarton Oaks (Harvard University) 634, 680, 772, 909, 971, 972, 982; Research Libraries and Collections, 478, 527, 601, 604
Dunlap, Joseph, 810
Dunlap, Lloyd A., 171
Dürer, Albrecht, 482, 483
Duschnes, Philip C., 241, 403

E. P. Dutton and Co., 25
E. V. Thaw and Co., 957
Eakins Press Foundation, 270, 298, 303, 305, 315, 341, 342, 343, 348, 352, 359, 367, 368, 397, 408, 511, 592, 598, 618, 630, 651, 681, 717, 732, 751, 767, 779, 879, 886
Eaton, Charles Edward, 543, 597
Eaton, Isabel Patterson, 597
Eberhart, Richard, 89, 100, 141, 178, 187, 233, 263, 312, 334, 343, 356, 420, 467, 488
Echols, Edward C., 459
Edgar Allen Poe Society, 931
Edmonds, Walter D., 109
Edwin Muir, 725
Eesti Kirjanike Kooperatiiv, 567
Eichenberg, Fritz, 209, 396
Einstein, Alfred, 764
Eisenhower, Dwight David, 7
Elder, John Petersen, 226
Eleutherian Mills Historical Library, 417
Eliot Church of Newton, 37
Eliot Porter and Bell Editions, 946

Elmslie, Kenward, 603, 726
Emerson Guild of Creative Arts, 518, 519
Emerson, William, 65
Eng, James M., 939
Episcopal Church, 93, 95
Errickson, Shirley, 197
Essex Institute, 738, 744, 760, 761, 825, 917, 974
Ettenberg, Eugene M., 529
Ettinghausen, Richard, 616, 772
Evans, Sir David, 411
Evans, Walker, 298
Everest, Allan S., 775
Ewan, Joseph, 390, 445, 646

Fadiman, Clifton, 714
Faison, S. Lane, Jr., 1006
Falcon, Thomas, 331
Fales, Martha Gandy, 68
Falter, John, 980
Far Gallery, 448
Farlow, Catherine H., 213
Farmington Historical Society, 740
Farnam, Anne, 917
Fast, Howard, 132
Feigenbaum, Rita F., 575
Feindel, William, 237
Feld, Stuart P., 426
Ferguson, Sanford B., 316
Ferris, Theodore Parker, 796
Filby, P. W., 161
Finlay, Ian Hamilton, 838
Fisher, Benjamin Franklin, IV, 931
Fleming, Harold, 322
Flower, Dean, 492
Focillon, Henri M., 457
Fogg Art Museum. *See* Harvard University
Folger Shakespeare Library, 653

Forbes, H. A. Crosby, 679
Ford, David, 423
Fordham University Press, 763
Forslund, David Erland Charles, 344
Forster, E. M., 397
Fort Ticonderoga Association, 96
Fortuine, Robert, 362
Foss, Edward G., 513
Foster, Frank C., 461
Foundation of the American Institute for Conservation, 881
Foursquare Press, 833
Fralin, Frances, 921
Frank Hallman, 669, 704, 709, 723
Franklin, Benjamin, 41, 167, 315, 436, 572, 628, 643
Freedberg, Anne Blake, 44
Freer Gallery of Art, Smithsonian Institution, 970
French Hill Press, 866
Freneau, Philip, 377
Frick, George, 646
Friedman, Ken, 905
Frost, Robert, 29, 182, 183, 288, 307, 308, 354, 503, 658, 659, 699, 823
Fuller, Timothy, 994

G. Felipe Dávalos, 604
G. K. Hall and Company, 167, 202, 486, 534, 572, 652, 753, 870
Gaertner, Johannes Alexander, 19, 275
Gallery Association of New York State, 896
Garden Club of America, 69
Gardner, Ray, 624

Garlick, Kenneth J., 965
Garo, Gene, 900
Garrett, Wendell D., 103
Garrigue, Jean, 270
Garvey, Eleanor M., 940
Gavin, William G., 154
Gebelein, J. Herbert, 762
Gehenna Press, 492
Gemming, Klaus, 436, 490, 956
Gensamer, Ted, 776
Gentleman, David, 365
Georgia Museum of Art, 426
Gerdts, William H., 276, 314
Getscher, Robert H., 871
Giles, Laura, 977
Gill, Brendan, 540
Gillies, Linda, 585
Glades Congress, 110, 115
Glazier, Lyle, 804
Gleason, Harold Willard, 433
Goddard College, 121, 230
Godine, David R., 263, 295, 463
Goff, Frederick R., 685
Golde, Arthur, 389
Golden, Herbert H., 423
Goldman, Marcus Selden, 415
Goldner, Nancy, 618, 630
Goldwater, Walter, 221
Gooch, Brad, 822
Good Lion, 535
Goodkind, Herbert K., 569
Goodrich, Lloyd, 443
Goodrich, Nathaniel L., 3
Goodyear, Frank H., 625
Gordan, Phyllis Goodhart, 606
Gordon, Ronald, 619, 687, 704, 831
Gorman, Joan H., 910
Gottfried, Rudolf B., 867, 966
Gottlieb, Gerald, 690
Grafton, Samuel, 520
Gralla, Howard I., 893

Grancsay, Stephen V., 154
Graphic Arts Workshop, 1
Graphic Crafts, Inc., 752
Gray, Vaughn, 405
Grear, Malcolm, 542
Greenberg, Alvin, 914
Greene, Jack P., 859
Greene, Stephen, 621
Greenly, Albert Harry, 21, 86
Grolier Club, 168, 217, 307, 550
Groten, Frank J., Jr., 448
Groth, John, 654
Groton School, Trustees of, 117, 757
Grushkin, Philip, 995
Guthorn, Peter J., 774
Guthrie, Ramon, 180

Haagen, Victor B., 179
Hadas, Moses, 324
Haines, Francis, 157
Hall, Ariel, 539
Hall, Donald, 74, 135
Hall, Edward Tuck, 338
Hall, Elton Wayland, 539, 656
Hall, Garrison Kent, 539, 982
Hall, Michael, 610
Hallock, Robert, 520
Halsband, Robert, 123
Hamilton, Edward Pierce, 52, 96
Hamlin, Elizabeth, 378
Hamlin, Wilfrid, 230
Hammerslough, Philip H., 575
Hancock, Marianne H., 781
Handlin, Oscar, 849
Hanna, Archibald, 864
Hanover Historical Society, 377, 428
Happel, Phillip, 964
Harding, Anne Borden, 508
Hardison, O. B., Jr., 486

Hareven, Tamara K., 941
Harper and Row Publishers, 533
Harris, Edward, 453
Harris, Elizabeth, 897
Harris, Joel Chandler, 696
Harris, John, 289
Hart, Mr. & Mrs. Ivan B., 158
Hart, James D., 783
Hartley, Marsden, 341
Harvard College Chapter of ΦBK,
    Alpha of Massachusetts, 102,
    345
Harvard College Fund, 747
Harvard Lampoon, Inc., 766
Harvard, Stephen, 648, 736, 788,
    889, 915, 943, 976, 1002
Harvard University, 204, 245,
    350, 590, 666; Adams House,
    103; Belknap Press, 127;
    College Library, 14, 48, 329,
    747; College Library Depart-
    ment of Printing and Graphic
    Arts, 12, 228, 293, 375, 383,
    509, 568, 755, 940; Fogg Art
    Museum, 11, 33, 35, 36, 48,
    55, 58, 77, 84, 98, 155, 156,
    170, 204, 254, 291, 487, 506,
    596, 706, 755, 865, 881;
    Houghton Library, 238,
    472, 819; Lowell House, 40,
    173; Medical Library, 227;
    Trustees, 527, 604; Univer-
    sity Libraries, 245, 400, 743;
    University Press, 143, 236,
    239, 326, 410, 481, 706
Harwell, Richard Barksdale, 696,
    702, 707
Hass, Robert, 588
Hatch, Francis W., 226
Hattis, Phyllis, 596
Hawley, Barbara, 544
Hawthorne, Nathaniel, 50, 313

Hayes, Miles V., Ph.D., 234
Hayim, Yosef, 765
Hazlehurst, F. Hamilton, 634
Heade, Martin J., 27
Heckman, J. Harrison, 781
Heckscher Museum, 862
Heffernan, Roy J., M.D., 299
Heitkamp, Peter, 789
Held, Julius S., 456
Helikon Press, 661
Heller, Erich, 528, 725
Henley, William Ernest, 976
Hennessey, Tom, 735
Henrikson, Carol, 806
Herrick, Phyllis, 815
Herrick, William F., 815, 903
Herring, Phillip F., 844
Herschberger, Ruth, 408
Herzl, Theodor, 397
Hewitt, Geof, 768
Hidy, Lance, 510
Higgins, Dick, 749, 829, 834,
    905, 993
Hill, Draper, 446
Hill School, 448
Hill-Stead Museum, Trustees of
    the, 285
Hilles, Frederick W., 437
Hillyer, Robert, 59
Historic New Orleans Collection,
    802
Hitchcock, Henry-Russell, 925
Hitchings, Sinclair, 62, 63, 122,
    213, 226, 271, 416, 520, 580,
    626
Hofer, Philip, 12, 16, 48, 53, 156,
    211, 228, 239, 293, 375, 608
Hoffman, Daniel, 668
Hoffmann, Felix, 528
Hokusai, 49
Holden, R. J., 731
Holden, Raymond, 126, 807

[288]

Holt, Rinehart and Winston, 288, 308
Hopkins, Ernest Martin, 286, 840
Horblit, Harrison D., 217
Horwitt, Pink, 549
Houghton Library, 328, 472, 819
House of Books, Ltd., 205
Hovey, Richard, 138
Howland, Llewellyn, 130
Hoyle, Pamela, 959
Hubbard, Harlan, 651
Hubert, Joseph P., 991
Hugo, Harold, 933, 1002
Huss, Richard E., 752
Hutchinson, Robert, 511
Hutton, Clarke, 655
Huxtable, Ada Louise, 342
Hyde Collection, 123, 152

Impressions Workshop, 858
Imprint Society, 436, 441, 444, 503, 557
Institute of Judaeo-Christian Studies, 198
International Exhibitions Foundation, 325, 388, 412, 484, 493, 505, 530, 559, 597, 633, 670, 698, 754, 805, 861, 869, 900, 965
Italmuse, Inc., 161
Ives, Charles, 352
Ives, Sidney, 819

J. B. Speed Art Museum, 610
J.D.R. 3rd Fund, 842
J. J. Augustin Publisher, 821, 924
J. S. Logan Foundation, 980
Jackson, William A., 238
Jaffé, Michael, 754
James, Schuyler, 839
James, Sydney V., Jr., 189

James, William, 352
Janus Press, 701
Jarrell, Randall, 85
Jasenas, Michael, 653
Jefferson, Thomas, 345, 367, 513
Jenkins Publishing Co., 864
Jensen, Merrill, 379
Jewett, Sarah Orne, 339
Jewish Publication Society of America, 697, 765
John and Mable Ringling Museum of Art, 177, 431, 745
John Carter Brown Library, Associates of the, 451, 473, 495, 657
John Hancock Mutual Life Insurance Company, 213
Johnson, Malcolm, 439
Johnson, Ruth Carter, 277
Johnson, Samuel, 152
Johnsonians, 437, 523, 975
Johnston, Frances Benjamin, 737
Jones, A. Ross, 522
Jones, Howard Mumford, 750
Jowett, Benjamin, 193

Kafka, Franz, 397, 725
Kainen, Jacob, 323
Kallen, Horace M., 193
Kallman Publishing Co., 427
Kanthos Press, 166
Kappell, Philip, 964
Karolik Collection of American Painting, 27, 146
Kaufman, Herbert, 575
Kazin, Alfred, 510
Kebabian, Paul B., 999
Keith, C. Freeman, 81, 450
Keith, Christopher, 488
Kennan, George F., 352
Kennedy, Benjamin, 645
Kennedy, John F., 352

Kernan, John Devereux, 679
Kerslake, John, 411
Kibre, Pearl, 812
Killion, Ronald, 614
Kimball, William Phelps, 489
King, B. A., 1002
King Ranch, 638
Kipling, Rudyard, 365
Kirschbaum, Walter R., M.D., 364
Kirstein, Lincoln, 341, 598, 630, 758, 879
Knight, Russell W., 761
Knopf, Alfred A., 22, 59, 114
Kollwitz, Cathy, 82
Korach, Mimi, 135
Korey, Marie Elena, 742
Kraemer, Ruth S., 688
Kramer, Hilton, 341
Kredel, Fritz, 324, 529
Kroeber, Bernd, 792
Kronenberger, Louis, 529
Krueger, Glee, 926
Kugler, Richard C., 711, 947
Kuhn, Charles L., 326
Kuhn, Walt, 235
Kunitz, Stanley, 588, 660
Kyle, John H., 70

Ladd, Gabrielle, 108
Laing, Diana Whitehill, 255
Lamb, Dana S., 175, 197, 268, 335, 490
Lamberton, Robert, 619
Lancaster [New Hampshire] Bicentennial, 207
Lancaster, Walter B., M.D., 39
Landreau, Anthony N., 401
Lane, Fitz Hugh, 38, 282, 650
Lane, Mills, 419, 499, 609, 612, 662, 673, 695, 715, 737, 823, 868

Lang, Andrew, 516
Lang, H. Jack, 937
Langdon, John Emerson, 106, 274, 429
Lankes, J. J., 29, 64
Lathem, Edward Connery, 107, 182, 183, 194, 286, 288, 307, 308, 377, 391, 491, 503, 524, 525, 581, 559, 799, 843, 876, 885
Lavalle, John, 262
Lea, Thomas, 638
Lear, Edward, 14, 484
Learning Research Association, Inc., 394
Leavens, Robert French, 243
Leavitt and Peirce, 87, 224
Leavitt, Dorothy Hall, 791
Lee, Edward Brown, Jr., 458
Lee, George, 532
Lee, Sherman E., 208
Leeds University Oriental Society, 278
Leeper, John Palmer, 210
Lehmann, Phyllis Williams, 613, 821
Lehmann-Haupt, Hellmut, 741
Lehrer, Ruth Fine, 701
Leighton, Margaretha Gebelein, 762
Lenox, Massachusetts, The Town of . . . , 405
Leonard, Chilson H., 330
Leonard, William Ellery, 636
Levenson, Jay A., 483
Levertov, Denise, 817
Lewis, David, 480, 619, 687
Lewis, R. E., 416
Lewis, Wilmarth S., 740
Library of Congress, 171, 764, 784
Liebert, Herman W., 473, 937

Limited Editions Club, 132, 193, 257, 313, 345, 365, 398, 455, 516, 528, 529, 561, 624, 636, 654, 655, 682, 712, 714, 725, 731, 776, 792, 857, 949, 976
Lincoln, Abraham, 171, 327, 713, 732
Lindsay, Vachel, 348, 352
Lipke, William C., 999
Little, Bertram K., 474
Little, David Bain, 118, 271
Littmann, Edwin R., 604
Livingston, Jane, 921
Lloyd Hills Press, 9
Lodge of St. Andrew, 368
Loehner, Conrad A., M.D., 496, 507
Logan, Sheridan A., 980
London, Jack, 624
Long House, Inc., 258, 327, 384
Longstreet, Augustus B., 696
Longwell, Dennis, 939
Lord, Arthur Hardy, 37, 243
Louisiana State University, 97; University Press, 70
Louttit, T. Robley, 997
Loveridge, Rosabel N., 181, 216, 300
Low, Joseph, 455
Low Memorial Library, 830
Lowry, Walker, 671, 683, 803, 875, 891
Lund, Marilan, 661, 969
Lunenburg Historical Society, 877
Lunenburg Village School, 310
Lynn Warde, 132
Lyons, Elizabeth, 158

M. Knoedler and Co., 55, 358, 460
McBride, Henry, 341

McCann, Anna Marguerite, 936
McCarter, William H., 51
McCarthy, Mary Wedemeyer, 564
McCary, Ben C., 555
McClary, Nelson, 311
McClelland, Donald, 457
McCollough, Charles, 319
McCord, David T. W., 226, 262, 271, 302, 434, 747, 797, 852, 856, 873, 923, 987
McCorison, Marcus A., 191, 347, 444
McCracken, Ursula E., 591
McCrillis, John O. C., 714
McCully, Marilyn, 935
McCurdy, Michael, 557
McDonald, Thoreau, 1
MacDougall, Elisabeth B., 634, 772, 909
McGill University Press, 237
McGrath, Robert L., 547
McGuire, William, 812
McIlvaine, Jane, 311
McIntyre, Ruth A., 163
McKeon, Edith. *See* Abbott, Edith McKeon
McKibbin, David, 45
McKitterick, David, 996
McLanathan, Richard B. K., 27, 31, 38, 42, 60, 104
McLean, Elizabeth Bancroft, 136
McLoughlin, William G., 859
McMichael, James, 920
McNulty, Kneeland, 858, 861
MacPhail, Ian, 445
MacSherry, Charles, 158
Mackie, Louise W., 616
Mahoney, Charles A., 517
Maitin, Samuel, 858
Malcolm Grear Designers, 596
Mallarmé, Stephane, 515

Manchester, Vermont, The Town of . . . , 129
Manet, Édouard, 44, 515
Mann, Thomas, 528
Mariacher, Giovanni, 386
Markman, Sidney David, 279
Marsh, Daniel L., 384
Martin, Eric, 173
Martin, Florence Giffin, 508
Martin, Van Jones, 737, 868
Massachusetts General Hospital School of Nursing, Nurses Alumnae Association, 678
Massachusetts Historical Society, 411, 1003
Massachusetts Society of the Cincinnati, 212
Mathues, Francis J., 252, 361, 471
Mattila, Robert, 895
Mayer, Peter, 995
Mayhall, Jane, 305, 359, 592
Mayor, A. Hyatt, 341, 717, 813, 863
Mazur, Gail, 929
Mearns, David C., 171
Mediaeval Academy of America, 600
Medlicott, Alexander, Jr., 912
Megaw, Elektra, 206
Meiss, Millard, 640, 880
Melanson, John, 122, 126, 162, 259
Mellon, Paul, 533
Mendelssohn, Felix, 784
Meriden Gravure Company, 16
Meriden-Stinehour, Inc., 1002
Merrifield, Richard F., 708
Messerli, Douglas, 687
Metropolitan Museum of Art, 485, 585, 724, 814, 911, 936, 940

Meyer, Baron Adolphe de, 886
Micossi, Mario, 520
Middlebury College, 578, 675
Milbank, Robbins, 215
Milfort, Louis LeClerc, 555
Miller, Anita, 585
Miller, Arthur G., 604
Miller, C. William, 628
Miller, Perry 41
Milray, Elizabeth, 977
Milton (Mass.) Historical Society, 52
Milton (Mass.) Tercentenary Committee, 151
Milton, Peter, 858, 861
Mitchinson, David, 698
Modigliani, Amedeo, 98
Mongan, Agnes, 36, 98, 156, 487
Monteverdi, Mario, 505
Montgomery, Constance, 728, 729
Montgomery, Raymond, 728, 729
Montpelier, Vt., Secretary of State, 149
Montreal Museum of Fine Arts, 297
Moore, Lillian, 249
Moore, Marianne, 173
Moretus Press, 996
Morgan, Junius S., 453
Morin, Richard W., 15, 642
Morison, Samuel Eliot, 189, 224, 259, 730
Morison, Stanley, 200
Morita, Shiryū, 452
Morrison, Mary, 868
Morse, Mr. & Mrs. Earl, 170
Morse, Stearns, 50, 294
Morton Arboretum, 445
Moss, Elaine, 842
Mount Vernon Ladies' Association of the Union, 56

Plimoth Plantation, 163, 189
Plowman, E. Grosvenor, 438
Plowman, George T., 438
Plumb, J. H., 690
Poe, Edgar Allan, 44
Pontes, Crimilda, 309, 323, 386, 401, 457, 483, 616, 970
Pool, Angeline, 773
Pool, Beekman H., 201
Pool, J. Lawrence, 773
Poor, Robert J., 158
Porte, Joel, 225
Porter, Elliot, 889, 946
Portolan Press, 774
Pory, John, 189
Posada, José Guadalupe, 209
Potter, Beatrix, 293
Pound, Omar S., 430
Powers, Richard M., 257
Praeger Publishers, 443
Pratt Graphic Art Center, 209
Prentice, T. Merrill, 622
Prescott, William Hickling, 92
Presidio Press, 811
Price, Lucien, 226
Princeton University Art Museum, 290, 935; Library, 214
Printed Editions, 905, 950, 993
Professor P. H. Bear (pseud. Philip Hofer) 211
Proper, David R., 617
Providence Public Library, 266, 357, 934
Provident Institution for Savings, 304
Pulitzer, Joseph, Jr., 55, 84, 264
Purcell, Dennis W., 705
Purcell, Rosamond Wolff, 705

Radcliffe College, 987
Radway, Laurence I., 545

Raggone, Dean David Vincent, 489
Railton, Stephen, 672
Randall, Lilian M. C., 591
Randall, Richard H., Jr., 591
Rannit, Aleksis, 567
Rasieres, Isaack de, 189
Rassias, John A., 376
Ravenel, Gaillard F., 483
Ray, Gordon N., 769, 786
Readex Books, 969
Red Dust, Inc., 250, 322
Reece, B. Carroll, 258
Reece, Louise Goff, 258
Reed, Clara Stillman, 137
Reese, Trevor R., 556, 583, 649
Reese, William S., 864
Reichert, Victor E., 824
Reid, Robert R., 237
Renaissance Society of America, 18
Renner, Frederic G., 277
Research Publications, Inc., 954
Revere, Paul, 42
Rexroth, Kenneth, 414
Reyman, Vernon, 519
Reynolds, Graham, 533
Rhode Island Historical Society, 625
Rhys, Jean, 709
Rich, Harry A., 949
Richard R. Smith Co., 333
Richard, Oscar, 97
Richardson, Grace Stuart Jones, 537
Richardson, John, 957
Richardson, Smith, 691, 692
Riling and Lentz, 154
Ringling Museum of Art. *See* John and Mable Ringling Museum of Art
Rink, Evald, 417

Ripley, S. Dillon, 560
Robert Hull Fleming Museum, The University of Vermont, 701, 999
Robertson, Ian L., 172
Robinson, Franklin W., 494, 607, 869
Robinson, Kenneth Allen, 64
Robinson, Rowland E., 80
Rogers, Bruce, 26
Rogers, Horatio, M.D., 79, 686, 810
Rome, H. S. Payson, 474
Ron, Costely, 838
Rosenbach Foundation, 468
Rosenberg, Jakob, 254
Rosenberger, Frances Coleman, 785, 882, 884
Rosenfield, Rachel, 881
Rosenwald, Lessing J., 790, 978
Rossetti, Dante Gabriel, 976
Rossiter, Henry P., 539
Roth, Elizabeth E., 256
Rowe, Ann Pollard, 971
Rowfant Club, 937
Rowland, Thomas, 202
Royalton Historical Society, 718
Royalton, Vt.: Royalton Historical Society, 718
Royalton, Vt.: South Royalton Women's Club, 718
Royalton, Vt.: The Town of . . . , 718
Roylance, Dale, 447
Rubel, C. Adrian, 291
Rubens, Peter Paul, 31, 36, 456
Ruzicka, Rudolph, 53, 503, 677, 845
Ryder, Arthur W., 561
Ryskamp, Charles, 571, 579, 700, 733

Sachs, Mary Parmly Kones, 321
Sadik, Marvin S., 140, 355, 374, 748
St. Botolph Club, 464
St. Johnsbury, Vt., Athenaeum and Art Gallery, 337
St. Mark's School Alumni Association, 338
Saltonstall, William G., 83
Sample, Paul, 178
Sandage, Allan, 124
Sanderson, Edmund L., 66
Sandstrom, Harvey, 991
Santayana, George, 185, 225
Sargent, Elizabeth D., 622
Sargent, John Singer, 45
Sass, Lorna J., 724
Satenstein, Harvey, 67
Sayre, Robert F., 348
Schaffer, Anne-Louise, 970
Schatborn, Peter, 530
Schaubeck, R., 709
Scheide Library, 736
Schniewind, Carl O., 71
Schoff, James Stanley, 831
Scholder, Fritz, 988
Schubert, Franz Peter, 906
Schultz, Anne Markham, 928
Schuyler, James, 839
Scientific Society, 922
Scott, Lawrence, 173, 404
Scott, Sir Walter, 516
See, Pamela, 593
Seigfried, Laurance B., 67
Seitter, Waltraut, 664
Sendak, Maurice, 468
Senzaki, Nyogen, 782
Sexton, Anna M., 318
Seymour, Richard J., 351
Shahn, Ben, 35
Shakely, Lauren, 814
Shapley, Fern Rust, 956

Shaw, George Bernard, 655
Shaw, James Bryan, 412, 559, 586
Sherman, Stuart C., 266, 357, 934
Shillito, Charles, 202
Shimano, Eido, 782
Shooter's Press, 991
Shore, Robert, 714
Siber, Helmut, 112
Signet Society, 185
Silk, Mary Dodge, 73
Sill, Gertrude Grace, 910
Silver, Rollo, 548
Silverman, Maxwell, 540
Simmonds, Harvey, 413, 794
Simonds, Philip B., Governor, 479
Simpson, Alan, 837, 848
Sisson, Clinton, 897
Skaggs, Charles E., 624
Skole, Bertha, 549
Smith Clove Press, 851, 874, 894, 908
Smith College, 366, 593, 599, 613, 984; Alumnae Association, 664; Friends of the, 492; Museum of Art, 78, 82, 99, 131, 158, 223
Smith, Datus C., 363, 552
Smith, Donald E. P., 394
Smith, Dorothy Hunt, 363, 552
Smith, Judith M., 394
Smith, Philip Chadwick Foster, 744, 887, 979
Smith, William Bentinck, 743
Smith, William Stevenson, 13
Smithsonian Institution Press, 147, 203, 208, 246, 289, 309, 323, 386, 457, 560
Society for French Historical Studies, 927
Somerset Club, 186
Sorrentino, Gilbert, 615

Soule, Allen, 149
Sparse Grey Hackle (pseud.), 522
Spee Club, 61
Spiller, Robert E., 257
Spitzmiller, Frederick, 737
Springfield, Mass., Museum of Fine Arts, 809
Srimati, Y. G., 561
Stahl, Ben F., 949
Staley, Allen, 871
Stampfle, Felice, 485, 586, 641, 689, 990
Stanlis, Peter J., 712
Stanton, Samuel Ward, 174
Starbuck, George, 902
Stebbins, Theodore E., Jr., 407
Stechow, Wolfgang, 482
Stefansson, Evelyn. See Nef, Evelyn Stefansson
Stegner, Wallace, 313
Steinberger, John, 361
Sterling and Francine Clark Art Institute, 554; Trustees, 977
Sterling, John C., 242
Stevens, Henry, 346
Stevens, William Bacon, 546
Stevenson, Robert Louis, 976
Stinehour Press, as publisher, 15, 19, 50, 62, 63, 80, 81, 86, 102, 107, 112, 162, 176, 180, 183, 273, 275, 281, 310, 318, 320, 346, 425, 439, 450, 631, 768, 773, 787, 788, 789, 800, 804, 806, 943, 967
Stowe, Mrs. H. B., 637
Strachan, Alan, 655
Strades, Diana, 913
Strange, Mary Alsted, 508
Strauss, Walter A., 481
Streeter, Nellie M., 877
Strider, Robert E. L., 476
Strong, Roy, 325

Wentzell, Jane, 216
Wesleyan College, 756
West, Eleanor, 780
West, Herbert Faulkner, 17
Westholm Publications, 64, 91
Weyerhaeuser, Carl A., 292, 442, 538
Whaling Museum, 623
Wheatland, David P., 350
Whicker, Harold Wave, 328
White, Christopher, 828
White, Lewis F., 313
Whitehill, Walter Muir, 110, 143, 224, 226, 248, 260, 304, 422, 474, 580, 629, 677, 761, 933
Whiting, H. Kneeland, 174
Whitman, Walt, 352, 389, 510, 672
Whitney Museum of American Art, 443
Whittemore, Bradford Adams, 212
Wick, Peter A., 28, 226, 509
Widmayer, Charles E., 840
Wildenstein, Inc., 360
Wilkins, Ruth S., 679
Willa Muir, 725
Willard, Nancy, 368
Willey, Samuel Hopkins, 24
William L. Clements Library. *See* University of Michigan
Williams, Alexander Whiteside, 186, 421
Williams College, 406, 1006; Museum of Art, 960; Trustees, 977
Williams, Eunice, 360
Williams, Gerald, 231
Williams, T. Harry, 97
Williams, Tennessee, 205
Willis, Thomas, 237
Wilmerding, John, 282, 504
Wilson, Adrian, 792
Wilson, John, 520

Wilson, Marc F., 846
Wilson, Nigel, 600
Wiltse, Charles M., 498
Windolph, F. Lyman, 501, 563, 589, 647
Winkfield, Trevor, 839
Winterthur Museum, 68
Witten, Laurence C., II, 812
Wolf, Edwin, 2nd, 742
Wong, Roberta, 626
Wood, David H., 405
Woodruff, William, 427
Woods, Shirley E., 735
Woolf, Virginia, 704
Woolmer/Brotherson, Ltd., 817
Wragg, Thomas S., 325, 412
Wright, Gertrude B., 269
Wright, Louis B., 786
Wright's Silver Cream, 617
Wroth, Lawrence C., 53, 495
Wunder, Richard, 675
Wyeth, Andrew, 155, 156

Yale Center for British Art, 828
Yale University, 447; Art Gallery, 532, 893; Department of Anthropology, 370; Library, 221, 576, 811; Press, 239, 588
Yates, Elizabeth, 674
Yerushalmi, Yosef Hayim, 697, 765
Yonemura, Ann, 970
Youmans, Charles L., 32

Z Press, 603, 722, 726, 822, 832, 838, 839, 944, 945, 992
Zahn, Carl, 60, 142, 146, 544
Zukofsky, Celia, 951
Zukofsky, Louis, 904
Zurcher, Suzette M., 71
Zweig, Janet, 963
Zweig, Martha, 787

1200 COPIES PRINTED
AT MERIDEN-STINEHOUR PRESS
LUNENBURG, VERMONT